This excellent new book by   ly
spiritual, and very practica   d
pastorally sensitive book w   u
have ever wondered about   a
must-read for you. It will prove especially helpful for ng
to grow in prayer and experience all that Jesus has for them.

—MIKE BICKLE
DIRECTOR, INTERNATIONAL HOUSE OF PRAYER
OF KANSAS CITY

In an engaging way Sam Storms addresses a wide range of questions about the gift of tongues. Systematically and carefully, yet graciously and fairly, he examines the various interpretive options, providing readers of any persuasion better understanding of the range of perspectives on this issue. Most importantly he also provides solid and, I believe, persuasive guidance in choosing the answers most consistent with the biblical witness.

—CRAIG S. KEENER
F. M. AND ADA THOMPSON PROFESSOR OF BIBLICAL STUDIES,
ASBURY THEOLOGICAL SEMINARY

The more controversial a subject is, the more wisdom, care, and clarity are needed in addressing it. Which makes it great news for all of us that Sam Storms has written a book on the gift of tongues, bringing straightforward and biblical answers to thirty important questions. Even those who disagree with some of his conclusions will benefit from being walked through the issues by such a thoughtful and experienced pastor-scholar. A super guide to a sometimes-divisive topic.

—ANDREW WILSON
TEACHING PASTOR, KING'S CHURCH LONDON

Sam Storms has blessed the church with his book *The Language of Heaven*. I urge the Reformed, Evangelicals, Catholics, Charismatics, and Pentecostals to read this book. You will not be able to put it down. It is engaging, thorough, biblical, convincing, sensible, and scholarly, and yet simple. You will not find a better treatment on this subject.

—Dr. R. T. Kendall
Minister of Westminster Chapel, London
from 1977–2002

This is the best book I've read on the gift of tongues. But it is more than that. It is a great book on the spiritual life. With the wisdom of a skillful theologian and the tender heart of a pastor, Sam leads us to a God who longs for us and wants us to feel His affection.

—Jack Deere
Author of *Surprised by the Power of the Spirit*

Dr. Sam Storms has asked all the right questions and provided solid, Bible-based, eminently practical answers about a very important topic. Tongues-speakers will be enriched by his in-depth exposition of the Scriptures, while those who have rejected tongues will be challenged to reconsider their views and embrace the Spirit's fullness in their lives. Praying in tongues has helped shape my own walk with God, and I'm so glad a solid theologian like Sam Storms has provided us with a timely manual at a critical time in church history.

—Dr. Michael L. Brown
President of FIRE School of Ministry,
Author of *Playing with Holy Fire: A Wake-up Call to the Pentecostal-Charismatic Church*

THE
LANGUAGE
OF
HEAVEN

SAM STORMS

CHARISMA
HOUSE

Most CHARISMA HOUSE BOOK GROUP products are available at special quantity discounts for bulk purchase for sales promotions, premiums, fund-raising, and educational needs. For details, write Charisma House Book Group, 600 Rinehart Road, Lake Mary, Florida 32746, or telephone (407) 333-0600.

THE LANGUAGE OF HEAVEN by Sam Storms
Published by Charisma House
Charisma Media/Charisma House Book Group
600 Rinehart Road
Lake Mary, Florida 32746
www.charismahouse.com

Library of Congress Cataloging-in-Publication Data:
An application to register this book for cataloging has been submitted
to the Library of Congress.
International Standard Book Number: 978-1-62999-607-3
E-book ISBN: 978-1-62999-608-0

19 20 21 22 23 — 987654321
Printed in the United States of America

Dedicated to

Jackie Pullinger

*With profound, heartfelt appreciation
for your Christ-exalting life and
sacrificial ministry to the weak and broken.*

CONTENTS

ACKNOWLEDGMENTS

As I THOUGHT about the people responsible for this book being published, my mind turned first to Jason McMullen of Charisma House. Jason was relentless (without being pushy!) in his encouragement of me to write this book. He was the first to see the potential in it, and I am grateful for his pursuit of me to provide this resource to the body of Christ. Thank you, Jason!

I should also say thanks to Debbie Marrie, vice president of Product Development at Charisma House, who has been incredibly supportive of my writing and remarkably helpful in keeping me pointed in the right direction.

A huge debt of gratitude is due to Adrienne Gaines, my editor. She worked tirelessly to make this book easier to read and to hold me accountable for proper citation of sources. Editing is often a thankless job done behind the scenes. So I want to make certain that Adrienne is properly thanked (!!!) and brought into the well-deserved limelight for all she did to make *The Language of Heaven* better than it would otherwise have been.

I also want to express my gratitude to the elders of Bridgeway Church in Oklahoma City. These men have supported my writing ministry in every conceivable way. Had they not given me time and opportunity to research and write, this book would never have seen the light of day.

Finally, as always, I must thank my wife of forty-seven years,

Ann. Her prayers for me (often in tongues!) have been the foundation for my work and ministry all these many years. She always
speaks words of encouragement and love, especially at those times
when I questioned the importance of what I was doing. I love you,
Annie!

—SAM

Introduction

TONGUES: A GOOD GIFT FROM THE FATHER OF LIGHTS

L IKE MANY PEOPLE, I grew up loving Christmas. I couldn't wait until Christmas morning when my sister and I would tear into the many gifts our parents had worked so hard to purchase for us. Even more enjoyable was when I became a parent of two daughters and experienced the satisfaction of blessing them with gifts they so passionately desired.

My sister and I were, as best I remember, always appreciative of what our parents gave us. And my own daughters were likewise grateful. If they ever felt disappointment, they never let on to me or my wife, Ann. But I can easily envision how I would have felt if they had. If, after opening a particular gift that I personally picked out for them, they responded by frowning at it, expressing virtual contempt for what I thought was in their best interests, only then to cast it aside and never take it up again, I confess that I would have been heartbroken. Perhaps those of you who are parents have experienced precisely this scenario, and you know the awkward feeling that comes with watching your children treat your best efforts at blessing them with utter disregard and disdain.

I don't think it's much of an exaggeration to suggest that this is what a large portion of the body of Christ has done with the spiritual gift of speaking in tongues. Because our heavenly Father loves us, has our best interests in view, and wants to bless us beyond anything we could ever deserve, He carefully conceived, crafted, and then lovingly bestowed on His children the gracious gift of tongues. Yes, it's a gift. Yes, it was God's idea, not that of any human being. And yes, God thought up and generously poured out on His children a gift that sadly so many of us have frowned upon, made fun of, tried to explain away, and largely ignored.

Try to imagine how that makes our heavenly Father feel. How would it make you feel if out of love you designed a special gift for your children, only to have them laugh at it, mock it, and then cast it aside? Speaking in tongues, or what I call the language of heaven, was *God's idea.* He thought it up. He invented it. He graciously bestowed it upon the church. And how have so many responded? Some with utter contempt, making statements such as, "But it's so weird." Or perhaps something like: "It's actually useless. It doesn't make much sense to me. I have no desire to receive this gift, and I'll do whatever I can to discourage others from making it an object of their prayer requests to God."

The gift of tongues and those who regularly practice praying in the Spirit do not have a good reputation among many outside the Charismatic movement. Those who practice this gift are thought by many to be mushy-minded and spiritually uncoordinated. They are perceived as incapable of chewing their theological gum and walking in a straight line at the same time. I've been told on several occasions that people who pray words they do not understand are probably intellectual lightweights who prefer feeling to thinking. Such Christians are likely averse to deep and rigorous engagement with the Scriptures and avoid theological argumentation at all costs.

Of course, I can only speak for myself, but I have found the gift of tongues to be a tremendous boost to my spiritual zeal and an immensely effective way of deepening my relationship with Jesus. Contrary to the caricatures many have of this gift, I can tie my shoelaces, balance my checkbook, drive a car, and hold down a job, and I rarely ever drool!

A CLANGING CYMBAL?

So why is talking about speaking in tongues not what one might call polite dinner conversation, especially in more conservative evangelical circles? Speaking in tongues is considered only a notch or two above snake-handling (or in the opinion of some, below it) and the drinking of deadly poison! If you're courageous enough to admit you speak in tongues, you will likely be met with looks of confusion or incredulity. "What did you say? You speak in tongues? You? But you always struck me as being normal, and you always appeared to love studying the Bible and engaging in rigorous theological debates. But tongues? Ah, you're kidding, right?"

The gift of tongues is often treated like the proverbial "red-headed stepchild" in the family of God. We can't completely dismiss its presence, but we regard it as something regularly found only among doctrinally weak-minded Christians who are emotionally unstable at best. What accounts for this reputation in the Bible-believing world?

Some of you may be tempted to think I'm being overly negative in even asking this question. You may think no one really cares much about the issue these days, especially since the spiritual gift of prophecy has usurped tongues as the most controversial of all spiritual gifts. But I assure you that the prejudice against tongues is alive and well. Whereas prophecy is looked on as a potential threat to the sufficiency of Scripture, tongues is just plain weird. It's only people who lack self-control and have little regard for their public image who admit to possessing and making use of this spiritual gift.

So why do so many people twitch nervously and sweat profusely at the thought of someone speaking in tongues? Why do they carefully hide the cover of this book lest someone sitting close by get a glimpse of the title? Why do they make certain to place the book facedown when they pause their reading? As you'll discover later in the book, there are numerous ways to answer this question, but here I want to focus on only two.

First, the disdain many have toward tongues is primarily the result of a misunderstanding of what is likely the most famous of all biblical texts on tongues. I'm sure you know it well:

> If I speak in the tongues of men and of angels, but have
> not love, I am a noisy gong or a clanging cymbal.
> —1 CORINTHIANS 13:1

Who wants to be a "noisy gong or a clanging cymbal"? No one, obviously. But the image (or sound) of tongues in this passage has often served to lodge in the hearts of many a deep dislike of the gift, or at least a healthy fear of it.

But Paul isn't denouncing or denigrating tongues. Far less is he making fun of the gift. His criticism is aimed at tongues devoid of love. He's talking about tongues pursued and practiced selfishly, without regard for others. He's talking about tongues being sinfully used to promote oneself or to draw attention to one's spirituality, as over against others who are "lesser" Christians because they haven't been blessed with the gift. The same would apply equally to every other spiritual gift. Any and all of the *charismata* that are exercised in the absence of love for others and a commitment to their spiritual welfare could easily become a noisy and offensive intrusion into the life of the local church. The only reason Paul mentioned tongues in particular is that the Corinthian church abused this gift more than any other.

So what do you think Paul would say if our speaking in tongues was motivated by love, thoroughly characterized by humility and consideration for others, and done for the praise and glory of God? I think Paul would have said something like this:

> If I speak in the tongues of men and of angels, and do so in a loving, gentle, and merciful way, I am a glorious and melodious sound, a virtual symphony of sweet music that is pleasing and satisfying to all who might hear me. If I never make use of my gift to put others down but only to serve them and build them up in their faith, what a marvelous and beautiful blessing this would be for everyone!

So let's be sure we don't take what Paul says about the selfish abuse of tongues and apply it to the loving and others-oriented use of tongues.

A second reason many harbor a deep-seated prejudice against tongues is the careless and unbiblical way in which tongues is flaunted in corporate gatherings without the benefit of interpretation. We've all seen it. And we've all cringed as the speaker appears to flaunt his or her "anointing" by delivering what we are told is a crucial message from God. The only problem is that this "message" is never interpreted for the benefit of those who hear it. It grieves me to say it, but some Charismatics give every appearance of simply not caring what Paul says in 1 Corinthians 14 about how tongues is to be exercised when God's people are gathered in corporate assembly. Perhaps they are thinking we've moved beyond the need for or relevance of such guidelines. Maybe the thinking is that what may have been important for first-century church life, one simply doesn't obtain in the twenty-first century. Or perhaps they think there are times when the Spirit comes in such power and the prompting one feels within is so overwhelming that to insist on interpretation would be to quench the Spirit or to grieve Him.

It really matters little what justification they may provide for violating Paul's instructions. There is no excuse, at any time, for intentionally violating the guidelines set forth in Scripture for the exercise of spiritual gifts. The conclusion of some on the cessationist side of the debate is that any alleged spiritual gift that is subject to such obvious abuse and mishandling cannot be of any value or hold any validity in the life of the church today.

So let me be clear about something in this book before we get started. I will do my very best to stay rooted in and tethered to the inspired and infallible Word of God. I will strive to justify my conclusions based on what Scripture says. I realize that some in the professing Christian community believe this is too restrictive, that it puts limitations on what God might choose to do in our day that the church so desperately needs. I do not share that fear. My fear in fact is that once we step outside the governing rule of the Bible, we are subject to all manner of deception and abuse.

God doesn't speak out of both sides of His mouth. He didn't say something about the nature and operation of tongues in the first century only then to reverse Himself and render those guidelines superfluous for us in the present day. The Bible is our functional authority when it comes to the gift of tongues (or any other gift, for that matter). I am governed by and submissive to its teaching. Its guidelines and the boundaries it articulates are no less applicable and essential in the contemporary church than they were in the early days of church life in the middle of the first century. I trust that my commitment to the functional authority of Scripture will be evident on every page that follows.

MAINTAINING A BIBLICAL PERSPECTIVE

As we prepare to explore this spiritual gift called speaking in tongues, let's make a commitment not to repeat the error of the Corinthians. Among their many problems, their immaturity was most readily seen in the way they overvalued tongues, as if it were the most important gift from God and a sure and certain indication that those who had received it were extraordinarily blessed and highly spiritual. As you'll hear me say repeatedly throughout this book, tongues is neither the best gift nor the worst gift. It is simply a gift like all the others.

When the apostle Paul exhorts us all to "earnestly desire the spiritual gifts" (1 Cor. 14:1), he means *all* spiritual gifts, not just tongues and not just prophecy. Some gifts are more overtly miraculous, while others are seemingly mundane. But nowhere does the New Testament place a value judgment on any particular gift based on that distinction. We must resist the temptation to exalt tongues above teaching, or to place a higher value on mercy than on prophecy, or to put healing above evangelism. This may seem to you as if I'm speaking out of both sides of my mouth. After all, I haven't written a book on the gifts of administration or giving or exhortation. So if tongues isn't special, why is it deserving of book-length treatment? That's a fair question.

Unlike the many other spiritual gifts, tongues is uniquely controversial (of course, prophecy, healing, and words of knowledge can just as readily provoke heated debate). And it is often misunderstood. On top of it all, sadly, tongues has the potential to be horribly divisive. I have never yet heard of a church split that cited as the principal cause a dispute over the legitimacy of teaching or serving others. But countless are the times I've heard of angry arguments and eventual divisions in the body of Christ because of the gift of tongues.

Now, let me bring a word of clarity to that last statement. *The problem isn't tongues.* The problem isn't that there is something inherently defective or divisive in this gift. The problem is always our sin, our ungodly ambition, our judgmental attitude, our tendency to exalt ourselves above others as if God loves us more based solely on the gifts He has given us. We must be careful that we do not swing to either end of the spectrum. At one extreme is the belief that we should focus on tongues because it is the inescapable mark of God's unique blessing. At the other end is the equally misguided belief that tongues is dangerous and not worth the effort it takes to understand it correctly and practice it to the building up of others and the glory of God. My aim is to shed biblical and pastoral light on this gift so it might operate in the lives of God's people in a way that all are encouraged and blessed and built up by it.

We're now ready to dive into the deep end of the pool and explore this phenomenon called speaking in tongues. Before we do, let me say something briefly about the way I've structured this book. My hope and prayer is that all of you will start at the beginning and read consecutively through each chapter. I believe that in doing so, you will more greatly profit than if you merely skip around. However, in attempting to answer what I believe are *the thirty most crucial questions* about this spiritual gift, some of you may wish to cherry-pick, as it were. Each question and its answer stand independently and can be read in any order you prefer. So if you see a question in the list of thirty that is especially intriguing, feel free to jump ahead and dive in there. Or you may find it helpful to move back and forth. Read in whatever order you believe will prove most beneficial to your growing understanding of this gift, because understanding is what we're after. So however you choose to read the following pages, enjoy!

Chapter 1

MY FIRST EXPERIENCE
OF SPEAKING IN TONGUES

THERE IS NOTHING in my early life that might suggest I would be a good candidate for speaking in tongues. In fact, precisely the opposite is true. Although I was raised in a godly home where both my parents were fervent Christians and my only sibling, a sister four years my senior, was likewise born again, our lives were far removed from anything remotely Charismatic. Before I entered the University of Oklahoma in 1969, my family had attended a Southern Baptist church in whatever city in which we lived. While in college in Oklahoma City I was quite active in an independent Baptist church whose entire pastoral staff was comprised of graduates of Dallas Theological Seminary, an institution I would later attend that is widely known for its dispensational and cessationist theology.

Southern Baptists up to that point in time were rarely known to be involved in what had come to be known as the Charismatic

Renewal.[1] We all believed in the Holy Spirit, but little was said of Him or His ministry aside from His work in producing what is known as the new birth. If our Pentecostal and Charismatic brethren were ever mentioned, and it was quite rare for them even to be noted in polite conversation, they were held up for ridicule and disdain. They were known as "gibberers" in my house, those who regularly spoke in mindless and meaningless gibberish.

It wasn't until the summer of 1970, following my freshman year at the University of Oklahoma, that I had my first encounter with Charismatic Christians. Although he wasn't enthusiastic about it, my father granted me permission to participate in a summer evangelistic project in Lake Tahoe, Nevada, sponsored by what was then known as Campus Crusade for Christ (now Cru). Most of the thirty-five or so who were present worked a job during the day and engaged in either a Bible study or street and beach evangelism at night. I worked the entire summer at a Shell gas station across the street from the place where all of us lived. There wasn't much excitement in that, except for Fridays, when the motorcycle gangs from Sacramento and San Francisco would descend upon that resort city. Their first stop upon entering the outskirts of Tahoe was to fill up at my service station. I thank God for the courage and opportunity to share the gospel with a few of them before the summer ended.

My perspective on the church and Christians as a whole was profoundly shaken that summer. This was due, in no small measure, to a visit I made to the campus of the University of California, Berkeley. You must remember that this was the late spring, early summer of 1970. It was a time of hippies, the Vietnam War and its protestors, the Kent State shootings, hallucinogenic drugs, and the emergence of what came to be known as the Jesus movement. While in Berkeley, I spent a couple of days with those who called themselves the Christian World Liberation Front, or CWLF. Let me assure you that nothing in my nineteen years as a Southern

Baptist from Oklahoma prepared me for the radical, offbeat approach to Christianity I encountered there! Although my exposure to the CWLF was brief, I was challenged in a positive way to be a bit more open and tolerant of those who worshipped and lived out their life in Jesus in ways that differed from my own.[2]

My spiritual life was deeply impacted at the close of my summer in Tahoe when I attended a meeting at which Lutheran pastor Harald Bredesen was scheduled to speak. I had never heard of him before that night but soon learned he was one of the early leaders of the Charismatic movement. In the course of the evening he mentioned a book by John Sherrill titled *They Speak With Other Tongues*. The story Bredesen told of Sherrill's experience wasn't even remotely similar to my life in God. But he had my attention. I stayed after the Bible study was over and spoke with Bredesen for a few minutes. He gave me a copy of Sherrill's book, and I read it immediately.

In almost complete defiance of my spiritual experience at that point in time, the issue of speaking in tongues immediately became an obsession with me. As my time of ministry in the beautiful Sierra Nevadas concluded, I returned to the University of Oklahoma to continue my studies as a sophomore. My plans at that time were to join the staff of Crusade following graduation. Little did I realize that Crusade's "unofficial official" policy regarding Charismatic experience was quite negative. Speaking in tongues, as I would soon discover, was off-limits.

For the first two months of my sophomore year I followed the same routine every night, Monday through Sunday. At ten o'clock each night I would walk two blocks from my fraternity house to the playground of the McKinley elementary school, where I would spend anywhere from thirty minutes to an hour praying earnestly that if the gift were real, God would give it to me. I wasn't exactly sure what I was praying for. Nevertheless, for several weeks I spent each night pleading with God for some indication of His will for me concerning this gift.

I can't say that I ever expected anything to happen. My skepticism toward spiritual gifts like tongues was deep-seated and pervasive. As already noted, my education and experience in Christianity, at least to this point, was decidedly cessationist. One thing is certain: I was not "primed," so to speak, either psychologically or spiritually, for what eventually happened.

HIJACKED BY THE SPIRIT

One night in October of 1970, as I sat at the foot of a large tree in that school playground (the tree, by the way, is still there!), quite without warning my normal, somewhat-routine prayer was radically interrupted. It's important for you to understand that I didn't experiment with speaking in tongues. I made no attempt to pray "banana" backward over and over again. Often people instruct those without the gift simply to start speaking whatever syllables or words pop into their minds. That may well be good advice, but I did nothing of the sort. I made no conscious effort to alter my speech patterns.

It was as if my normal English prayers were hijacked by the Spirit. I suddenly began speaking forth words of uncertain sound and form. Once again, I didn't start out by consciously muttering a few senseless syllables that then gave way to a more coherent linguistic experience. It was more like a spiritual invasion in which the Spirit intruded on my life, interrupted my speech patterns, and "gave...utterance" (Acts 2:4).

There was a profound and utterly unexpected intensification of my sense of God's nearness and power. I distinctly remember feeling a somewhat detached sensation, as if I were separate from the one speaking. I had never experienced anything remotely similar to that in all my life. While this linguistic flood continued to pour forth, I carried on a separate dialogue within my own mind: "Sam, what are you saying? Are you speaking in tongues?" It was the first time I had ever experienced the sensation of thinking in one language while speaking in another.

I realize how odd this may sound. It will strike some of you as delusion. Trust me when I say I completely understand that reaction. The closest way I can come to describing what happened is that it felt as though the veil between my life on earth and the realities of heaven had been removed. The sense of the supernatural invading the natural was virtually tangible. Nearly half a century has passed since that October evening, and nothing I've seen, sensed, or felt during that time can remotely compare with what I experienced on the playground of that elementary school.

My initial reaction to something so unfamiliar and new was a strange mixture of both fear and exhilaration. I don't recall precisely how long it lasted, but it couldn't have been more than a couple of minutes. I was confused, but at the same time I felt closer to God than ever before. At the time, I didn't have theological categories to describe what happened. My Pentecostal friends would probably insist that this was my baptism in the Holy Spirit and that my speaking in tongues was the "initial physical evidence" that this event had actually occurred. After all, I had been born again a decade earlier, when I was around the age of nine.

As you will discover later in this book, I believe Spirit baptism is simultaneous with conversion. In other words, I believe the New Testament teaches that all believers are baptized in the Spirit at the first moment they turn in faith to Jesus Christ. I have no desire to quarrel with (much less divide from) those who differ with me on this point. I honestly don't think it's that big of a deal. What's important is whether our post-conversion encounters with the Spirit are real. Does the New Testament give us reason to believe we can experience a greater and more powerful outpouring of the Spirit than what we received when we first believed in Jesus? In my opinion, yes. Whether we call this event "Spirit baptism" or "Spirit filling" or "Spirit anointing" is entirely secondary to the more pressing question of whether the Holy Spirit is actually doing something in us or on our behalf beyond what happened at conversion.

As I reflect on that October evening, I'm more inclined to view it as a powerful filling of the Holy Spirit rather than Spirit baptism (although, as you can tell, I'm open to being convinced otherwise). Having said that, I must confess that when I look for words to describe it, the only thing that comes to mind is immersion and saturation, a sense of being inundated or flooded with the presence of God.

Those who have had a similar experience know why I struggle to describe what happened. My relationship with God to that point had been largely, if not entirely, intellectual. I'm not questioning the reality of my salvation. I'm simply saying that aside from a few emotional moments in church as a young boy, and the miraculous healing of a migraine headache when I was eleven years old, I had no tangible awareness of a dimension of reality beyond what I could encounter through the five senses. But on the night in question it was as though the barrier that separated my being from the being of God was lifted. My spirit was engulfed by the Spirit of God. Neither before nor since that day have I felt so directly, empirically, and undeniably in touch with the realm of the supernatural.

Although the onset of tongues was unexpected, I consciously chose to stop speaking. I jumped to my feet, returned to my fraternity house filled with excitement, and called a friend who was on staff with Campus Crusade for Christ. I didn't tell him what had happened, only that I needed to speak with him immediately. Thirty minutes later I sat down in his car and said, "You'll never guess what happened tonight."

"You spoke in tongues, didn't you?" he asked, almost deadpan.

"Yes! How did you know? It was great. But I don't understand what it means."

This man cared deeply for me and had no intention of offending me or obstructing my Christian growth. But what he said next affected me for years to come.

"Sam, you do realize, don't you, that you will have to resign your position as student leader and give up any hope of joining staff when you graduate. Campus Crusade doesn't permit people who speak in tongues to hold positions of authority. Of course, if you don't do it again, there's no need for us to tell anyone. Everything can be the same as it was before."

I was crushed and profoundly confused. I remember feebly and fearfully trying to speak in tongues the next night, but nothing happened. Not wanting to forfeit my position in the ministry on campus, I concluded that it must have been something other than the Holy Spirit. I never thought it was demonic, although many of my friends did. I explained it away as a momentary emotional outburst that I'd be better off forgetting. I rarely spoke of the incident in the years following, fearful of the disdain of my friends who looked with suspicion on anyone remotely associated with or showing interest in the gift of tongues. Needless to say, I didn't speak in tongues again for twenty years!

I think it's important to point out that deep within my heart I always knew the experience was a genuine encounter with the Spirit of God. My agreement with those who explained it (away) by appealing to psychological factors was prompted less by conviction than by my fear of incurring their ridicule or, worse still, losing their friendship. I also believe that my attempt to write it off as a momentary, one-time phenomenon better left in the past was offensive to God and a clear instance of quenching the Holy Spirit.

Following graduation in May of 1973, my wife and I immediately moved to Dallas to begin my study at Dallas Theological

Seminary (DTS) in preparation for ministry. I loved my time at DTS. The fact that my theological trajectory has taken a different turn from what I was taught at Dallas does not in any way diminish the respect I had then and have today for the education in God's Word DTS provided. But the entire faculty was committed to the belief that certain spiritual gifts, such as speaking in tongues, were restricted to the first century of the early church.[3] I was taught in virtually every class that once the first generation of apostles died out, so too did the gift of tongues. Out of respect for my instructors I embraced this perspective and taught it faithfully throughout the first fifteen years of my public ministry. But all the while my personal experience from several years earlier was lingering in the back of my mind and haunting me with the reminder of what God had done.

I have written elsewhere of my transition from a cessationist who regularly mocked Charismatic practices to a continuationist who not only believes in but regularly pursues and practices the full range of spiritual gifts.[4] Here I would only point out that my theological transition from an evangelical cessationist to an evangelical continuationist or Charismatic began sometime in late 1987 with my reading of D. A. Carson's book *Showing the Spirit: A Theological Exposition of 1 Corinthians 12–14*. But I digress.

Slightly more than twenty years subsequent to that October experience in the McKinley School playground, in November of 1990, I attended the annual meeting of the Evangelical Theological Society in New Orleans. While there I spent time with Jack Deere, a close friend and former classmate at DTS. Jack is the author of *Surprised by the Power of the Spirit* and *Surprised by the Voice of God*, both excellent biblical refutations of cessationism. Jack taught Old Testament and Hebrew at DTS for twelve years before being dismissed because of his embrace of continuationism. At the time of our visit in New Orleans he was serving as an associate of John Wimber's at the Anaheim Vineyard in California.

At dinner one night I shared with him my journey and told him about what had happened back in the fall of 1970, hoping to gain additional insight into the nature of my experience and what God's will for me might be. He then reminded me of something the apostle Paul said to young Timothy: "For this reason I remind you to fan into flame ["kindle afresh" in the NASB] the gift of God, which is in you through the laying on of my hands" (2 Tim. 1:6). Jack then laid hands on me and asked the Lord to kindle afresh in me this gift He had bestowed so many years before.

This verse in 2 Timothy is important. It tells us that one may receive a spiritual gift only to neglect and ignore it. The imagery Paul uses is helpful. He describes a spiritual gift in terms of a flame that needs to be continually fanned. If it is not understood, nurtured, and utilized in the way God intended, the once brightly burning flame can be reduced to a smoldering ember. He says in essence, "Take whatever steps you must: study, pray, seek God's face, put it into practice, but by all means stoke the fire until that gift returns to its original intensity."[5]

I took Paul's advice to Timothy and applied it to my own case. Every day, if only for a few minutes, I prayed that God would renew what He had given but I had quenched. I prayed that if it was His will, I would once more be able to pray in the Spirit, to speak the heavenly language that would praise and thank and bless Him. (See 1 Corinthians 14:2, 16, 17.) Unlike my first experience with tongues, I didn't wait for some sort of divine seizure but in faith began simply to speak forth the syllables and words the Spirit of God brought to mind.

Nearly thirty years have passed now since God renewed His precious gift in my life. Praying in the Spirit is by no means the most important gift. Neither is it a sign of a spirituality or maturity greater than that of those who don't have this particular gift. On the other hand, no gift of God is to be despised, ridiculed, or suppressed. If no less a man than the apostle Paul can say, "I thank

God that I speak in tongues more than all of you" (1 Cor. 14:18), who are we to despise this blessed gift of God?

As I said in the introduction, this book is built around the asking and answering of what I believe are the thirty most crucial questions regarding speaking in tongues. So let's begin.

Chapter 2

TONGUES IN SCRIPTURE

THE BOOK OF ACTS is often a battleground for any number of issues related to the Holy Spirit and local church life. That certainly is true when it comes to the spiritual gift of speaking in tongues. Therefore, it is here that we begin our study of what the New Testament says about this gift. It often comes as a surprise to many that tongues is explicitly mentioned in only three chapters in Acts, the most extensive of which is Acts 2 and the events associated with the day of Pentecost. So it is there that we begin.

1. What happened on the day of Pentecost?

Pentecost is the day in the church calendar that typically comes on the fiftieth day after the Sabbath of Passover week.[1] As you probably know, it was on the day of Pentecost in Acts 2 that the Holy Spirit was poured out on the followers of Jesus. We shouldn't take this to mean that the Spirit was inactive or absent before Pentecost. But a decidedly new and more expansive dimension to His activity and empowering presence in believers began on that day.

Pentecost was the event that fulfilled the prophecy of Jesus to His disciples in Luke 24:49. "And behold," Jesus said, "I am sending the promise of my Father upon you. But stay in the city until you are clothed with power from on high." Clearly, then, the focus of Pentecost is *the coming of the Holy Spirit*, His indwelling presence in our lives, and the power He brings to enable us to do what we otherwise could never accomplish.

As we begin our exploration into the nature and practice of speaking in tongues, it only seems fitting that we should begin with Acts 2 and the events that transpired on the day of Pentecost. Several questions immediately come to mind. For example, *where* did this event occur? We know they were in Jerusalem. According to Acts 2:2, they were all gathered together in a "house" (cf. Acts 1:12–26), whose we don't know.

What exactly happened? Let me respond to this question with two answers. First, the events of Pentecost were *a singular phenomenon in history*. In other words, *there is only one day of Pentecost* when the Holy Spirit was poured out on the people of God. It was historically unique, which means it is not correct to speak of people elsewhere throughout the world, down through the centuries, each experiencing their own Pentecost. However, it is equally important to remember that although the day of Pentecost and the outpouring of the Holy Spirit could only happen once, as a singular event in redemptive history, the effects or aftermath or fruit of the Spirit's coming are experienced at all times throughout the course of church history. Let me try to explain this in simple terms.

We are told in Acts 2:2 that when the Spirit came, "a sound like a mighty rushing wind" filled the house where they were gathered. Many suggest this makes perfect sense given the fact that *pneuma*, the Greek word for *Spirit*, is also the Greek word for *wind* or *breath*. The word *wind* is a recurring sign of or reference to the Spirit (e.g., John 3:8; Ezek. 37:9–14). However, perhaps we shouldn't make too much of this since the Greek word for *wind* in

Acts 2:2 is not *pneuma* but *pnoē*. In any case, we do not expect that this same sound of "rushing wind" will occur again each and every time someone receives the power of the Spirit.

Likewise, we are told in Acts 2:3 that "tongues as of fire" appeared to everyone and "rested" on each one of them. A more literal translation of Acts 2:3 would be that these tongues of fire were "divided" and "rested on each one of them." This is massively important because under the old covenant, before the coming of Jesus, the Spirit ministered corporately and only came on selected individuals personally (kings, priests, prophets, and military commanders, for instance). In the new covenant the Spirit now comes upon and resides within each believer individually. This is the "democratization" of the Spirit!

This point is reinforced in Acts 2:17, where Peter quotes the prophecy of Joel to the effect that when the Spirit comes, He will be poured out "on all flesh," that is to say, not just on kings, prophets, and priests but on every child of God: every man and woman, every son and daughter, young and old. Look closely at the extent of the Spirit's presence in Acts 2:17–18: "all flesh," meaning irrespective of *age* ("old men" and "young men"), without regard to *gender* ("sons" and "daughters" and "male servants" and "female servants"), with no thought or special favors given to *social rank* ("servants"), and on people of every *race* ("all flesh"; cf. Acts 2:39; i.e., both Jew and Gentile). So it would appear that flames of "fire" in the shape of the human tongue rested on the head of each person present. This was to serve both as a sign of God's powerful presence and as a sign of the gift of speaking in tongues that was to follow.

These two sensory phenomena of both sound and sight were a one-time occurrence that marked the Spirit's entrance into the life of all God's people. Whereas I would never say that God couldn't do this yet again, I don't live with the expectation that He will. I think these two sensory phenomena were uniquely tied to the one event of the Spirit's coming at Pentecost.

Having said that, and this is my second response to the question I asked above, what the disciples of Jesus experienced as a result of the Spirit's descent is something we most assuredly should expect and pray for. The Spirit Himself comes only once. He is now here. He doesn't need to repeat His arrival as occurred on Pentecost. But what He did among the disciples at Pentecost in the first century He most certainly has continued to do among all God's people in every subsequent century.

Look again at the opening words of Acts 2:17. There Peter, quoting Joel, tells us that what was happening then on the day of Pentecost is something that is to characterize "the last days." Let me emphasize the word *characterize*. Some have tried to argue that the events that occurred on the day of Pentecost back in the first century were designed solely to launch or inaugurate or jump-start the age of the new covenant. Now, make no mistake, the coming of the Spirit in power on Pentecost most assuredly did launch or jump-start the new covenant age in which we now live. But what the Spirit did on that day centuries ago is also designed by God to characterize the experience of God's people throughout the course of this age until Jesus comes back.

We must never forget that the "last days" Joel had in view when he uttered this prophecy back in the late seventh or early sixth century BC was the entire present age in which we now live. In other words, the "last days" began on the day of Pentecost and extend all the way until Jesus returns. The "last days," or the era of the new covenant, have now extended for nearly two thousand years. (See 2 Timothy 3:1; Hebrews 1:1–2; 9:26; James 5:3; 1 Peter 1:20; 1 John 2:18; cf. also 1 Corinthians 10:11 and 1 Timothy 4:1.) Most Christians make the mistake of thinking that when the New Testament speaks of the "last days," it has in view the final few years of human history immediately preceding the second coming of Christ. Thus, what we read in Acts 2:17–21 is a description of what the Holy Spirit does in, through, and on behalf of God's people throughout the entire course of this present age.

SPEAKING IN TONGUES ON THE DAY OF PENTECOST

There is some dispute among scholars as to who constituted those who "were dwelling in Jerusalem" on the day in question. They are described as "Jews, devout men from every nation under heaven" (Acts 2:5). Some argue that the word translated "were dwelling" suggests these were Jews of the Diaspora who had returned to live in Jerusalem, perhaps even choosing to retire there. Others contend that they were among the nearly one million Jewish pilgrims who had come to Jerusalem to celebrate the Feast of Pentecost. The likelihood is that both are true, the crowd consisting of both resident Jews who had migrated back to Jerusalem and visitors from the many nations listed in Acts 2:9–11.

Did all the disciples speak simultaneously? Theologian Eckhard Schnabel believes not, insisting in his commentary on the Book of Acts that "since people in the crowd understood both the languages being spoken and the content of what was being said (v. 11), presumably the believers spoke one after the other."[2] There is no way to be certain on this point, and it does not affect our understanding of the phenomenon either way.

The reaction among those present that day is described in Acts 2 with a variety of different terms. According to verse 6, they were "bewildered." In verse 7 we read that they were "amazed and astonished." The word *amazed* is used again in verse 12 together with the word rendered "perplexed." Finally, in verse 13 Luke describes them as "mocking" the disciples or subjecting them to ridicule or scorn. The charge that they were "filled with new wine" (v. 13) suggests they mistakenly took the energetic joy and freedom of the disciples as an indication of inebriation.

On the other hand, "a perhaps more plausible explanation takes the reaction of the 'scoffers' as a sarcastic insult that does not care whether the accusation can be correct."[3] In either case, as Schnabel points out, "the hostile reaction of a minority is not a contradiction to what Luke has said about the people in the crowd who understand the words uttered in their own language. Either these are people who do not recognize any of the languages spoken—perhaps Jews who have always lived in Jerusalem—or their taunts are directed against the exuberant joy of the believers who praise God with loud voices and ostentatious conviction (v. 4)."[4]

Were the "tongues" spoken on the day of Pentecost an example of *xenolalia*, which is to say, the ability to speak real human languages? In my opinion, yes, they were. This seems to be a justified conclusion based on several things we see in this passage. For example, we read of the variety of nations represented (Acts 2:8–11), which would certainly suggest this. The word translated "tongue" (*glōssa*) in Acts 2:3 refers either to the literal organ in our mouths or to real human language. Observe also that the word *language* (Acts 2:6, 8, which is the Greek word *dialektōs*, meaning dialect) points to human languages known throughout the world (cf. Acts 1:19; 21:40; 22:2; 26:14).

Can this phenomenon still occur today? Absolutely, yes. But in my opinion it happens quite rarely. Don't be misled by what I just said. I said speaking in tongues that are genuine, human languages the speaker never studied is quite rare today. I've heard quite a few personal testimonies from missionaries who have had such experiences as they encountered people whose language they hadn't learned.[5] But I'm persuaded that the spiritual gift of speaking in tongues that continues throughout church history and is so widespread today is the Spirit-prompted ability to pray and praise God in a heavenly dialect, possibly even an angelic language that is not related to anything spoken on earth, such as German, Swahili, Mandarin, or English.

In other words, I believe the vast majority of instances where speaking in tongues occurs today are best explained as the Holy Spirit personally crafting or creating a special and unique language that enables a Christian to speak to God in prayer, praise, and thanksgiving. This gift is not a human language that one might encounter in some foreign country but a Spirit-empowered capacity to speak meaningful words that are only understood by our triune God: Father, Son, and Holy Spirit.

Could it be the case that some of the disciples present that day had previously studied and mastered one or more of the "dialects" represented by the pilgrims in Jerusalem? It is highly unlikely, especially in view of what Luke says in Acts 2:4. There he declares that they "began to speak in other tongues as the Spirit gave them utterance." This would strongly suggest that "the words they utter are not of human origin but have been 'given' [*didōmi*] by the Spirit."[6] The biblical text simply will not permit us to account for this phenomenon in any way other than by the miraculous intervention of the Holy Spirit.

Some insist that the tongues in Acts 2 were not human languages. They contend that Luke is describing not the hearing *of* one's own language but the hearing *in* one's own language. In other words, as J. Rodman Williams has argued, what occurred at Pentecost wasn't so much a miracle of speaking but a miracle of hearing. "At the same moment that 'other tongues' were spoken through the Holy Spirit, they were immediately translated by the same Holy Spirit into the many languages of the multitude."[7] Thus there was no identifiable linguistic content or structure to what the disciples said. What made their speech intelligible wasn't the fact that they were speaking in the actual languages of the people present at Pentecost but rather the work of the Spirit in the minds of the latter by which they were enabled to "hear" these utterances in their native tongues. Three times in Acts 2 Luke tells us that those present were "hearing" (v. 6) them speak in their own language. Again, they ask: "And how is it that we hear, each of us in his own native language?" (v. 8). Finally, they said: "we hear them telling in our own tongues the mighty works of God" (v. 11). Thus, Williams argues that there is *both* a miracle of "speech"—other, different, spiritual tongues—*and* a miracle of "understanding," each facilitated by the Holy Spirit.[8]

If this view is correct, a miraculous *charisma* of the Holy Spirit (namely, the gift of interpretation) was given to every *unbeliever* present on the day of Pentecost. But as D. A. Carson has noted, it is Luke's purpose "to associate the descent of the Spirit with the Spirit's activity *among the believers,* not to postulate a miracle of the Spirit *among those who were still unbelievers.*"[9] Nothing in the text explicitly speaks of the Holy Spirit descending on the crowd but rather on the disciples. Or, as Max Turner puts it, surely Luke "would not wish to suggest that the apostolic band merely prattled incomprehensibly, while God worked the yet greater miracle of interpretation of tongues in the *un*believers."[10] One should also note that "Luke reports their speaking 'other languages' before mentioning that anyone hears them (2:4)."[11]

Later in this book I will undertake to demonstrate from the text of Scripture that the tongues-speech in Acts 2, on the day of Pentecost, is not the same as the tongues-speech in 1 Corinthians 12–14. The tongues-speech here in Acts 2 was genuine, previously unlearned human languages whereas the tongues-speech in 1 Corinthians 12–14 is either an angelic dialect or a heavenly language crafted by the Spirit for each individual believer to whom God chooses to supply this gift.

Finally, as far as Acts 2 and Pentecost are concerned, we are told by Peter, who is using the prophecy of Joel in the Old Testament, that God's people will "prophesy," "see visions," and "dream dreams" (vv. 17–18). It isn't the purpose of this book to demonstrate why these experiences continue to occur in the life of the church today. But it should be obvious to all who are reading that I am a continuationist, which is to say I believe all these gifts and activities of the

Holy Spirit continue throughout the present church age and will continue to be operative right up until the time Jesus returns to this earth.

WHAT IS THE MEANING OF PENTECOST?

So what then is the meaning of Pentecost? I'll be brief. First, we should recognize that this is *not* the first appearance of the Holy Spirit in human history. However, it is the first appearance of the *fullness* of the Spirit to empower and permanently indwell and encourage and enable all of God's people individually.

Furthermore, the events of Pentecost are the fulfillment of three prophetic words: first, the prophecy of Joel 2:28–32 (in accordance with the terms of the new covenant); second, the prophecy of John the Baptist in Matthew 3:11–12; and third, the prophecy of Jesus Himself in John 14:16 concerning the "other Comforter." On the one hand, Pentecost is the pouring out of the Holy Spirit by the risen and exalted Lord Jesus Christ. Listen to Peter's words in Acts 2:32–33:

> This Jesus God raised up, and of that we all are witnesses. Being therefore exalted at the right hand of God, and having received from the Father the promise of the Holy Spirit, he [Jesus] has poured out this that you yourselves are seeing and hearing.

But Pentecost is not simply the Holy Spirit coming to the church but Christ Himself coming to the church in the person of the Holy Spirit. (See John 14:18 and Romans 8:9–10.)

Pentecost has also been described as the birthday of the church, the universal body of Christ. People often ask the question: When did the church begin? What was its birthday? The simplest answer is the day of Pentecost, when the risen Lord Jesus Christ poured out the Spirit and formed His people into a living, spiritual organism called the body of Christ, the church.[12]

Students of Scripture have also observed that Pentecost is the reversal of Babel. We read in Genesis 11 that at Babel God confused human languages and "dispersed" the nations "over the face of all the earth" (Gen. 11:8). We see precisely the reverse taking place at Pentecost, when the language barrier was overcome as a sign that God would now gather the nations together in Christ. At Babel, as someone has said, "earth proudly tried to ascend to heaven," while at Pentecost "heaven humbly descended to earth."[13]

THE POWERFUL WORK OF THE
SPIRIT WHO CAME AT PENTECOST

I want to conduct a very quick overview of the Book of Acts so you may see what the Holy Spirit does. In other words, this is why the Holy Spirit was given.

First, the Holy Spirit fills and empowers God's people to boldly proclaim the truth of the gospel. When Peter was asked by what power the man lame from birth had been healed, we read this:

> Then Peter, filled with the Holy Spirit, said to them...
>
> —ACTS 4:8

This was in fulfillment of something Jesus Himself prophesied back in Matthew 10:19–20:

> When they deliver you over, do not be anxious how you are to speak or what you are to say, for what you are to say will be given to you in that hour. For it is not you who speak, but the Spirit of your Father speaking through you.

The Holy Spirit was already indwelling Peter, but on this occasion *an extraordinary impartation of power* was needed. We read of much the same thing later in Acts 4.

> And when they had prayed, the place in which they were
> gathered together was shaken, and they were all filled
> with the Holy Spirit and continued to speak the word of
> God with boldness.
>
> —ACTS 4:31

Don't miss the causal connection between being filled with the Spirit and speaking or proclaiming the gospel of God fearlessly or boldly (e.g., Acts 5:32; 6:10; 9:17–19; 13:9–11; 18:25). This was especially the case when Stephen was testifying to the religious leaders about Jesus. In the face of certain death Stephen found courage, power, and boldness to unashamedly proclaim the truth of the gospel. How did he do it? Here is what we read in Acts 7.

> Now when they heard these things they were enraged,
> and they ground their teeth at him. But he, full of the
> Holy Spirit, gazed into heaven and saw the glory of God,
> and Jesus standing at the right hand of God. And he said,
> "Behold, I see the heavens opened, and the Son of Man
> standing at the right hand of God."
>
> —ACTS 7:54–56

In other words, we may be filled with the Spirit in a spiritual emergency. This is an immediate and special endowment of power to fulfill an especially important and urgent task. Thus, someone who is already full of the Spirit may experience a further or additional filling. That is, no matter "how much" of the Holy Spirit one may have, there's always room for "more."[14] (See Acts 4:8, 31; 13:9; and Luke 1:41, 67.)

Second, the empowering, indwelling presence of the Holy Spirit was essential for God's people to carry out the wide varieties of ministry for which they were responsible. One example of this is seen in Acts 6 where one of the qualifications for serving as a deacon in the local church is that a person be "full of the Spirit"

(v. 3; see also Acts 11:23–24; 13:52). Even elders are identified, equipped, and appointed by the Holy Spirit. Paul said this to the elders of the church in Ephesus:

> Pay careful attention to yourselves and to all the flock, in which the Holy Spirit has made you overseers, to care for the church of God, which he obtained with his own blood.
> —ACTS 20:28

Third, the ability to perform signs, wonders, and miracles is explicitly said to be the work of the Holy Spirit in and through God's people. For example:

> And Stephen, full of grace and power, was doing great wonders and signs among the people.
> —ACTS 6:8; CF. ACTS 4:30; SEE ALSO 10:38

In the writings of Luke the word *power* is almost always a synonym for the Holy Spirit.

Fourth, it is the Holy Spirit who speaks to God's people and provides guidance to them regarding where, when, and to whom ministry should be extended. The explanation for why Philip preached to the Ethiopian eunuch is explicitly stated:

> And the Spirit said to Philip, "Go over and join this chariot."
> —ACTS 8:29; SEE ALSO ACTS 8:39; 10:19–20; 11:12

The Spirit's role in providing guidance for missionary and evangelistic outreach is clearly seen in Acts 13:2 and 4:

> While they were worshiping the Lord and fasting, the Holy Spirit said, "Set apart for me Barnabas and Saul for the work to which I have called them."...So, being sent out by the Holy Spirit...

Likewise, we read in Acts 16 of how Paul was redirected into Macedonia.

> And they went through the region of Phrygia and Galatia, having been forbidden by the Holy Spirit to speak the word in Asia. And when they had come up to Mysia, they attempted to go into Bithynia, but the Spirit of Jesus did not allow them.
> —Acts 16:6–7; see also 15:28; 19:21; 21:22–23

Fifth, it was by means of the power of the Holy Spirit that God's people would prophesy and speak in tongues. We read in Acts 11:27–30 of prophets who traveled from Jerusalem to Antioch:

> And one of them named Agabus stood up and foretold by the Spirit that there would be a great famine over all the world (this took place in the days of Claudius).
> —Acts 11:28; see also Acts 21:4, 10–11

> And when Paul laid his hands on them, the Holy Spirit came on them, and they began speaking in tongues and prophesying.
> —Acts 19:6

This is but a small sampling of what we find in Acts that is the work of the Holy Spirit who came at Pentecost. And there is no reason to think the Spirit who indwelled, empowered, and filled these early disciples will not do the same for us today.

2. Where else in Acts did people speak in tongues?

Many are quite surprised to discover that apart from what we've just seen in Acts 2, there are only two other occasions where the gift of tongues is explicitly mentioned in the Book of Acts.[15] We shouldn't conclude from this that tongues was rare or unimportant.

In fact, we shouldn't draw any firm conclusions concerning the relative importance of tongues based on the silence we find in Acts. Tongues may well have been present on other occasions, but we can't know that with any degree of certainty. It's just as likely that the gift of tongues was absent. So I'll resist the temptation to speculate and simply direct your attention to Acts 10 and 19, where tongues are explicitly mentioned.

In Acts 10 we read about the spread of the gospel beyond the borders of Israel into the Gentile community. By means of a visionary experience the Gentile centurion Cornelius was instructed to invite Peter to his house in Caesarea. Peter likewise had seen a vision designed to overcome his prejudice against Gentiles (v. 28). When Peter entered the house of Cornelius, he began to preach to him the gospel of salvation by faith in Jesus Christ. This is a monumental development in the Book of Acts and especially in the cross-cultural expansion of the church beyond the borders of ethnic Israel.

The Holy Spirit didn't wait until Peter was finished with his sermon before falling on "all who heard the word" (v. 44). Presumably the Gentiles had come to faith in the message Peter preached quite early on in their encounter. The Jewish believers who had accompanied Peter to Caesarea were astounded "because the gift of the Holy Spirit was poured out even on the Gentiles" (v. 45). How did they know this? On what basis did they draw the conclusion that these Gentiles had received the Spirit even as they had? It is because "they were hearing them speaking in tongues and extolling God" (v. 46).[16]

We are immediately confronted with a question: Is this a description of two separate phenomena of speech or only one? That is to say, did they first speak in tongues and then also, after that, speak in their native language, extolling and glorifying God? Or were they "extolling God" by means of their tongues-speech? In other words, is this a case of praise in tongues in which the content of the tongues-speech was worship? The latter is more likely. But this does raise several additional questions.

There is nothing in Acts 10 to suggest that the tongues-speech of Cornelius and his friends was actual human languages. In Acts 2 it is quite otherwise, given the presence of countless individuals from a variety of nations and linguistic backgrounds. Most cessationists simply assume that what occurred in Acts 10 is identical to what we find in Acts 2. But an assumption is not an argument. What *reasons* are there, derived from the text of Scripture itself, that would lead us to this conclusion?

If their tongues-speech was identical to what occurred at Pentecost and consisted of foreign human languages that neither Cornelius nor his companions had previously studied, how would Peter and the other Jewish believers have known this? Schnabel suggests that "Hebrew or Aramaic was [likely] among the languages being spoken—languages that Cornelius or some of his friends may not have been able to speak but languages that Peter and his friends from Joppa would have understood."[17] But this is nowhere stated or implied in the narrative. David Peterson, on the other hand, insists that what happened at Pentecost was unique and singular: "There is no indication in the [New Testament] that this ever happened again."[18] He proceeds to argue that "the glossolalia in 10:46 and 19:6 is more likely to have been the phenomenon described in 1 Corinthians 12–14, which required interpretation."[19]

Much is left unstated in this passage. At minimum Peter and his companions heard enough that sounded sufficiently parallel to what happened at Pentecost that the only reasonable conclusion was that Cornelius and his friends were similarly blessed with the Spirit's presence and gifting. It's entirely possible, but purely speculative on my part, that following their tongues-speech, a conversation ensued in which Peter and his companions queried the Gentiles as to what had happened, asking questions designed to

THE LANGUAGE OF HEAVEN

identify the nature of their experience. Or it may be that the Spirit granted the Jewish believers the gift of interpretation so they might know what was being spoken by the Gentiles.

Of course, our primary concern here is whether this story supports the idea that when anyone receives the Holy Spirit for the first time, he or she will invariably speak in tongues. That they most assuredly did on this occasion is beyond dispute. Those who endorse this view also point to Acts 11:17, where Peter recounts the incident to Jewish believers in Jerusalem. His conclusion is this: "If then God gave the same gift to them as he gave to us when we believed in the Lord Jesus Christ, who was I that I could stand in God's way?" However, the "same gift" most likely is the Holy Spirit Himself, not tongues, for we know that Peter and the disciples had "believed in the Lord Jesus Christ" long before Pentecost but did not speak in tongues until that day.

There simply is too little evidence from this passage to draw any firm conclusion one way or the other. It is entirely possible that the gift of tongues was given to all these Gentile believers because that is what happens when a person is converted and receives the Spirit. But it is equally possible that the gift of tongues was given in this instance to mark the colossal implications of the gospel reaching cross-culturally beyond Israel into the world of Gentiles. If the latter is true, then we should not expect that every time a person believes in Jesus and receives the Spirit, he or she can expect to speak in tongues. In this case tongues was a unique phenomenon marking this redemptive/historical transition in the spread of the gospel and the building of the church of Jesus Christ.

The third and most likely final incident involving tongues-speech is found in Acts 19:1–7. We should read the text together:

> And it happened that while Apollos was at Corinth, Paul
> passed through the inland country and came to Ephesus.
> There he found some disciples. And he said to them, "Did

34

you receive the Holy Spirit when you believed?" And they said, "No, we have not even heard that there is a Holy Spirit." And he said, "Into what then were you baptized?" They said, "Into John's baptism." And Paul said, "John baptized with the baptism of repentance, telling the people to believe in the one who was to come after him, that is, Jesus." On hearing this, they were baptized in the name of the Lord Jesus. And when Paul had laid his hands on them, the Holy Spirit came on them, and they began speaking in tongues and prophesying. There were about twelve men in all.

Some argue from this passage that these are Christian men who had not yet received the Holy Spirit. It is only after Paul prays for them (i.e., subsequent to their faith) that they are "baptized in the Spirit." I believe this interpretation is largely fueled by the erroneous translation of Acts 19:2 in the King James Version (emphasis added): "Have ye received the Holy Ghost *since* ye believed [or *after* you believed]?" The correct translation is found in the English Standard Version, New American Standard Bible, and New International Version (emphasis added): "Did you receive the Holy Spirit *when* you believed?" Paul's question in Acts 19:2 is designed to uncover what kind of "belief" or "faith" they had experienced. If their belief was "saving," Christian belief, then they would have received the Holy Spirit (Rom. 8:9). The fact that they had not received the Holy Spirit proved to Paul that their "belief" was not "Christian" belief. Says New Testament scholar James Dunn, author of *Baptism in the Holy Spirit*:

> "It was inconceivable to him [Paul] that a Christian, one who had committed himself to Jesus as Lord in baptism in his name, could be yet without the Spirit. This is why the twelve had to go through the full initiation procedure. It was not that Paul accepted them as Christians with

an incomplete experience; it is rather that they were not Christians at all. The absence of the Spirit indicated that they had not even begun the Christian life."[20]

Their response, "No, we have not even heard that there is a Holy Spirit" (Acts 19:2), does not mean they had never before so much as heard of the Spirit's existence. The Holy Spirit is frequently mentioned in the Old Testament, and John the Baptist's own words to his followers (among whom these people included themselves) were that the Messiah would baptize in "Spirit" and fire. The point is that although they had heard John's prophecy of Messianic "Spirit baptism," they were not aware of its fulfillment. In other words, *they were ignorant of Pentecost.*

But if these people were not "Christian" disciples, what kind of disciples were they? G. R. Beasley-Murray, author of *Baptism in the New Testament*, offers this explanation:

> There is...nothing improbable in the existence of groups of people baptized by followers of John the Baptist and standing at varying degrees of distance from (or nearness to) the Christian Church. There must have been many baptized by John himself, who had listened to the preaching of Jesus and His disciples, who had received the gospel with more or less intensity of conviction and faith and regarded themselves as His followers, yet who had no part in Pentecost or its developments....In Paul's eyes these men were not Christians—no man who was without the Spirit of Jesus had any part in the Christ (Rom. 8:9). Probably Luke himself did not view them as Christians; his employment of the term...disciples, is a gesture in recognition that they were neither on a level with unbelieving Jews, nor classed with pagans. They were men who had paused on the way without completing the journey, half-Christians, occupying a zone of territory that could exist

only at that period of history when the effects of John's labors overlapped with those of Jesus.[21]

Thus, when Paul discovers they had not received the Holy Spirit, he knows immediately they are not Christians. Upon realizing that they were but disciples of John, Paul proclaimed Jesus, in whom they believe, at which point they received the Holy Spirit.

Our primary concern is whether their reception of tongues provides us with a paradigm or pattern for what should happen in the case of all at the moment they first come to saving faith in Jesus and receive the Holy Spirit. The first problem is that they not only speak in tongues but also begin to prophesy (Acts 19:6). Few, if any, argue that the ability to prophesy is the invariable evidence of having received the Spirit. So why would we believe that tongues is? But more important still is the fact that, as noted earlier, these "disciples" lived in a salvation-historical time warp that cannot be reproduced beyond the time of the New Testament. They lived in the overlap between the ages that is not found subsequent to their lifetime.

It would, therefore, be unwise to draw any definitive or dogmatic conclusions about the relation of tongues to reception of the Spirit based solely on their experience. Thus, I concur with Craig Keener, who argues that "Luke reports such phenomena to assure us that these disciples received the Spirit (especially the dimension of cross-cultural empowerment), and probably not to imply that tongues necessarily must accompany Spirit reception in every individual instance."[22]

Chapter 3

TONGUES AND SPIRIT BAPTISM

CONSIDERABLE CONTROVERSY HAS centered around the question of the relationship between speaking in tongues and Spirit baptism. Many in the classical Pentecostal tradition insist that Spirit baptism is an experience separate from and subsequent to saving faith or one's initial conversion to Christ. The physical evidence, so to speak, of this "second blessing" of the Spirit is that one will speak in tongues.

Perhaps the most well-known body of believers who argue in this way is the Assemblies of God. This view is clearly articulated in points 7 and 8 of their "Statement of Fundamental Truths" (emphasis added):

> 7. THE BAPTISM IN THE HOLY SPIRIT
> All believers are entitled to and should ardently expect and earnestly seek the promise of the Father, the baptism in the Holy Spirit and fire, according to the command of our Lord Jesus Christ. This was the normal experience

of all in the early Christian Church. With it comes the enduement of power for life and service, the bestowment of the gifts and their uses in the work of the ministry.

+ Luke 24:49 [KJV/NIV]

+ Acts 1:4 [KJV/NIV]

+ Acts 1:8 [KJV/NIV]

+ 1 Corinthians 12:1–31 [KJV/NIV]

This experience is *distinct from and subsequent to* the experience of the new birth.

+ Acts 8:12–17 [KJV/NIV]

+ Acts 10:44–46 [KJV/NIV]

+ Acts 11:14–16 [KJV/NIV]

+ Acts 15:7–9 [KJV/NIV]

With the baptism in the Holy Spirit come such experiences as:

+ an overflowing fullness of the Spirit, John 7:37–39 [KJV/NIV], Acts 4:8 [KJV/NIV]

+ a deepened reverence for God, Acts 2:43 [KJV/NIV], Hebrews 12:28 [KJV/NIV]

+ an intensified consecration to God and dedication to His work, Acts 2:42 [KJV/NIV]

+ and a more active love for Christ, for His Word and for the lost, Mark 16:20 [KJV/NIV]

8. THE INITIAL PHYSICAL EVIDENCE OF THE
BAPTISM IN THE HOLY SPIRIT
The baptism of believers in the Holy Spirit is witnessed
by the initial physical sign of speaking with other tongues
as the Spirit of God gives them utterance.

* Acts 2:4 [kjv/niv]

The speaking in tongues in this instance is the same in
essence as the gift of tongues, but is different in purpose
and use.

* 1 Corinthians 12:4–10 [kjv/niv]
* 1 Corinthians 12:28 [kjv/niv]¹

There are three crucial elements in this view. First, there is the
doctrine of *subsequence*. Spirit baptism is always subsequent to and
therefore distinct from conversion. The time intervening between
the two events may be momentary or conceivably years. Second,
there is an emphasis on *conditions*. Depending on whom you read,
the conditions on which Spirit baptism is suspended may include
repentance, confession, faith, prayers, waiting ("tarrying"), seeking,
yielding, etc. The obvious danger here is in dividing the Christian
life in such a way that *salvation* becomes a *gift* to the *sinner* whereas
the *fullness of the Spirit* becomes a *reward* to the *saint*. Third, and
most controversial of all, they emphasize the doctrine of *initial evidence*. The initial and physical evidence of having been baptized in
the Spirit is speaking in tongues. If one has not spoken in tongues,
one has not been baptized in the Spirit. Those in the Assemblies do
not deny that a person may be saved without speaking in tongues.
But tongues is itself the evidence that one has also been baptized
in the Spirit.²

3. Does the gift of tongues always and invariably follow Spirit baptism as its initial physical evidence?[3]

So does the New Testament, and especially the Book of Acts, support the answer given by the Assemblies? In other words, does Spirit baptism happen for all Christians at the moment we first come to faith in Jesus, or does it occur as a separate event, sometime subsequent to conversion? We might as easily ask: Is Spirit baptism an *initiatory* experience for *all* Christians or a *second-stage* experience that only *some* receive?[4] And is speaking in tongues the initial physical evidence of this experience?

Non-Charismatic evangelical believers are almost unanimous in insisting that Spirit baptism is simultaneous with conversion and therefore is the experience of all Christians. The late Martyn Lloyd-Jones, who for many years served as pastor at Westminster Chapel in London, identified Spirit baptism with the "sealing" of the Holy Spirit described in Ephesians 1:13. He believed this was an experiential or "felt" event that occurs sometime after regeneration. Its purpose was to impart a profound, inner, direct assurance of salvation. It also produces power for ministry and witness, joy, and a sense of God's glorious presence. But neither Lloyd-Jones nor others who take this view make any connection between the "sealing" of the Holy Spirit or Spirit baptism and the impartation of spiritual gifts, including tongues.[5]

Generally speaking, many Charismatics today, and certainly all who self-identify as classical Pentecostals, endorse the two-stage doctrine of subsequence. Not all of them, however, believe Spirit baptism is suspended on conditions that the believer must fulfill. And not all believe every Spirit-baptized Christian will necessarily speak in tongues.

The late C. Peter Wagner was perhaps the first to speak of yet another movement that he called the Third Wave. The "first wave" of the Holy Spirit was the revival at the turn of the twentieth century that occurred at Azusa Street. This outpouring resulted in the formation of most classical Pentecostal denominations, such as the Assemblies of God. The "second wave" of the Spirit is typically dated to the early 1960s, when Charismatic experience spread beyond classical Pentecostal groups into more mainstream Protestant denominations such as Southern Baptists, Episcopalians, Methodists, and Presbyterians, just to mention a few. According to Wagner, the "third wave" refers to the spread of Charismatic gifts into nondenominational or independent Evangelical churches. The Association of Vineyard Churches, led by John Wimber until his death in 1997, is a good example of Third Wave Christianity.[6]

Most Third Wave believers insist that all Christians are baptized in the Holy Spirit at the time of their new birth. However, they would also insist on multiple, *subsequent* experiences of the Spirit's activity. At any time following conversion the Spirit may yet "come" or "fall upon" the believer with varying degrees of intensity. The person who has been a Christian for years may still experience an empowering or anointing of the Spirit that is typically referred to as a "filling." This filling of the Spirit may lead to the impartation of a new spiritual gift or extraordinary boldness in witnessing to unbelievers, or even, as Lloyd-Jones said, a deeper and more emotionally intense assurance of salvation.[7]

THE APOSTLE PAUL ON SPIRIT BAPTISM

The apostle Paul explicitly refers to Spirit baptism only once, in 1 Corinthians 12:13. Here is the English Standard Version translation of this text: "For in one Spirit we were all baptized into one body—Jews or Greeks, slaves or free—and all were made to drink of one Spirit." Others prefer to translate the opening phrase as "by one Spirit," suggesting that the Spirit Himself is the One who baptizes believers into Christ or unites them with Him for salvation. This view can be portrayed as follows:

At conversion → Holy Spirit → baptizes ALL → "into"
Jesus Christ → salvation

Most Pentecostals and many Charismatics then argue that at
some time subsequent to conversion Jesus baptizes some, but not
necessarily all, believers in the Holy Spirit to empower and equip
them for ministry. This scheme would look like this:

After conversion → Jesus Christ → baptizes SOME → "in"
Holy Spirit → power

Some justify drawing this distinction by pointing to the seemingly awkward phrase in 1 Corinthians 12:13, "in one Spirit...into
one body." But what may sound strange in English makes perfectly good sense in the original Greek text. Paul is simply saying
that every believer has been baptized by Jesus in the Spirit, the
result of which is that every believer is now a member of the same
spiritual body.

We see this same use of terminology in 1 Corinthians
10:2—"all were baptized *into* Moses *in* the cloud and *in* the sea"
(emphasis added). The "elements," as it were, in which the people
were immersed or with which they were surrounded and overwhelmed are the *cloud* and the *sea*. The reference to Moses indicates the new life of participation in the old covenant, of which
he was the leader, and the fellowship of God's people during that
time of redemptive history.

There is an important point of Greek grammar that needs to
be noted. In every other text in the New Testament where Spirit
baptism is mentioned, the preposition *en* is used, typically translated as the English word *in*. This directs our attention to the element in which one is, as it were, immersed or with which one is
inundated. The Holy Spirit is never said to be the agent or cause
of this baptism. The Holy Spirit is He in whom we are engulfed or

the "element" with which we are saturated.[8] Jesus is always the One who does the work of baptizing, and the Spirit is always the One in whom or with whom we are immersed and saturated.

Some have tried to argue that whereas 1 Corinthians 12:13a refers to conversion, 1 Corinthians 12:13b describes a second, post-conversion work of the Holy Spirit. But this is more likely an example of the sort of parallelism that is a common literary device employed by the biblical authors. The same reality (immersion or baptism in the Spirit) is portrayed by the use of two different metaphors. Furthermore, the activity portrayed in the two phrases extends to the same group of people. It is "we...all" who were "baptized into one body" and "we...all" who "were made to drink of one Spirit." All believers, therefore, were baptized, or immersed, in the Holy Spirit and were "made to drink of one Spirit" when they first came to faith in Jesus. And this work of being baptized in the Spirit and given of Him "to drink" was brought about by Jesus Himself.

What is it, then, that effects our incorporation into the spiritual organism of the body of Christ, the church? It is our experience of being immersed in the Spirit, being engulfed or inundated by His abiding presence in our hearts. Some have suggested that this experience described by Paul is an allusion to several Old Testament texts that portray the outpouring of the Spirit on the land and its people in the age to come. For example:

> ...until the Spirit is poured upon us from on high, and the wilderness becomes a fruitful field, and the fruitful field is deemed a forest.
>
> —ISAIAH 32:15

For I will pour water on the thirsty land, and streams on the dry ground; I will pour my Spirit upon your offspring, and my blessing on your descendants.

—ISAIAH 44:3

And I will not hide my face anymore from them, when I pour out my Spirit upon the house of Israel, declares the Lord GOD.

—EZEKIEL 39:29

Thus our conversion or reception of the Spirit when we trust Christ for salvation is analogous to the outpouring of a sudden flood or rainstorm on parched ground, transforming dry and barren earth into a well-watered garden (cf. Jer. 31:12). Gordon Fee points out that

> such expressive metaphors (immersion in the Spirit and drinking to the fill of the Spirit)…imply a much greater experiential and visibly manifest reception of the Spirit than many have tended to experience in subsequent church history.…Paul may appeal to their common experience of Spirit as the presupposition for the unity of the body precisely because, as in Gal. 3:2–5, the Spirit was a dynamically experienced reality, which had happened to all.[9]

In light of this I feel confident in drawing this conclusion. To be baptized in the Spirit by the Lord Jesus Christ is a metaphor designed to portray our reception of the Spirit at the point of conversion. All believers in Jesus are, as it were, submerged in the Spirit, who subsequently indwells each of us permanently. This is an experience that happens to *all* Christians, not some, and it happens at the time of our new birth. However, as noted earlier, this does not mean the activity of the Holy Spirit in our lives is restricted to the time of our conversion. The New Testament clearly describes a multitude of post-conversion encounters with the Spirit that are transforming, empowering, and designed to equip us for ministry. As I have often said, Evangelicals are *right* in affirming that all Christians have experienced Spirit baptism at conversion. They are *wrong* in minimizing (sometimes even denying) the reality of subsequent, additional experiences of the Spirit in the course of the Christian life. Charismatics are *right* in affirming the reality and importance of post-conversion encounters with the Spirit that empower, enlighten, and transform. They are *wrong* in calling this experience "Spirit baptism."

This conclusion has significant repercussions for an issue that I addressed earlier in this book, namely whether speaking in tongues is the invariable, initial physical evidence of being baptized in the Spirit. We must remember that in 1 Corinthians 14:5 Paul expressed his wish that all would speak in tongues. This doesn't make much sense if he believed they did. Why wish for something that is already and always true? But if all believers in Corinth (and elsewhere) had been baptized in the Spirit but not all believers in Corinth spoke in tongues, it would rule out the idea that tongues is always the initial physical evidence of Spirit baptism.[10]

THE DOCTRINE OF SUBSEQUENCE

I am often asked why those in the Pentecostal and Charismatic traditions came up with the doctrine of tongues as an experience that is separate from and subsequent to conversion. The best explanation I've seen is provided by Gordon Fee.[11]

First, Fee points to the dissatisfaction of many with the lethargy and lifelessness of their own Christian experience and that of the church corporately. The coldness, cowardice, and routine of religion sparked in them a passion, thirst, and hunger for more of God, for more of what they saw New Testament Christians experience. Second, this in turn evoked a desire for a deeper and truly transformative experience. Many were thus undeniably touched by the presence of God. A life-changing encounter with God brought new power, renewed commitment, a zealous rededication to holiness of life, and deepened love. Third, this experience was clearly subsequent to their conversion (often years after they were saved). Therefore, it was something different from the new birth or justification or anything else associated with their initial saving encounter with Christ. Fourth, as has often been said, these were a people with an experience in search of a theology. Turning to the Bible to identify and justify what had occurred, they found what they believed was a threefold precedent for what had happened to them (which will be discussed in this chapter). The final step was simply to identify what happened to them as the "baptism in the Holy Spirit."

So where in the Bible, if at all, do Pentecostal believers find support for the idea that Christians may receive a greater fullness and more expansive power of the Holy Spirit that occurs separately from and sometimes long after the moment of conversion, an experience that they feel justified in labeling Spirit baptism? There are generally three instances to which they point. We will look at each in chronological order.

The experience of Jesus

This argument may strike some as odd, and rightly so. The point is that the conception of Jesus in the womb of the Virgin Mary and His subsequent physical birth supposedly correspond with or are analogous to the born-again experience of a child of God. And since it was some thirty or more years later that Jesus was anointed and filled with the Holy Spirit (see Acts 10:38 and the other descriptions of His baptism by John), we should likewise expect to receive the Spirit's power following, but not simultaneous with, our spiritual birth or regeneration. In other words, it seems that Jesus was "baptized in the Spirit" when the dove descended upon Him in the

River Jordan in order to equip and empower Him for His public ministry. So shouldn't the same reality apply to us? Shouldn't we experience this spiritual baptism subsequent to our conversion to equip and empower us for ministry as well?

There is an important truth in this suggestion that we shouldn't overlook. Although the Holy Spirit surely indwelled Jesus before His public ministry, there was an extraordinary anointing that occurred when John the Baptist immersed Him in the water of the River Jordan. This is clearly asserted by Luke in Acts 10:38. But we can't overlook the fact that Luke refers to this as an anointing with the Spirit, not a baptism. John the Baptist himself made it clear that whereas he baptized in water, Jesus "will baptize you with the Holy Spirit and fire" (Matt. 3:11; see also Mark 1:8; Luke 3:16; and John 1:33). In other words, far from being "baptized in the Spirit," Jesus is Himself the One who does the baptizing!

This argument also breaks down when we remember that Jesus, unlike you and me, didn't stand in need of salvation. In fact, He alone is the Savior! Jesus didn't need to be born again. There was never a time in His earthly experience when He was "dead in…trespasses and sins" (Eph. 2:1). Simply put, Jesus never experienced anything remotely similar to our conversion. That is why it is unbiblical to speak of any particular incident in His life as being *separate from and subsequent to conversion*. God the Father "anointed Jesus of Nazareth with the Holy Spirit and with power" to enable Him to do "good" and to heal "all who were oppressed by the devil" (Acts 10:38).

We also stand in need of this empowering presence, but the New Testament never portrays the empowering of Jesus by the Spirit as analogous to our being baptized in the Spirit. As best I can tell, there is no biblical evidence to suggest that what the Father did for the Son at the inauguration of His public ministry reflects a normative, divinely ordained will for "subsequence" in the lives of Christ's followers. I'm happy to acknowledge that there is an analogy between the experience of Jesus and the experience of the Christian: we desperately stand in need of the power of the Holy Spirit to do the works of Jesus. But there is no biblical justification for identifying this with Spirit baptism. In Acts it is more appropriately called the "filling of the Spirit."

The experience of the first disciples

A similar argument is made based on the experience of the first disciples of Jesus. According to this view, the disciples were born again or regenerated (i.e., they were saved) when they received the Spirit on the day Jesus appeared to them following His resurrection. But it wasn't until the day of Pentecost, a day that was separate from and subsequent to their new birth, that they were baptized in the Spirit. Here is the text in question:

> On the evening of that day, the first day of the week, the doors being locked where the disciples were for fear of the Jews, Jesus came and stood among them and said to them, "Peace be with you." When he had said this, he showed them his hands and his side. Then the disciples were glad when they saw the Lord. Jesus said to them again, "Peace be with you. As the Father has sent me, even so I am sending you." And when he had said this, he breathed on them and said to them, "Receive the Holy Spirit. If you forgive the sins of any, they are forgiven them; if you withhold forgiveness from any, it is withheld."
>
> —JOHN 20:19–23

The problem with this argument is that this experience following the resurrection of Jesus was not their conversion. It was not the moment when they were first saved. Jesus told them while in the Upper Room that they were already "clean" (John 13:10). He earlier exhorted them to rejoice that their names were already written down in heaven (Luke 10:20). Peter had openly testified that Jesus was the Christ (Matt. 16:16–17; John 16:30). In His high priestly prayer in John 17:8–19 Jesus described them as already belonging to the Father. And it would seem that John 20:21–22 is more concerned with the disciples' commission to ministry than with their new birth experience ("even so I am sending you," v. 21).

We must acknowledge that John 20:22 is a difficult passage. Some believe that this constituted a *preliminary* impartation of the Spirit in anticipation of the complete gift that would come at Pentecost. We know from Luke 24:49 that the followers of Jesus would not receive the fullness of divine power (i.e., the Holy Spirit) until the day of Pentecost. Perhaps, then, John 20 is describing a *transitional empowering* of the disciples to sustain and energize them during the interval between Christ's resurrection and the coming of the Spirit at Pentecost. The case has also been made that no impartation of the Spirit literally occurred in John 20; this was simply an acted parable, that is to say, a symbolic promise of the coming power of the Holy Spirit that would finally occur on the day of Pentecost.

So it does not seem the experience of the disciples provides us with a normative pattern for our own personal baptism in the Spirit. How could it, given the fact that the disciples' experience could not have been other than it was? The fact of the matter is that they couldn't have been baptized in the Spirit when they believed, because they believed long before Spirit baptism was even possible. Henry Lederle put it this way:

> This conclusion is…underscored by the fact that the apostles began believing in Jesus (in some or other form at least) before the Spirit was poured out on the church on the day of Pentecost. This places them in a situation different to every Christian living after Pentecost. It was thus necessary that the apostles experience the new freedom and life

in the Spirit which came with Pentecost in a unique way because they could not experience it before it had come (prior to Acts 2).[12]

Wayne Grudem concurs and explains it this way:

They [the first disciples] received this remarkable new empowering from the Holy Spirit *because they were living at the time of the transition between the old covenant work of the Holy Spirit and the new covenant work of the Holy Spirit.* Though it was a "second experience" of the Holy Spirit, coming as it did long after their conversion, it is not to be taken as a pattern for us, for we are not living at a time of transition in the work of the Holy Spirit. In their case, believers with an old covenant empowering from the Holy Spirit became believers with a new covenant empowering from the Holy Spirit. But we today do not first become believers with a weaker, old covenant work of the Holy Spirit in our hearts and wait until some later time to receive a new covenant work of the Holy Spirit. Rather, we are in the same position as those who became Christians in the church at Corinth: when we become Christians we are all *"baptized in one Spirit into one body"* (1 Cor. 12:13)—just as the Corinthians were, and just as were the new believers in many churches who were converted when Paul traveled on his missionary journeys.[13]

The experience of individuals in Acts

Advocates of the doctrine that Spirit baptism is separate from and subsequent to conversion will then appeal to three groups of people in the Book of Acts: the Samaritans, Cornelius and the Gentiles, and the Ephesian disciples.

THE SAMARITANS

Although the precise terminology "Spirit baptism" or "baptism in the Spirit" is not found in Acts 8:4–24, this text is often cited as providing us with a precedent for what we can experience. There we read of how Philip the evangelist traveled to Samaria and preached the gospel with wonderful results. Signs and wonders were performed, and many "believed" in Jesus. But something in their experience was missing. We are told that Peter and John traveled to Samaria and prayed for these people "that they might receive the Holy Spirit, for he had not yet fallen on any of them, but they had only been baptized in the name of the Lord Jesus" (vv. 15–16).

Everyone concedes that Acts 8:16 is one of the most unusual statements in the entire book. It is the only record in the entire New Testament of people believing in Jesus Christ, being baptized in water, and yet not receiving the Holy Spirit. Was this normative for all Christians in the early church? And is it something we should expect to happen in our day as well?

Of all the texts cited by classical Pentecostals to support the reality of a second reception of the Holy Spirit, separate from and subsequent to the initial work by which people become believers in Jesus, this one is the most explicit. It comes as no surprise, therefore, that they identify this second experience as the "baptism in the Holy Spirit" despite the fact that Luke nowhere uses that terminology. However, we have to reckon with the fact that Luke appears to suggest that the Holy Spirit had not fallen on them *at all* (Acts 8:16). Thus, would not what occurs in verse 16 be their first reception of the Spirit, not the second? My point is simply that the Samaritans had not as yet experienced a *first* coming of the Spirit, something prerequisite to their experience of a subsequent or *second* coming.

Another view is that the Samaritans had truly received the Holy Spirit but had not experienced His charismatic gifts or manifestations. It isn't the Spirit *Himself* they lacked, so goes the argument, but only His supernatural gifts. Much has been made of the fact that the words "Holy Spirit" in this narrative lack the definite article, thus pointing not to the person of the Spirit per se but to the power or operations of the Spirit, i.e., His gifts. However, James Dunn and others have demonstrated that no significant theological conclusions can be drawn from the presence or absence of the definite article.[14] Furthermore, we read in Acts 8:15–19 that it is the Holy Spirit, not His gifts, who comes when the apostles lay on hands.

A few have suggested that we should account for this unusual scenario by recognizing that the Holy Spirit only comes through the laying on of hands. But this would not account for Acts 2:38, where no mention is made of anyone's hands being laid on anyone else. If it were only a matter of the laying on of hands, couldn't Philip have done it? When Paul was converted (Acts 9), there was no reference to anyone laying hands on him to receive the Spirit. The same is true in the story of Philip leading the Ethiopian eunuch to the Lord (Acts 8:26–40). Finally, the coming of the Holy Spirit is nowhere else connected in Acts with the laying on of hands (aside from the incident in Acts 19, which will be discussed later in this chapter). But perhaps the difference here is the presence of "apostolic" hands. But if that were the case, why do we not see in Acts a record of the apostles travelling from city to city and church to church in order to lay hands on everyone who had come to faith in Jesus? The notion that the experience of Spirit baptism was somehow suspended on the imposition of apostolic hands is simply not found in Acts or elsewhere in the New Testament.

There is one final view found in the writings of only a minority of scholars. Some argue that the reason the Samaritans had not received the Holy Spirit is because they were not yet saved. Conversion had not yet occurred. Simply put, they weren't born again. Their response to the preaching of Philip was one of mass hysteria as they were caught up in the euphoria and spiritual excitement of the moment. They may have given intellectual or mental assent to the truth of the gospel, but they had not trusted Jesus in heartfelt commitment.

This view stumbles on the clear assertion of Acts 8:14 that they had "received the word of God." The same wording is found in Acts 2:41 and Acts 11:1, where genuine conversion is in view. Also, Acts 8:12 is quite clear about the nature and object of their faith: "they believed Philip as he preached good news about the kingdom of God and the name of Jesus Christ." Again, Luke uses the same terminology in Acts 16:34 and Acts 18:8 to describe genuine, saving faith in God. And if the Samaritans were not saved, why didn't Peter and John preach the gospel upon their arrival? Instead they prayed for the Samaritans to receive the Spirit.

And if Philip had failed to make clear the precise nature of the gospel, we would have expected the apostles to correct the problem through additional teaching (as Priscilla and Aquila did with Apollos in Acts 18:26). One more point noted by several commentators is that they were baptized *into* the name of Jesus (Acts 8:16). This phrase was common in commercial transactions when a property was transferred or paid "into the name" of someone else. Thus a person baptized "into the name of Jesus" is saying: "I have passed into *His* ownership; Jesus owns me lock, stock, and barrel. He is my Lord."

There is, I believe, a much more cogent explanation for this admittedly unusual scenario. The answer is found in the hostility that existed between Jews and Samaritans. Let's not forget that Acts 8 records the first occasion when the gospel extended not only outside Jerusalem but inside Samaria. Sadly, we are all familiar with the racial hostilities that too often mar our existence today. It wasn't much better in the ancient world when it came to the relationship between Jews and Samaritans.

There were several reasons for the mutual disdain in which they held each other. The Jews accused the Samaritans of disrupting the unity of God's people following the death of Solomon in 922 BC. Samaritans were considered "half-breeds" for having intermarried with Gentiles. Upon the Israelites' return from exile in Babylon, the Samaritans resisted Jewish efforts to rebuild the temple. In fact, the latter chose to erect their own temple on Mount Gerizim. (You may recall the interaction between Jesus and the Samaritan woman on the proper place to worship in John 4:20.) There was also an incident around AD 6, during the Passover, when certain Samaritans scattered the bones of a dead man in the court of the temple in Jerusalem, an act of defilement that enraged the Jews and only intensified their animosity.[15]

The situation had degenerated so badly that Jews publicly cursed Samaritans and prayed fervently that God would never save any of them. All of us are familiar with what has come to be known as the parable of the good Samaritan. To Jewish ears "good Samaritan" would have been a shocking contradiction in terms. And then there was the occasion when the Jewish leaders addressed Jesus in this manner: "Are we not right in saying that you are a Samaritan and have a demon?" (John 8:48). I suspect that if the Jews themselves had a choice between the two, they might prefer to be demonized rather than be a Samaritan!

Finally, it's important to remember that Samaria was located between Galilee to the north and Judea to the south. The Jewish disdain for Samaria was so bitter that when they had to travel from Galilee to Judea, or vice versa, they would first travel due east and then south (or north, as the case may be) in order to avoid even having to set their feet on Samaritan soil!

Now try to imagine the chaos and uproar that would have been provoked had the Samaritans believed in the gospel independently of the church in Jerusalem. Something needed to be done to ensure unity, lest schism or division emerge. Frederick Bruner explains:

The Samaritans were not left to become an isolated sect with no bonds of union with the apostolic church in Jerusalem. If a Samaritan church and a Jewish church had arisen independently, side by side, without the dramatic removal of the ancient and bitter barriers of prejudice between the two, particularly at the level of ultimate authority, the young church of God would have been in schism from the inception of its mission. The drama of the Samaritan affair in Acts 8 included among its purposes the vivid and visual dismantling of the wall of enmity between Jew and Samaritan and the preservation of the precious unity of the church of God.[16]

All this suggests that the otherwise unprecedented withholding of the Holy Spirit from these Samaritan believers was orchestrated by divine providence. The delay was designed to give the leaders of the church in Jerusalem, specifically Peter and John, time to make the journey into Samaria so they might visibly and personally place their imprimatur or stamp of approval on the preaching of the gospel there (Acts 1:8). Given the long-standing racial and religious animosity between Jews and Samaritans, God determined that steps should be taken to prevent a disastrous split in the early church. This would easily account for the temporary and altogether unusual delay of the coming of the Spirit. An unprecedented situation demanded quite exceptional methods.

That being said, honesty demands we admit this incident poses questions about the reception and experience of the Holy Spirit that may have to remain unanswered. Although I believe my explanation for the suspension of the Spirit in the case of the Samaritans is cogent, and more likely than any other account, we are still left with the undeniable fact that certain individuals were born again, trusted in Jesus, were made members of the body of Christ, and yet had not received the Holy Spirit.

CORNELIUS AND THE GENTILES

The second example cited from the Book of Acts concerns the story of Cornelius and the Gentiles (Acts 10; 11:12–18). Following the events in Acts 8, this is the second monumental extension of the gospel beyond the boundaries of Jewish exclusivism. Those who would find in the experience of Cornelius an example of Spirit baptism, separate from and subsequent to salvation, point to the fact that he appears at first glance to have already been converted when Peter arrived at his house. (See Acts 10:2, 35.) If this were the case, his reception of the Holy Spirit in Acts 10:44–48 might well constitute a second blessing, or a post-conversion baptism in the Holy Spirit. But I'm persuaded that Cornelius was not truly converted before Peter's arrival.

One reason for this is found in Peter's retelling of the incident in Acts 11:14. The angel who appeared to Cornelius told him that Peter "will declare to you a message by which you *will be* saved" (emphasis added). In order to be saved, Cornelius had to hear the message Peter would proclaim. Note also the future tense: "will be saved." If Cornelius and others in his household would believe, they would be saved, a clear indication that they were not yet truly converted. God granted these Gentile believers the "repentance that leads to [eternal] life" when they believed Peter's proclamation, not before.

One possible objection to this is in Acts 10:35. There we read that before Cornelius had heard the gospel, he was regarded as "acceptable" to God. How do we account for this? John Piper's explanation is the best:

> My suggestion is that Cornelius represents a kind of unsaved person among an unreached people group who is seeking God in an extraordinary way. And Peter is saying that God *accepts* this search as genuine (hence "acceptable"

in verse 35) and works wonders to bring that person the gospel of Jesus Christ the way he did through the visions of both Peter on the housetop and Cornelius in the hour of prayer....So the fear of God that is acceptable to God in verse 35 is a true sense that there is a holy God, that we have to meet him some day as desperate sinners, that we cannot save ourselves and need to know God's way of salvation, and that we pray for it day and night and seek to act on the light we have. This is what Cornelius was doing. And God accepted his prayer and his groping for truth in his life (Acts 17:27), and worked wonders to bring the saving message of the gospel to him. Cornelius would not have been saved if no one had taken him the gospel.[17]

My sense, then, is that Cornelius and the other Gentiles who accompanied him were not saved until they heard Peter preach the gospel to them. It was then, at the time of their conversion, that they were baptized in the Holy Spirit, not at some time subsequent thereto.

THE EPHESIAN DISCIPLES

Our last example comes from Acts 19:1–10 where Paul encountered "some disciples" at Ephesus. The argument of most Pentecostals is that these were born-again, Christian believers who quite obviously had not yet received the fullness of the Spirit's presence and power. Paul prays for them, "the Holy Spirit came on them, and they began speaking in tongues and prophesying" (Acts 19:6). I argued in the previous chapter that this explanation is highly unlikely, given the fact that this story pertains to a unique group of disciples of John the Baptist whose experience cannot be repeated beyond the time of the transition from the old covenant into the new covenant.

It should be obvious by now that I don't believe any of these events in Acts contradicts or undermines the truth that Spirit baptism occurs for all Christians at the time of conversion. Likewise, speaking in tongues is not the invariable sign that a person has been baptized in or filled with the Holy Spirit. I should probably also direct your attention to numerous other instances in Acts where true conversion is portrayed and yet neither Spirit baptism nor tongues is mentioned (2:37–42; 8:26–40; 9:1–19; 13:44–52; 16:11–15, 25–34; 17:1–10, 10–15, 16–33; 18:1–11, 24–28).

However, we have not yet determined whether tongues is a gift that God wishes to grant to all believers. Even though tongues may not be the expected experience of everyone who is baptized in the Spirit, perhaps speaking in tongues is a spiritual reality that all followers of Jesus should expect to receive. I will address this specific question later in chapter 11.

Chapter 4

TONGUES AND FOREIGN LANGUAGES

OPPOSITION TO THE contemporary validity of the spiritual gift of tongues has always been intense. Among the arguments brought to bear against tongues today, there is one that stands above them all. Some insist that tongues was a so-called "sign" gift designed to testify to the authenticity of the gospel message proclaimed by the first-century apostles. Others contend that God intended tongues to serve exclusively as a declaration to Jewish unbelievers that their judgment for rejecting Jesus as Messiah was near. I've actually encountered a handful of cessationists who argue that the gift of tongues was revelatory. That is to say, it was one way in which God revealed infallible truths that were to serve as foundational for the life of the universal body of Christ down through the centuries. As such, it could only be operative before the time the canon of Scripture was closed.[1]

But the single most oft-cited argument against tongues in the present day is the insistence that all legitimate, biblical tongues-speech was a human language, spoken somewhere in the world, but previously unknown to the person to whom the gift was given. The second stage in this argument comes from the observations of linguistic experts who tell us that their study of contemporary tongues-speech proves that none of it is a known human language. So there is the argument: all New Testament tongues-speech was human languages, contemporary tongues-speech is not; therefore, and contemporary tongues-speech is not biblical but some form of psychological emotivism or nonsense gibberish. This, then, leads us to the fourth of our thirty crucial questions about speaking in tongues.

4. Are tongues always human languages previously unlearned by the speaker? If not, what kind of language is speaking in tongues?

Once again it is important to understand the argument cessationists use in their opposition to contemporary tongues-speech. They point, and rightly so, to the fact that in Acts 2 the tongues spoken on Pentecost were actual human languages the disciples had never before studied or learned. But they then argue, wrongly so, that all tongues-speech, wherever else it may appear in the New Testament, must be identical with that at Pentecost. In other words, Acts 2 is believed to govern all other instances of this spiritual gift. Whatever is true in Acts 2 regarding tongues must be true in every other case of its occurrence.

But there is no discernible reason we should believe this. It is an assumption without an argument. Perhaps it would be an argument that carries a bit more weight if there were no evidence elsewhere in the New Testament that tongues may come in a variety of species or expressions, both known human languages and heavenly speech that is crafted by the Holy Spirit for those believers to whom the gift is given. Furthermore, if the cessationist argument is to hold up, we would need to be shown that the other occurrences of tongues in Acts (and in 1 Corinthians) are parallel to Acts 2 and display the same characteristics. But this is precisely what is lacking. We now turn to the evidence that tongues outside of Acts 2 is *not* known human languages but rather another linguistic expression crafted by the Spirit or perhaps even one of the possible numerous dialects spoken by the angelic hosts.

First, if tongues-speech is always in a foreign language intended as a sign for unbelievers or as an evangelistic tool, why are the tongues in Acts 10 and Acts 19 spoken in the presence of only believers? This is precisely what I mentioned in chapter 2. Again, if tongues is always in an actual human language so it might serve to communicate the gospel to unbelievers, why are no unbelievers present in Acts 10 and Acts 19? Why would the Spirit energize or lead believers to speak in tongues in the absence of the very folk for whom this alleged evangelistic tool is designed?

Second, Paul describes various "kinds," or species, of tongues in 1 Corinthians 12:10 and 12:28. His words suggest there are differing categories of tongues-speech, perhaps human languages, angelic dialects, and heavenly languages that are uniquely formed by the Spirit for each person to whom the gift is granted.

Those who insist that all tongues-speech is necessarily a human language of some sort push back and argue that in saying tongues come in a variety of kinds or species, Paul means there are a variety of human languages such as English, French, Japanese, Mandarin, etc. But who would ever have suggested that all tongues-speech was only one specific human language? In other words, we already know from Acts 2 that when tongues appeared at Pentecost, it came in the form of differing human dialects. It seems highly unlikely, then, that Paul would have labored to point out that tongues is never just one human language but a multiplicity of such.

It is true, of course, that the countless dialects or languages that humans around the world speak when communicating with one another constitute at least one kind or species of tongues, namely, human languages. But another kind or species would be nonhuman languages, such as the variety of ways in which angels might communicate with one another or with God. I find it almost impossible to believe that among the myriads and myriads of angels they all speak only a single language. But however many different languages the angels employ, they would all be subsumed under the rubric of one species or kind, namely, angelic speech.

What I'm contending for is that yet another species or kind of tongues is the sort the Holy Spirit constructs or enables a human being to speak in the course of his or her prayer and praise to God. Each of these expressions of tongues would be unique to each individual, all of which, however, would together constitute yet another kind or species of tongues.

Third, perhaps the most persuasive argument against tongues being known human languages is what Paul says in 1 Corinthians 14:2. There he asserts that whoever speaks in a tongue "speaks not to men but to God." Now, ask yourself this question: What is a human language, whether it be Russian or German or Norwegian? Is it not a means by which one human being communicates with or speaks to another human being?

The answer, of course, is yes. But Paul very clearly denies this is what is happening when a person speaks in tongues. This person is most decidedly *not* doing what human language typically does. To speak in tongues is *not* to speak to other humans. Rather it is a way of speaking directly to God. Therefore, the species or kind of tongues Paul has in view in 1 Corinthians 12–14, unlike the species Luke describes in Acts 2, is not a human language.

Fourth, and very much related to the previous point, if tongues-speech is always a human language, how could Paul say that when one speaks in tongues, "no one understands him" (1 Cor. 14:2)? If tongues are human languages, many could potentially understand, as they did on the day of Pentecost (Acts 2:8–11). This would especially be true in Corinth, a multilingual, cosmopolitan port city that was frequented by people of numerous dialects. Thus, "if Paul came speaking in tongues, in a non-Greek or non-Latin language, he surely would have been able to communicate with someone."[2]

Try to imagine a scenario in which a person with the gift of tongues in Corinth stands up and uses his Spirit-empowered ability to speak, let's say, in the language of the Parthians. (See Acts 2:9.) Paul might then take advantage of the situation to teach on the subject. "What you've just heard," says Paul, "is one expression of the gift of tongues. And since what he just said is mysterious and incoherent in the absence of interpretation, he obviously was not speaking to you and me but to God alone." At this point a visitor to the service might stand up and say: "Wait a minute, Paul. With all due respect, you are wrong. What he said was not mysterious or incoherent. I understood perfectly what he said. He was, after all, speaking my own native language!"

This hypothetical scenario is not all that hypothetical. In fact, if tongues in Corinth were always a known human language, it could conceivably happen again and again anytime a person who spoke that particular language was present. My point is simply that Paul would be repeatedly wrong in saying that "no one understands" the person speaking in tongues. Conceivably, and not hypothetically, numerous individuals would understand what was being said, just as they did on the day of Pentecost. Clearly, then, the tongues Paul envisioned being given to Christians in Corinth (or any other city of that day and time) was not identical to the tongues given at Pentecost. They were in fact a different species or kind of tongues, namely, the sort that cannot be understood by any human being unless supernaturally enabled to understand by means of the spiritual gift of interpretation.

Fifth, one reason no one understands what is being said in tongues is because "he utters mysteries in the Spirit" (1 Cor. 14:2). Those who stand opposed to the legitimacy of tongues today contend that the word *mysteries* in 1 Corinthians 14:2 refers to what

Paul had in mind in Ephesians 3:2–6 when he spoke of the "mystery of Christ," to wit, that "the Gentiles are fellow heirs, members of the same body, and partakers of the promise in Christ Jesus through the gospel." There is no mistaking the fact that the word *mystery* (singular) here in Ephesians 3 is a technical term for the truth concerning Gentile salvation, something largely hidden during the time of the Old Testament but now revealed to Paul and to us. Or, as New Testament scholar Anthony Thiselton defines it, the word denotes "what was once hidden but has now been disclosed in the era of eschatological fulfillment ([see 1 Cor.] 2:1, 7; 4:1; 15:51)."[3] But Thiselton also goes on to point out that "every writer uses terminology in context-dependent ways that may modify a more usual meaning," and that is evidently what Paul is doing here.[4] In other words, we must look first and foremost at how an author uses a word in a specific context to determine its meaning. And there are several reasons Paul's use of the word in 1 Corinthians 14:2 is different from how he uses it in Ephesians 3.

First, it is significant that in verse 2 the word is plural, *mysteries*, not singular as in Ephesians 3. There was a singular and deeply profound mystery that was made known to Paul concerning Gentile salvation and equality in the body of Christ. But there are multiple mysteries to which those who speak in tongues give utterance. This use of the word means something unintelligible, something incomprehensible, something that is not known to us unless brought into the vernacular by means of the gift of interpretation. The content of the tongues-speech remains a mystery to all because it is a species of heavenly language evoked by the Holy Spirit and spoken back exclusively to God Himself.

Second, no such descriptive information concerning the content of the mysteries is given in 1 Corinthians 14. In Ephesians 3 we are told explicitly what the mystery was. It was the "mystery of Christ" (Eph. 3:4) and the manner in which His death and resurrection and the inauguration of the new covenant have brought

Gentiles into equal standing in the covenants of promise. But this is far and away different from 1 Corinthians 14:2, in which we find "mysteries" that "no one understands." We understand the mystery of Christ, but no one understands the mysteries uttered by the tongues-speaker. Clearly we are dealing with two different senses in which the word *mystery* may be used. Paul is not speaking of doctrinal or ethical truths that comprise the foundation on which the church of Jesus Christ is built but simply of utterances that are unknown to those who hear them because they are spoken in a tongue that "no one understands."

Third, we should consider other texts where *mystery* is used in the sense of something unknown, something whose meaning is difficult to decipher or comprehend, something the meaning of which is beyond us unless it is revealed. Paul writes in 1 Corinthians 13:2 of prophecy and says that even though he may "understand all mysteries," it is useless without love. John spoke of the "mystery of the seven stars," which he then explains to his readers as being a reference to "the angels of the seven churches" (Rev. 1:20). He likewise refers to the "mystery of the woman" or the "great prostitute" who oppresses the people of God (Rev. 17:1, 7). Her identity is a mystery, or something unknown until such time as John explains it.

New Testament scholar Paul Gardner also points out that the gist of 1 Corinthians 14:2 "is simply that the person who speaks 'in a tongue'...cannot be understood by normal people but only by God because what he speaks is a 'mystery' given him by God's Spirit."[5] But if tongues is always a known human language, then countless numbers of "normal people" would be able to understand what is being spoken. Anyone who spoke the particular language being uttered by the tongues-speaker would instantly recognize his or her own native dialect and make sense of its meaning. It would hardly be a mystery to him or her.

Fifth, if tongues-speech is always in a human language, then the gift of interpretation would be one for which no special work or enablement or manifestation of the Spirit would be required. Anyone who was multilingual, such as Paul, could interpret tongues-speech simply by virtue of his educational talent. No supernaturally energized gift of the Spirit was needed by those who were present in Jerusalem on the day of Pentecost. Since the tongues in Acts 2 were human languages, any and all who spoke a particular language could instantly recognize what was being said. But Paul clearly describes the gift of interpretation of tongues as one that is sovereignly and supernaturally given to some believers (1 Cor. 12:8–10).

Again, try to envision this not-unlikely scenario in first-century Corinth. At a corporate meeting of the church a person stands up and begins to speak in tongues. Upon that person finishing, another person stands up and provides a clear and intelligible interpretation or rendering of the meaning of what was said. One of the elders at Corinth then might respond by saying, "Let us praise God for the way His Holy Spirit has imparted a supernatural and miraculous gift of interpretation so we might benefit and be built up by what was said in tongues." At that moment the man who provided the interpretation could conceivably stand up and say: "Well, not exactly. I can speak several languages. I've studied them intently and have lived in a variety of places. So when I heard the brother speak in a tongue, I instantly recognized what he was saying by virtue of my exceptional education."

But is this what we read in 1 Corinthians regarding interpretation? It would appear that Paul believed this to be a miraculous gift by which a man or woman is enabled by the Holy Spirit to understand and communicate the truth of an utterance that otherwise they would not comprehend. However, if all tongues-speech is some human language spoken somewhere in the world, a great many people who hear it would be capable of making sense of what is said without any help or gifting from the Spirit at all. In addition, if tongues-speech is always a human language, it makes no sense for Paul to suggest that interpretation should be prayed for (1 Cor. 14:13) since the ability to translate a foreign language comes through instruction and rote practice, not prayer.

Sixth, in 1 Corinthians 13:1 Paul refers to "the tongues of men and of angels." While he may be using hyperbole, he just as likely may be referring to heavenly or angelic dialects for which the Holy Spirit gives utterance. Stop and ask yourself this question: What language do angels speak? Or again, Do all angels speak the same language? Surely you don't believe angels speak only English! When the angel spoke to Daniel in Daniel 10, he would have had to speak either Hebrew or Aramaic. When the angel spoke to Peter in Acts 12, it was most likely in Greek. It would appear that angels are capable of speaking in whatever human language is needed to communicate with the human they are addressing.

Now, how many angels are there? We don't know, but several biblical texts speak of myriads upon myriads or ten thousand upon ten thousand. If each believer has a "guardian" angel (and this is by no means certain; see, however, Hebrews 1:14), and there are, as some experts say, 2.3 billion Christians in the world,[6] that would mean there are at least 2.3 billion angels. I can't prove that, but I suspect there are likely even more. All of us would agree that angels communicate. They hear from God, they interact with humans, and they interact with one another. Assuming angels differ in power, rank, and role,[7] does it not seem highly likely that they communicate in a variety of dialects suitable to their identity and station as angelic beings? So when Paul speaks of the "tongues of angels" in 1 Corinthians 13:1, we should not be at all surprised. Could it be possible, then, that he actually envisions angelic tongues as one species or kind of tongues the Spirit enables human beings to speak when they pray and praise God?

Gordon Fee cites evidence in certain ancient Jewish sources that the angels were believed to have their own heavenly languages or dialects and that by means of the Spirit one could speak them.[8] In particular we take note of the *Testament of Job* 48–50, where Job's three daughters put on heavenly sashes given to them as an inheritance from their father, by which they are transformed and enabled to praise God with hymns in angelic languages.

Some have questioned this account, however, pointing out that this section of the *Testament* may have been the work of a later Christian author. Yet, as New Testament scholar Christopher Forbes points out, "what the Testament *does* provide...is clear evidence that the concept of angelic languages *as a mode of praise to God* was an acceptable one within certain circles. As such it is our nearest parallel to *glossolalia*."[9] The fact that tongues are said to cease at the second coming of Christ (1 Cor. 13:8) leads Anthony Thiselton to conclude that it *cannot* be angelic speech, for why would a heavenly language terminate in the eschaton?[10] But it would not be heavenly speech per se that ends, but heavenly speech on the part of *humans* designed to compensate *now* for the limitations endemic to our fallen, pre-consummate condition.

Craig Keener, F. M. and Ada Thompson Professor of Biblical Studies at Asbury Theological Seminary, cites a document from Qumran, the site where the Dead Sea scrolls were discovered, that claims different angels lead the heavenly worship on successive Sabbaths making use of different languages. He suggests that since these angels are called "princes," it is possible they are those whom God appointed to oversee the nations whose languages they employ. (See Dan. 10:13, 20–21; 12:1.)[11]

Seventh, some say the reference in 1 Corinthians 14:10–11 to earthly, foreign languages proves that all tongues-speech is also human languages. But Paul's point is that tongues function *like* foreign languages, *not* that tongues *are* foreign languages. He is saying the hearer cannot understand uninterpreted tongues any more than he can understand the one speaking a foreign language. If tongues *were* a foreign language, there would be no need for an *analogy*.

Eighth, Paul's statement in 1 Corinthians 14:18 that he "speak[s] in tongues more than all of you" is evidence that tongues are not foreign languages. As theologian Wayne Grudem notes, "If they were known foreign languages that foreigners could understand, as at Pentecost, why would Paul speak more than all the Corinthians in private, where no one would understand, rather than in church where foreign visitors could understand?"[12]

Ninth, if tongues-speech is always a human language, Paul's statement in 1 Corinthians 14:23 wouldn't necessarily hold true. His argument in this passage is that if tongues is to be used in the corporate assembly of God's people, there must be accompanying interpretation. Otherwise if "outsiders or unbelievers enter, will they not say that you are out of your minds?" My response is, not necessarily if the tongues being spoken are languages known throughout the world at that time. If that were the case, any unbeliever who knew the language being spoken would more likely conclude the person speaking was highly educated rather than out of his mind.

WHAT, THEN, ARE TONGUES?

We have seen that there are a variety or differing species of tongues. On some occasions, such as at Pentecost, they are actual human languages spoken somewhere in the world, dialects such as those employed by Parthians and Medes and Elamites and people from Cappadocia, just to mention a few. (See Acts 2.) On other occasions, primarily in the daily experience of local churches throughout the ancient world and in our day as well, they may be one of the many dialects spoken by the angelic hosts.

But more times than not I suspect the tongues Paul had in mind in 1 Corinthians 12–14, the tongues in which I regularly speak and pray today, is a heavenly language, a language that derives from the supernatural enablement of the Holy Spirit. It is not a language that anyone on earth could study in grad school or encounter while on a mission trip to a remote third-world country. Thus, it is not itself in the same category of such languages as English or German or Swedish, but it functions to communicate desires, requests, and declarations of praise and thanksgiving that God fully grasps. Therefore, we can say that tongues is linguistic, in the sense that it is genuine speech that communicates information. Or as author and theologian Robert Graves has said, tongues is "structured, articulate speech."[13] Remember: Paul says the one speaking in tongues is speaking to God and later will contend that uninterpreted tongues is a form of giving thanks to God (1 Cor. 14:16–17). So there is substantive content to what is being spoken. But it comes in a form uniquely and especially crafted or shaped by the Holy Spirit, who is its source. Thus the only way that either I or any other human might know what is actually being said is if the same Holy Spirit provides the interpretation.

There is no question, then, that tongues-speech conveys meaning. If tongues-speech is meaningless, it would be a futile and fruitless experience. The purpose of tongues-speech is to communicate with God (1 Cor. 14:2). That neither the speaker nor those listening understand what is being said (unless, of course, the gift of interpretation should accompany it) is no objection to the legitimacy of tongues. It only matters that God understands, that the "coded" speech of the believer contains meaningful, substantive truths that are known to God because they have their source in God. Therefore, I agree with New Testament scholar David Garland when he says that "Paul understands it [tongues] to be a language inspired by the Spirit and not a noncognitive, nonlanguage utterance. It is not simply incoherent babbling in the Spirit.... Tongues consist of words..., which, though indecipherable, are not meaningless syllables strung together."[14]

Chapter 5

THE PURPOSE OF TONGUES, PART I

IN THIS CHAPTER we'll take up four more of our thirty crucial questions, beginning with the issue of whether God intended tongues to be used primarily for the evangelism of unbelievers.

5. Is the gift of tongues primarily designed for the evangelism of unbelievers?

This shouldn't take up much of our time since I already addressed it in the second chapter. But it never hurts to remind ourselves repeatedly of what the Bible says.

As we saw in our discussion of events on the day of Pentecost, Jesus' disciples most assuredly spoke in actual human languages they had never before learned. And the massive crowd of Jewish pilgrims present that day were astonished when they heard them "speak in his own language" (Acts 2:6). But what is spoken by means of this miraculous gift is not evangelism. It is worship or praise or adoration. The disciples are heard to be declaring "the mighty works of God" (Acts 2:11).

Contrary to what many cessationists argue, there is no evidence that tongues-speech in Acts 2 (or elsewhere) served an evangelistic purpose. Nowhere does any biblical author encourage the use of tongues when unbelievers are present in order to win them to saving faith in Christ. Later, in Acts 10, one of only two other instances of tongues-speech in Acts, Luke uses the related verb form of the word *megaleios* used in Acts 2:11, which is translated "extolling God" (Acts 10:46; see 19:17 where it is said "the Lord Jesus was extolled"). Also against the notion that tongues were evangelistic is the fact that when they were spoken at Pentecost, the hearers were left in complete confusion, some openly ridiculing the phenomenon.

Thus, when tongues occurred at Pentecost, the people present didn't hear an evangelistic message but doxology or worship. This is consistent with what Paul says in 1 Corinthians 14 where he describes tongues as a vertical communication with or to God. As we will shortly see, tongues is either prayer to God, praise to God, or a way in which the believer gives thanks to God. In Acts 2 it is only Peter's preaching that brings salvation. (See Acts 2:22–41.) Thus, we see that the primary purpose of tongues-speech is to *address* God (whether it be in praise or prayer; see 1 Cor. 14:2, 14), not men.

Furthermore, if, as the cessationist argues, tongues was primarily an evangelistic sign-gift for unbelieving Jews or was designed to communicate the gospel to non-Christians, why were only believers present in two of its three occurrences in Acts? Let me ask the same question in slightly different terms. In Acts 10 the only people present when Cornelius and his companions spoke in tongues were the Jewish believers who had accompanied Peter to Caesarea. There simply was no occasion for tongues to serve an evangelistic purpose given the obvious absence of unbelievers. The same holds true in Acts 19. The only person explicitly identified as being present when the disciples of John the Baptist spoke in tongues was the apostle Paul. Even if there were traveling companions with him, they would have been followers of Jesus. So again we see that tongues was present but unbelievers were not. It simply will not hold up to scrutiny to say that tongues is an evangelistic instrument.

Furthermore, if tongues-speech is always a foreign language designed by God to be used in sharing the gospel with unbelievers, why does Paul describe his exercise of this gift in his private devotions when no one else is present to hear him? (See 1 Corinthians 14:14–19.) In the previous chapter we looked closely at 1 Corinthians 14:2. This verse carries application for this question as well: If God designed tongues to enable believers to speak to other people in their own language, why would Paul say in 1 Corinthians 14:2 that the person who speaks in tongues does not speak to men but to God? Evangelism is speaking to men. But tongues is speaking to God.

I'm sure you are wondering what I will say about 1 Corinthians 14:22, where Paul declares that tongues are a sign for "unbelievers." Doesn't this mean he viewed the purpose of tongues as declaring the gospel to those who don't know Christ? No, in fact, it doesn't. But you'll have to be patient and wait for my discussion of that passage (unless you wish to turn to chapter 10 right now).

6. Is it OK to seek personal edification by speaking in tongues?

Here's a simple question for you that has an equally simple answer: Why are you reading this book? In fact, why do you read *any* book? I suppose someone might answer by saying, "I'm reading it to be informed. I'm curious about what you have to say concerning this gift." OK, that's entirely legitimate. But I suspect that deep down inside you are reading this book as you would any book in order to build yourself up in your Christian faith. You want to grow as a Christian and be knowledgeable about the things of God. You have a deep desire to improve your relationship with Jesus and be more conformed to His image. You long to be more Christlike in order that you might be a more effective witness to others and to be better equipped to encourage them and love them and instruct them. To be brief, you are reading this book in order to edify yourself!

Those who stand opposed to the exercise of tongues today typically appeal to what Paul said in 1 Corinthians 14:4. There he says, "The one who speaks in a tongue builds up himself, but the one who prophesies builds up the church." They then respond to this statement by saying that since spiritual gifts are given to benefit, bless, and build up *others* and the "common good" (see 1 Corinthians 12:7), and tongues serves to benefit, bless, and build up *oneself*, it should be avoided at all costs.

But Paul's words in 1 Corinthians 14:4 are not an indictment or an accusation against the use of uninterpreted tongues. *Self-edification is a good thing!* It's just not the best thing. As I noted, you are reading this book in order to edify yourself! You attend a Sunday school class in order to edify or strengthen your faith. You attend good Christian conferences hoping to be built up and strengthened in your relationship with God. And it's good that you do. That is a good and godly motive. You read the Bible to be edified. You practice spiritual disciplines to be edified. You will undoubtedly purchase books in your local Christians bookstore and read them in order to be edified. Not only is self-edification a good thing, but for you to avoid what might enhance and deepen your walk with Christ is a bad thing!

If you still aren't convinced, consider that *we are commanded to edify ourselves.* In Jude 20–21 we read this: "But you, beloved, building yourselves up in your most holy faith and praying in the Holy Spirit, keep yourselves in the love of God."[1] Here in Jude 20 the word translated "building...up" is built on the same root as the word translated "building up" in 1 Corinthians 14:4. If anything, it is an intensified version of the same verb. Whether "praying in the Holy Spirit" in Jude 20 is a reference to praying in tongues is an issue we'll take up later in this book. But the point is simply that we are obligated, required, and commanded to do what we can, with the help of the Holy Spirit, to edify and build up and strengthen ourselves spiritually.

Therefore, *self-edification is only bad if it is done as an end in itself.* But if you are built up in Christ in order that you in turn might be more effective in building up others, then it is certainly a good and godly thing. So it is good to take whatever steps you can to edify yourself, to build up and strengthen your soul. But it is good primarily so that you might be better able and equipped to build up others. That is why Paul said back in 1 Corinthians 12:7 that every spiritual gift has as its ultimate and primary goal "the common good," that is, the spiritual benefit and blessing of others in the church.

One more thing should be noted. As we will shortly see, Paul describes his own private prayer life in 1 Corinthians 14:18 as consisting, in large part, of speaking in tongues. Gardner is surely spot-on in his commentary on 1 Corinthians when he says, "Paul would hardly admit to using this gift privately if he regarded it as an entirely self-serving activity that necessarily puffs up the individual."[2] That is to say, if self-edification through speaking in tongues were inherently evil or dangerous, Paul would no doubt have labored to avoid it and would most assuredly not have spent any time in his private devotional life praying in this manner.

I'm quite certain that many reading this book will be asking themselves this question: How precisely does praying in a heavenly language that one does not understand serve to build up the speaker? Somewhat surprisingly, neither Paul nor any other biblical author bothers to tell us. They provide no explanation. But that doesn't mean there isn't good reason to believe tongues does in fact edify and strengthen the one who prays. We know this because Paul will tell us in 1 Corinthians 14:14–18 that despite the fact that his mind is "unfruitful" (i.e., incapable of comprehending what is said, as we read in verse 14), he is determined to continue both praying and singing in tongues. He would not have resolved to perpetuate this spiritual practice if he didn't believe it would bear good fruit in his life.

So how then does prayer in tongues build us up? I wish I could direct your attention to several explicit statements in the New Testament that answer the question. But neither Paul nor anyone else appears to be overly concerned with the matter. That they do edify us, even if in ways we can't explicitly identify, seems to be enough for the apostle. But that doesn't mean we can't suggest a few possible ways in which this is done. I would only remind you that what follows comes from personal experience, not Scripture. That doesn't mean my comments are contrary to Scripture; only that the Word of God is silent on the subject.

Perhaps the first thing to be noted is that since tongues is a form of prayer and praise, we should expect it to strengthen the believer in much the same way prayer and praise in one's native language regularly does. The fact that the latter is intelligible and tongues unintelligible may lead you to think the comparison between the two is baseless. But this objection, once more, is built on the assumption that intelligibility is a necessary prerequisite to edification. However, as we've seen, Paul would differ. Although his mind is unfruitful when he prays, praises, and gives thanks in tongues, he is determined to make use of this gift in his private devotional life. The point is that simply because we cannot fathom how something unintelligible serves to sanctify and edify the believer does not mean it doesn't or can't.

When I pray in English, I'm greatly encouraged to know that my deepest desires, fears, needs, and hopes are being communicated to God. This is no less the case when I pray in tongues. My confidence rests in the reality of the Spirit's work in making known to the Father precisely what my heart feels and longs for.

When I pray in tongues, I often (but not always) experience a sense of nearness to God that I don't ordinarily have at other times. James assures us that if we will draw near to God, He will draw near to us (Jas. 4:8). We can draw near to God in countless ways—in worship, in obedience, in ordinary prayer, etc. Praying in tongues is by no means the only way, but it is assuredly an important way for those who have this gift. In fact, I often find that when praying in tongues, the circumstances, noises, and even people that tend to distract me from single-minded focus on God are absent, or at least they are minimized. It is especially during those seasons in life when God seems distant and far removed that praying in the Spirit serves to reignite in my heart the assurance that He is in fact closer than the skin on my bones.

In Ephesians 3:14–21 Paul prays for several things, all of which pertain to our *sensible experience* of the love of Christ. He prays that we might be internally strengthened by the Spirit so that Christ might dwell in our hearts. But how can that be if we have *already* received Christ into our hearts when we were born again? The only viable explanation is that Paul is referring to an *experiential enlargement* of what is already theologically true. He wants us to be strengthened by the Spirit so that Jesus might exert a progressively greater and more intense personal influence in our souls. The result of this expansion of the divine power and presence in our hearts is the ability to "comprehend...what is the breadth and length and height and depth" of Christ's love for us (Eph. 3:18). This is Paul's way of saying God intends for us to feel and experience and be emotionally moved by the passionate affection He has for us, His children. Theologian and New Testament professor D. A. Carson, in my view, is right on target when he says:

> This cannot be merely an intellectual exercise. Paul is not asking that his readers might become more able to articulate the greatness of God's love in Christ Jesus or to grasp with the intellect alone how significant God's love is in the plan of redemption. He is asking God that they might have the power to grasp the dimensions of that love

in their experience. Doubtless that includes intellectual reflection, but it cannot be reduced to that alone.[3]

But how are we to compute such love? What are its dimensions? Does it come in meters or miles? Do we measure it in yards or pounds? Does Paul intend for you to think in terms of mathematical proportions, as if to suggest that God loves you one hundred times more than He loves the angels or fifty times less than He loves a purportedly godlier Christian? Quite the contrary, says Paul. There is a width and length and height and depth to Christ's love for you that goes beyond human measurement. The immensity and magnitude of that love is incalculable. Its dimensions defy containment. It is beyond knowing. Yet Paul prays that we might *know* it! This deliberate oxymoron serves to deepen what is already too deep to fathom. British scholar Andrew Lincoln summed it up best by saying, "It is simply that the supreme object of Christian knowledge, Christ's love, is so profound that its depths will never be sounded and so vast that its extent will never be encompassed by the human mind."[4]

I'm not suggesting that only those Christians who pray in tongues can experience this reality. By no means! This is the inheritance and indescribable blessing of all those who have been born again, regardless of what spiritual gifts they either have or don't have. My point is simply that in my personal experience of praying and praising in tongues, I have found this truth to be extraordinarily powerful and transformative. The Spirit awakens in me an almost tangible sense of the affection that my heavenly Father has for me. The indwelling presence of the risen Christ becomes more (although certainly not less) than a doctrinal affirmation. And the "fullness of God" with which I am "filled" (Eph. 3:19) is among other things a sensible blessing that alerts and awakens me to the deeply personal and intimate fellowship I have with God.

Prayer in tongues has also served to intensify in me the truth of

1 Peter 1:8 in ways that I never knew before. Peter speaks of loving Christ, believing Christ, and rejoicing in Christ "with joy that is inexpressible and filled with glory." Again, please know that I'm not restricting this truth only to those who pray and praise in tongues. I'm merely describing the heightened manner in which I experience this love, faith, and joy when I praise God in tongues. It is truly "inexpressible"! No ordinary human vocabulary can find the terminology to articulate my joy and the gratitude I feel for all God is for me in Jesus. My prayer language provides me with a means of giving heartfelt expression to these deeply personal and intimate affections for my Savior.

I've also discovered, and others frequently bear witness to the same, that tongues builds up or intensifies one's faith. When I struggle with doubt or find myself overcome with anxiety or perhaps even fear that all I've believed is a myth, I resort to speaking to God in my prayer language and find that the Holy Spirit re-energizes my confidence and puts my heart at rest.

I suspect that my experience is not unlike that of most Christians. There are times when my heart grows cold and the pressures and disappointments of life combine to snuff out the flame of the Spirit's presence. But when I devote myself to extended times of praying in tongues, I soon discover that my sensitivity to the Spirit's work of conviction has returned. One practice that has proven especially powerful is to precede my time of study of God's Word with a season of praying and praising in tongues. In fact, I often find myself praying in tongues simultaneously with a deep immersion into the truths of the written Word. This should not surprise us, as the Word and the Spirit have forever been wedded by God in a glorious convergence. One without the other is a recipe either for hardness of heart or unbridled fanaticism.

Contrary to what many have concluded, *tongues is not an assertion of my strength but of weakness*. It is my confession to God that my mind suffers from the limitations of finitude and the human boundaries of what I'm capable of understanding. Thus tongues is always a declaration of utter dependence on the Holy Spirit, not only in terms of what He knows needs to be communicated in prayer but also of the supernatural power I desperately need to overcome the downward drag of my sinful flesh.

To the extent that Romans 8:26–27 at least includes tongues,[5] it serves to give expression to our groaning for the consummation of God's redemptive purposes on our behalf. The groaning described by Paul is the inescapable consequence of living under the curse and laboring in a body given to fleshly impulses and vulnerability to decay and death. Praying in the Spirit is one way in which God provides me with a foretaste of the day of redemption when the groaning of God's children together with the groaning of the material creation will give way to the celebration of complete victory.

Some have mistakenly concluded that the gift of tongues is a sign either of triumphalism or escape, when in fact it is neither. Because tongues is often viewed as the line of demarcation between Pentecostal/Charismatic believers and the rest of those who self-identify as Evangelicals, some of the former have sinfully concluded that they belong to an elitist body of believers who know and experience more of God's favor than others. At the other end of the spectrum are those who employ the gift of tongues to avoid having to face the challenges and conflicts that come with living in a fallen and broken world. The fact is that tongues is simply one way among many by which the Spirit empowers and encourages us to walk not around but through the valley of the shadow of death without fear or hesitation.

7. What does Paul mean when he says the person who prophesies is greater than the one who speaks in tongues? Is tongues inferior to prophecy?

If we are to answer this question, we need to see the passage in its context. Here is what Paul wrote:

Pursue love, and earnestly desire the spiritual gifts, especially that you may prophesy. For one who speaks in a tongue speaks not to men but to God; for no one understands him, but he utters mysteries in the Spirit. On the other hand, the one who prophesies speaks to people for their upbuilding and encouragement and consolation. The one who speaks in a tongue builds up himself, but the one who prophesies builds up the church. Now I want you all to speak in tongues, but even more to prophesy. The one who prophesies is greater than the one who speaks in tongues, unless someone interprets, so that the church may be built up.

—1 Corinthians 14:1–5

Paul couldn't have been clearer on this point. In fact, it is his primary point in the whole of 1 Corinthians 14, namely, other people in the body of Christ can only be edified if they can understand what you are saying. Spiritual fruit is the result of comprehensible teaching and encouragement. Now, as we've just seen, the person who prays in tongues can be edified by the exercise. But no one else can, unless of course what is said in tongues is interpreted.

As Paul says, when you prophesy in the corporate gathering of the church, you do so in the language that everyone present can understand. That is why they experience "upbuilding and encouragement and consolation." Paul makes it quite clear that he wishes all Christians spoke in tongues (more on this in a subsequent chapter). And by this he must mean tongues in private devotions because he contrasts it with prophecy in the corporate assembly. This is why the one who prophesies is "greater." It is because through the person's gift the church is built up. However, if someone follows a tongue with an interpretation, people can be built up just as effectively as if they had heard a prophetic word.

So we should not take Paul's words here as an indictment against tongues. I encounter people all the time who think to themselves, and say to me: "Well, if the one who prophesies is *greater* than the one who speaks in tongues, the tongues-speaker must be *inferior* and perhaps even dangerous and therefore is to be avoided." But saying the one who prophesies is greater is not a criticism or a rejection of tongues. It is simply Paul's way of saying that when you compare intelligible prophecy with unintelligible tongues, only prophecy is of benefit to others in the gathered assembly of God's people. That is why it is "greater." But if tongues are interpreted, as Paul says in the middle of verse 5, it becomes the functional equivalent of prophecy. That doesn't mean interpreted tongues equals prophecy. They are and always remain two different gifts of the Spirit. It simply means prophecy is no longer "greater" than tongues because the tongue is interpreted and consequently just as intelligible and just as capable of edifying others as is prophecy. Interpreted tongues *function* equally as well as prophecy to build up the body.

So let me briefly sum up this point. The tongues Paul wishes all would speak (1 Cor. 14:5) is obviously the tongues he mentioned in the immediately preceding verse (1 Cor. 14:4). We know verse 4 is referring to uninterpreted tongues because Paul says that although he wishes all spoke in tongues, he prefers that they prophesy. And the reason for preferring prophecy over tongues is prophecy is immediately intelligible to all. It doesn't require interpretation. This preference for prophecy over tongues disappears, however, if the tongues-speech is the sort that is followed by interpretation. Then tongues function in the same way prophecy does by encouraging and edifying others in the body of Christ (1 Cor. 14:5).

8. Is tongues-speech an "ecstatic" experience?

Is tongues-speech an *ecstatic* experience? In his book on spiritual gifts cessationist Thomas R. Schreiner repeatedly refers to tongues as "ecstatic utterances,"[6] despite the fact that tongues is never once spoken of in this way in the New Testament. Although certain English translations may employ the adjective *ecstatic* to describe tongues, the word itself is nowhere found in the original Greek text to modify the nature of tongues.

Everything depends, as it should, on how the word *ecstatic* is defined. The *Concise Oxford English Dictionary* defines *ecstasy* as "an overwhelming feeling of great happiness or joyful excitement; an emotional or religious frenzy or trance-like state."[7] The principal definition of *ecstatic* is "blissfully happy; joyful; involving an intense mystical or trance-like experience."[8] *Webster's* is similar and defines *ecstasy* as "a state of being beyond reason and self-control" or a "state of overwhelming emotion" and "rapturous delight," and *ecstatic* as "of, relating to, or marked by ecstasy."[9] Many define *ecstatic* as a mental or emotional state in which the person is more or less oblivious to the external world. The individual is perceived as losing self-control, perhaps lapsing into a frenzied condition in which self-consciousness and the power for rational thinking are eclipsed.[10]

The Greek verb *existēmi* is used in seventeen verses in the New Testament and can be rendered either "to amaze" or "to confuse" someone. Twice it means "to be out of one's mind." (Interestingly enough, this was the charge brought against both Jesus in Mark 3:21 and Paul in 2 Corinthians 5:13.) It more commonly is translated "to be amazed" or "confused" or even "to be frightened." The noun *ekstasis* is used seven times in the New Testament and typically has the sense of "amazement" (Mark 5:42; Luke 5:26; Acts 3:10) or "astonishment" (Mark 16:8). Three times it is translated by the English Standard Version as "to fall into a trance" (Acts 10:10; 11:5; 22:17) during which the individual has a revelatory vision.

It must be clearly noted that neither the verb nor the noun is ever used to describe someone who is speaking, praying, or praising God in tongues. There is simply no indication anywhere in the Bible that people who speak in tongues lose self-control or become unaware of their surroundings or in any sense of the term fall into a trancelike state. Paul's instruction on how tongues should be used in the corporate assembly only makes sense on the assumption that the one speaking in tongues is in full control of his or her senses and therefore can start and stop speaking at will (1 Cor. 14:15–19, 27–28, 40; cf. 14:32). If they were not in complete control of their tongues-speech, Paul's exhortation would make no sense. They were not oblivious to their surroundings or to what others were saying. Anyone who claims that he or she could not refrain from speaking out in tongues is simply in error.

Thus, any suggestion that speaking in tongues entails an experience of mental detachment wherein a person becomes unaware of her surroundings and in varying degrees oblivious to sight or sound, is not biblical. Others define *ecstasy* as something akin to divine seizure in which the Holy Spirit overrides and usurps control of one's faculties of thought and speech. This isn't to deny or to in any way undermine the reality of spiritual trances in which the person is granted a vision from God. But nowhere in the New Testament is speaking in tongues associated with trances or uncontrolled frenzy or any such state of mind and spirit.

I think we can assume that Paul would say much the same thing when it comes to the spiritual gift of prophecy. He assumes the person prophesying is capable of recognizing from some form of signal that someone else had received a revelation and was ready to speak (1 Cor. 14:30). Clearly, then, she was not oblivious to her surroundings. The person prophesying is also expected to cease speaking upon recognition that another has received a revelation ("let the first be silent"). The prophet could both speak and keep silent at will. Also, the second prophet didn't burst into speech but somehow indicated to the first, then waited until she had stopped.

Paul says that all who prophesied could do so in turn, "one by one" (1 Cor. 14:31), indicating the sensible and voluntary control of their faculties. In 1 Corinthians 14:32 Paul says "the spirits of prophets are subject to prophets." He is referring to the many different manifestations of the one Holy Spirit through the spirit of each individual prophet. (See also 1 Corinthians 14:12.) This means the Holy Spirit will never force or compel a prophet to speak but subjects His work to the wisdom of each individual. The Spirit voluntarily submits in this one respect for the sake of order. This isn't a theological declaration that we are in some sense superior to or more powerful than the Holy Spirit. It isn't the nature of the Spirit to incite confusion or to coerce the will; thus He subordinates His inspiration to the prophet's own timing. This verse also answers a potential objection to Paul's instructions in 1 Corinthians 14:30, "If a revelation is made to another sitting there, let the first be silent." Someone might object by saying she was forced to prophesy (or perhaps even to speak in tongues), being unable to restrain herself and thus unable to defer to a second. Paul's answer is that the Holy Spirit remains subject to the prophets, never forcing one to speak in a disorderly or chaotic way. The Spirit is neither impetuous nor uncontrollable.

It seems reasonable and well-justified to view speaking in tongues in much the same way. The tongues-speaker could speak or be silent at will and was expected to follow a prescribed order of service in the exercise of the gift (1 Cor. 14:27–28), something out of the question if he or she were in any sense mentally disengaged from events in the meeting.

But let's return for a moment to *Webster's* secondary definition of *ecstasy* as the experience of "rapturous delight."[11] I can certainly see where one might think of tongues in this way. On numerous occasions when I speak in tongues, and even more so when I sing in tongues during the course of a Sunday worship service, I experience an elevated emotional state of being in which joy, peace, and love flood my heart beyond what I might feel at any other time. But I remain fully in control of all my senses and am never oblivious to my surroundings (although I must say there is what may be

THE LANGUAGE OF HEAVEN

considered a mild dissociation as the focus of my mind and affections is singularly set on God and all that He has done for me in Jesus). Thus tongues is often highly emotional and exhilarating, but that does not mean it is "ecstatic." In many instances praying in tongues "may be used with the same emotional outpouring elicited by opening a can of soup or feeding the cat."[12] So sometimes tongues is highly emotional while at other times it is not. But in no case is it ecstatic.

Chapter 6

THE PURPOSE OF TONGUES, PART II

THERE'S NO GETTING around the sad fact that Charismatic Christians, especially those who speak in tongues, are often viewed as theological lightweights. "If only you had more interest in biblical truths," some are inclined to say, "you wouldn't spend so much time praying in gibberish that neither you nor anyone else can understand. It seems you are so infatuated with spiritual experience that you disregard or rarely worry about what the Bible actually says."

I hope by now that you can see how misguided this is. My defense of the legitimacy of tongues-speech is rooted in and tethered to Scripture. If it isn't, you should ignore what I say. I highly prize the mind and rigorous theological reflection, and this is in no way threatened or compromised by the fact that I daily pray and praise God in tongues. This leads us to our next question.

9. Is speaking in tongues a sign of anti-intellectualism or a sign that people are afraid of deep theological thinking?

While we must engage intellectually with all that Scripture says, we must at the same time be careful to resist what I call *idolatry of the mind*. Needless to say (or perhaps I *do* need to say it), I'm not suggesting the mind isn't essential for Christian living. The mind is not our enemy. Our minds are to be constantly renewed (Rom. 12:1–2). It is through our minds that we understand who God is. There is no such thing as "mindless" Christianity. In fact, if you didn't make use of your mind, you would have no idea what I'm saying right now or have any capacity to evaluate whether it is true or false! And when people minimize the mind or treat it as a threat to true spirituality, they often end up in either godless living or a cult, or both. So let me explain what I mean by "idolatry of the mind."

What I have in mind (no pun intended) is the approach to Christian spirituality that argues nothing is of value unless it can be cognitively understood. And many of you are saying right now, "Yeah, that's right." Well, no, it isn't. Again, many opponents of the gift of tongues insist that nothing is of value in terms of its ability to build us up spiritually into the image of Jesus that does not pass through the cerebral cortex of the brain. Any notion that the Holy Spirit might engage with the human spirit directly, bypassing our cognitive thought processes, is anathema to most Evangelicals. If it is to be spiritually profitable, it must be intelligible.

Now, in one sense they have a very good point. In 1 Corinthians 14 Paul is concerned with what happens in the corporate gathering of the local church. When all God's people in a particular local congregation are gathered together, *everything should be intelligible* in order that all may be edified or built up. This is why Paul insists that if tongues is manifest in the corporate gathering, there must be interpretation. He never denies that something good and helpful is happening in the life of the person speaking in tongues.

But he rightly points out that it is entirely unhelpful for others if they don't understand what you are saying.

So we must recognize that there is a vast difference between the necessity of intelligibility for the sake of the entire body of Christ on the one hand, and on the other whether a Christian can be edified, blessed, and built up spiritually while speaking in uninterpreted tongues privately. Paul very clearly believed that tongues in the corporate assembly must be intelligible or interpreted for the sake of others who are listening. But he is equally clear that profound spiritual fruit is possible in the life of the individual believer when that person prays in tongues privately, when there is no interpretation.

Now, why do I say this? Several things in 1 Corinthians 14 lead me to this conclusion.

First of all, in 1 Corinthians 14:2 Paul writes this: "For one who speaks in a tongue speaks not to men but to God; for no one understands him, but he utters mysteries in the Spirit." The lack of understanding applies not only to those listening but also to the person speaking in tongues. Yet despite this lack of cognitive understanding of what is being said, the person "utters mysteries in the Spirit," and these utterances are obviously of benefit to the believer's prayer life. If they weren't, Paul would have prohibited the practice, which he didn't.

Second, Paul says the person who speaks in tongues is truly praying to God (v. 14), praising or worshipping God (v. 15), and thanking God (v. 16). But he also says this can be done while his "mind" is all the while "unfruitful" (v. 14). By the word *unfruitful* he means either "*I* don't understand what I am saying" or "*Other people* don't understand what I'm saying," or perhaps both. There is a strong likelihood that Paul is referring to his own comprehension or lack thereof. After all, he says, "*My* mind is unfruitful," not "Your mind is unfruitful" or "Their minds are unfruitful." In other words, Paul doesn't understand what he is praying or how he is giving thanks or in what manner he is worshipping. But praying, praising, and giving thanks is most certainly taking place! And all this at the same time he lacks cognitive awareness of what is happening.

The immediate response of many is to say: "Well, if one's mind is unfruitful, if one doesn't understand what one is saying, then it is worthless. Why would anyone find benefit or blessing in something he doesn't understand? Surely Paul's response to his mind being 'unfruitful' is to *stop* speaking in tongues altogether. Shut it down. Forbid it."

But that isn't Paul's conclusion. No sooner does he say his "mind is unfruitful" than he makes known his determined resolve: "I *will* pray with my spirit, but I *will* pray with my mind also; I *will* sing praise with my spirit, but I *will* sing with my mind also" (1 Cor. 14:15, emphasis added). We know Paul is referring to praying and singing in tongues because in the next verse he describes giving thanks with one's spirit as unintelligible to those who may visit the church meeting.

Many Christians are uncomfortable with reading Paul this way. They insist that if one's mind is unfruitful—that is to say, if one's mind is not engaged in such a way that the believer can rationally and cognitively grasp what is occurring—the experience, whatever its nature may be, is useless, perhaps even dangerous. Worse still, it might even be demonic. After all, if our minds are not engaged, what safeguards do we have against the encroachment of heresy? Subjectivism of this sort will serve only to diminish the centrality of Scripture in the life of the believing community.

I strongly disagree. If Paul had been fearful of *transrational* experience (which by the way is far and away different from being *irrational*), would not his next step be to repudiate the use of tongues altogether, or at minimum to warn us of its dangers? After all, what possible benefit can there be in a spiritual experience that one's mind can't comprehend? At the very least we should expect

Paul to say something to minimize its importance so as to render it trite, at least in comparison with other gifts. But he does no such thing.

A brief word is in order concerning my use of the word *transrational*. It may have caught some of you by surprise. First, let me be perfectly clear: there is nothing beneficial in being irrational. To be irrational is to be illogical or simply wrong in the conclusions one reaches or the beliefs one holds. Christianity as a whole is in many ways mysterious in the sense that it exceeds the limits of our finite minds. We simply don't perfectly and comprehensively understand everything. Only God does. Paul said as much in 1 Corinthians 13 when he conceded that "for now we see in a mirror dimly, but then face to face. Now I know in part; then I shall know fully, even as I have been fully known" (v. 12). But one does not have to know something exhaustively to know something is true. Our knowledge can be accurate, so far as it goes, without being comprehensive. I know the truth of the incarnation, that "the Word became flesh" (John 1:14). But I by no means understand all the immeasurable implications of this or even how it is possible for an infinite spiritual being to become a finite human being while remaining both infinite and spiritual.

So when I speak of something being transrational, I simply mean certain truths or experiences *transcend* our limited and altogether human intellectual capacity. They don't contradict or exclude anything else revealed in Scripture. But they certainly exceed it. And my point is that there can be certain spiritual experiences that we can't fathom or reduce to a nice, neat theological formula, yet they are profoundly beneficial and edifying in ways that we don't fully understand. This is certainly the case when it comes to speaking in tongues in one's private prayer closet.

I'll have more to say about this later in the book, especially Paul's comments in 1 Corinthians 14:14–19 and why this is rock-solid proof that he prayed in uninterpreted tongues in his private devotions. But for now suffice it to say that the apostle most assuredly believed that there was personal spiritual value in a practice that did not pass through the cognitive mechanism of his thinking brain.

Before leaving this subject, there is one more text that confirms my point. In Romans 8:26–27 Paul refers to an unusual experience of every believer in which the Holy Spirit "helps us in our weakness." I'll go into more detail about this in answer to yet another question later in the book, but clearly the apostle has in view a phenomenon that is not intelligible to us. He says that since we don't know what to pray for as we ought, "the Spirit himself intercedes for us with groanings too deep for words" (Rom. 8:26). If something is happening in us or on our behalf through the Spirit in such a way that it cannot be put into words, then clearly it is unintelligible. Words entail intelligibility. But this ministry of the Spirit either bypasses or in some manner exceeds our vocabulary and mental grasp. And yet it is obviously of tremendous spiritual value.

10. Is tongues-speech primarily directed to men or to God?

In an earlier chapter I answered this question, but in asking it again, I have something slightly different in mind. It is quite common in Charismatic churches for people to make use of tongues as a way of communicating, horizontally, a message to other Christians. One will often hear of a "message in tongues" that came during the course of a meeting.

But thus far it seems from what we've seen in Acts and 1 Corinthians that tongues is likely always either prayer, praise, or thanksgiving. In saying the person who speaks in a tongue "speaks not to men but to God" (1 Cor. 14:2), Paul is clearly telling us that tongues is a form of prayer. That is what speaking to God is! It is prayer, whether in the form of a request (petition), supplication, or intercession. As we'll see later in the book, speaking in tongues, and in particular singing in tongues, is a form of worship or extolling God and His mighty works. (See 1 Corinthians 14:14–15 and Acts 2:11; 10:46.) Tongues-speech is also a way in which a believer can give expression to his or her heartfelt gratitude or thanksgiving to God for what He has done (1 Cor. 14:16). More on this later.

My point in directing your attention to these texts is to ask the question, Is it biblical to describe tongues as a *message* directed horizontally to people rather than vertically to God? I've already briefly alluded to the fact that when tongues in the corporate assembly are interpreted, they become the functional equivalent of prophecy. That is to say, they serve to build up and encourage others in the same way prophecy does. But that doesn't mean they are in every sense equal to each other. When I hear someone praise God or pray to God, I am encouraged and even on occasion rebuked for my own lack of zeal and confidence in God's ability to answer. Are we not all blessed by the psalms, where David and others are recorded worshipping God and giving Him thanks? But these psalms are vertical in their orientation: they are directed to God, and we profit from them as we listen to or read someone else communicate to and with our heavenly Father.

So I'm not inclined to think of tongues as designed by God to function like teaching and prophecy. Tongues, instead, as already noted, is prayer, praise, and thanksgiving. That being the case, what we are hearing when someone speaks in tongues in a public setting is either their intercessory prayers or their worship of God. We should then expect the forthcoming interpretation to correspond to the tongues utterance. Otherwise we have good grounds for questioning if it is a genuine expression of the gift of interpretation.

If the interpretation of tongues is nothing more than prophecy, why bother with either tongues or interpretation if in the end we get what we otherwise, and more easily, would have gotten with a prophetic word alone? I agree that interpreted tongues *function* like prophecy insofar as they edify and encourage other believers (1 Cor.

14:5). But that is not to say that interpreted tongues are identical with prophecy. The latter would be true only if one assumes (and then proves) that tongues-speech is revelatory.

If what I've said is correct, it would suggest that the many so-called "messages" in tongues, ostensibly directed to people in the form of instruction, rebuke, or exhortation, have *not*, in point of fact, been properly interpreted. The correct equation would not be that tongues + interpretation = prophecy, but rather tongues + interpretation = prayer or praise or thanksgiving.

Having said all that, I should perhaps be more flexible in my understanding of what God can do through the gift of tongues. Is it possible that the Spirit can make use of a spoken word in tongues to convey a message of encouragement, counsel, instruction, or rebuke to another believer, or perhaps several believers? I think we should at least hold open the possibility that this can occur. But in doing so, it's important that we at least acknowledge that if it happens, it does so without explicit biblical sanction.

11. If tongues is primarily a form of prayer in words we don't understand, how can it be helpful to us in our relationship with God?

I certainly understand and appreciate the concern that gives rise to this question. Often when I begin to pray or sing in tongues, I find myself asking the same question over and over again: "God, I have no idea what I'm saying. Do You? I suppose I can only trust that my utterances make perfectly good sense to You. You are, after all, omniscient!"

People ask me this question about tongues more often than most others. They can make sense of why they pray in their native language. They know what they need and have no problem putting it into words that both they and others would comprehend. But when people are praying in tongues, they have no idea what the content of that speech is. Or do they?

The only way I know to answer this question is to describe my own practice. I don't have explicit biblical support for this, as if to say Paul or some other New Testament author says the same thing in some epistle. But given what I know of tongues and the nature of God, I think I'm on solid ground.

Before I pray in tongues, I rehearse in my mind—in English!—the many burdens on my heart. I identify people by name. I speak to myself of their needs and the love I have for them. If my heart is weighed down with the suffering and afflictions of people in my church, I try to mentally articulate them, and even on occasion speak them aloud. Of course, the first thing I do is then to pray in English. I may have a long list written down from which I operate. In any case, I pray as clearly and passionately as I can for as long as I can. But almost invariably I run out of energy. I run out of words. I run out of ways to give expression to their needs and my needs. I run directly into the reality that Paul mentions in Romans 8:26—I do not know what to pray for as I ought. I suspect that everyone reading this book, even those who are opposed to tongues in the church today, knows precisely what that feels like. It is frustrating. I often am overwhelmed with a sense of failure and both bodily and emotional weakness. What am I to do?

On the one hand, I put my trust and confidence in what Paul then says in Romans 8. He assures us all that the Holy Spirit happily compensates for our shortcomings and intercedes on our behalf with the Father, perfectly articulating in our place the needs we struggled to find words to express. Praise God for this glorious promise.

But I also respond to this problem by praying in tongues. Here is an example of what I typically say and do:

Heavenly Father, I come to You in the name of Jesus, Your Son and my Savior, and I do so in the power of the Holy Spirit. And I confess that I'm at my wit's end. I don't have

*anything left in my spiritual or intellectual tank. I've used
all the words I know. My dictionary is depleted! But I
believe I need to continue to pray for this person or that
circumstance. So, Father, here is my prayer. Here is the
working assumption on which I will proceed. I am going
to trust the Holy Spirit to grant me words of a heavenly
(or angelic) language that perfectly embody and express the
inarticulate groanings and shortcomings of my heart. If
You have laid these burdens on my heart and have stirred
me to pray on behalf of myself and these many others, I
will trust the Spirit to take the "mysteries" that I utter,
the verbal expressions that I don't understand, and shape,
form, and craft them into the precise requests You enjoy
answering. I confess that I don't know what I'm saying
when I pray in tongues. And honestly, Father, sometimes
I fear that it might be as nonsensical to You as it is to me.
But when that happens, I take myself in hand and rebuke
my own soul and preach to my heart with the reminder
that this gift You've given me is real and powerful and will
be used by the Spirit to make known to Your heart what is
on my heart. Thank You, Father, for hearing me in words
of this heavenly language.*

That's when I launch into prayer in tongues. It doesn't matter
how long or short it may be. But in most cases it extends for a
considerable period of time. In fact, almost without exception I
find myself praying well beyond the limits of what I could say if I
were speaking only in English. I will often be heard (unintention-
ally) praying in tongues while working at other tasks. I will pray
in tongues in the shower, while getting dressed, during breakfast,
while driving to work, as I fall asleep on my pillow, and at any
and all other times as well. There is never an inappropriate time.
And I never seem to run out of physical or spiritual energy to do

so. Tongues is truly energizing. I feel exhilarated and refreshed instead of exhausted and depleted. Such is the power of the Holy Spirit when we pray in and through Him and the gift He has bestowed.

So is prayer in unintelligible and uninterpreted tongues in private a spiritually beneficial activity? By all means, yes!

There is one more passage in Paul's discussion of this issue that should forever put to rest any concern about the substantive and spiritually beneficial blessing that comes from speaking words that one's own mind does not comprehend. In 1 Corinthians 14:14–17 Paul states without equivocation his determination to both pray in tongues and pray in the language that he and anyone listening could understand. The former he calls praying "with my spirit" and the latter praying "with my mind." He uses the word *mind* to convey the idea that he and others could understand what was being said. It's important, says Paul, that we not only pray with the spirit (i.e., in tongues) but also with the mind.

> Otherwise, if you give thanks with your spirit, how can anyone in the position of an outsider say "Amen" to your thanksgiving when he does not know what you are saying?
> —1 Corinthians 14:16

Now, notice carefully what is happening here. The "outsider" is a visitor to the service. Whether Paul intends us to understand this person to be a Christian or non-Christian is unclear. However, since he envisions this person saying "Amen" to your words of gratitude, it is probable that he has a born-again person in view. He also says this person can be "built up" if the individual could understand what you are saying.

But the primary thing I want you to see is that when you "give thanks" with your spirit, that is to say, in an uninterpreted tongue, you are truly giving thanks! There is substantive content to your words despite the fact that neither you nor the outsider knows what is being said. *God* knows what you're saying. *God* hears your expression of gratitude. But it is far better that when you are in the presence of others in the assembly of God's people, you "give thanks" with your "mind" so all can hear it, comprehend it, and say "Amen" in response to it.

Paul then adds this critically important statement:

> For you may be giving thanks well enough, but the other person is not being built up.
>
> —1 Corinthians 14:17

Do you see the importance of this? We are trying to determine whether it is beneficial, helpful, or meaningful to utter words in uninterpreted tongues, words your mind does not comprehend. Here Paul says, in effect, "Yes, by all means it is real and meaningful and substantive. You are truly saying 'thank You' to God. You are expressing heartfelt gratitude for all He has done and will do, despite the fact that your mind doesn't comprehend it." Don't race past this verse! When you speak or sing in tongues in your private devotional life, you are truly expressing your appreciation to God for His grace, love, and providential kindness, among other things. Of course, should other people hear you do this in the absence of interpretation, they won't benefit from it. That would require interpretation. But the fact that *they* can't be built up doesn't mean *you* can't! You can, and you are!

So the answer to our question, once again, is yes! Speaking and singing in tongues in private, even without interpretation, is real communication, genuine worship, and authentic gratitude to God!

12. Is tongues also a way to worship God?

The simple and straightforward answer is yes, by all means. We see this from a handful of biblical texts. We've already taken note of what happened at Pentecost. There the disciples spoke exuberantly in human languages they had not previously learned and in doing so were heard declaring "the mighty works of God" (Acts 2:11). To proclaim the many miraculous and merciful deeds God has done is to worship Him; it is to make known His gracious acts in delivering His people and in preserving them in times of trouble. The psalmist exhorts us to "sing to him, sing praises to him; tell of all his wondrous works!" (Ps. 105:2). "We recount your wondrous deeds," declares Asaph (Ps. 75:1), and he speaks for himself in saying, "I will ponder all your work, and meditate on your mighty deeds" (Ps. 77:12). Such expressions of praise and honor are found throughout the psalms.

This is what we also encountered in Acts 10 when Cornelius and his Gentile companions spoke in tongues. Whether they were "extolling God" (Acts 10:46) in tongues or merely did so in conjunction with their tongues-speech is unimportant. What we see consistently in these texts is that often when one makes use of his or her gift, either the content or consequence of it is the praise and worship of God.

When Paul tells us that the one who speaks in tongues addresses God, not man, this may well include more than prayer. Praise is, after all, no less God-oriented speech than is petitionary prayer. But there can be no mistake about the role of tongues as worship when we come to Paul's description of his own personal practice. When he states his resolve to make use of tongues despite the fact that his mind doesn't grasp what is being said, he includes this affirmation: "I will sing praise with my spirit" (1 Cor. 14:15). The word translated "sing praise" is from the verb *psallō*, which means to touch or strike the strings or chords of a musical instrument. Others render it "to play on a stringed instrument" such as a lyre (or in our day a guitar) or "to sing to the music of the harp."[1]

I'll address this in more detail later, but for now be it noted that Paul's gift of tongues took on more than one formal expression. He didn't merely "speak" in tongues but often would "sing" in tongues as well. What he might say in the course of his prayers, he could as easily set to music and worship God in a more melodious and perhaps even poetic manner. There is, then, no escaping the fact that Paul viewed tongues as one way to sing his praises to God. The question we must now face is whether he believed this could or should be done in the corporate gathering of God's people, not merely by himself but in unison with other gifted individuals. And if he believed this was permissible, did it require interpretation in the same way he insisted it must when it came to a spoken utterance in tongues? To that question we now turn our attention.

13. Is it permissible for people to sing in tongues in corporate worship?

One question I'm often asked, for which I don't have a definitive answer, is whether it is biblically permissible to sing in uninterpreted tongues in a corporate setting. Many would immediately say no and point to Paul's emphasis throughout 1 Corinthians 14:28, "But if there is no one to interpret, let each of them keep silent in church and speak to himself and to God [presumably, in private]."

Of one thing I'm sure. If the corporate gathering in view is an official church service, the point of which is to edify other believers (see 1 Cor. 14:26), uninterpreted tongues is not permissible. This is what accounts for Paul's demand for silence in 1 Corinthians 14:28. But people will often suggest possible exceptions to this rule. In certain Pentecostal denominations it is almost standard practice for the pastor or worship leader, at some point in the course of corporate praise, to encourage everyone present to sing aloud in the Spirit, that is, in tongues. Rarely if ever is this followed with interpretation. And how could it be? If dozens, perhaps even hundreds, of people are singing in tongues at the same time, it would be utterly impossible for an interpretation of each utterance to be given.

For example, Mark Cartledge, an Anglican theologian and scholar of Pentecostal and Charismatic Christianity, describes his experience at three separate New Wine conferences in the earlier years of the twenty-first century, at which anywhere from five thousand to eight thousand people were in attendance. New Wine is a ministry outreach based in the UK and comprised largely of Anglicans who are committed to the contemporary validity of all spiritual gifts. According to Cartledge, there was typically a time when the worship leader would sing into the microphone in tongues and encourage others to do so as well. "It is interesting to observe," says Cartledge, "that I have never heard anyone give an audible message in tongues followed by interpretation."[2] The explanation given to Cartledge for this was that the gathering was too large to facilitate interpretation. Furthermore, the gathering was not a church service but a summer conference at which only believers were expected to be present. Might this, then, be an exception to the otherwise important rule that tongues always be followed by interpretation?

It is not uncommon in Charismatic church gatherings for the person leading worship to occasionally break from the song that all are singing in English (or in whatever language they all typically speak) and begin to sing in tongues on his or her own. No one else does. Sometimes it is hardly noticeable, but in most cases it is obvious what is happening. The leader will typically say that he or she was caught up in the euphoria of praise and very easily and naturally transitioned from singing in English to singing in tongues. Again, though, similar to what happened at the New Wine gathering, there is rarely if ever time given to ask for an interpretation.

What should we say if the gathering is one at which only believers are in attendance? What if the purpose of the meeting is not instruction or exhortation but praise and intercession? One of Paul's concerns is that uninterpreted tongues will confuse any unbelievers who may be present. (See 1 Corinthians 14:22–23.) But if the meeting is, if you will, a meeting of believers, perhaps even a small-group gathering in someone's home, that possibility no longer exists. In such settings the unintelligibility of uninterpreted tongues, whether spoken or sung, is no obstacle to achieving the purpose for which people have congregated and therefore would not violate Paul's counsel.

This is by no means a definitive answer. I also realize it is in large measure an argument from silence. I'm only suggesting that we be cautious about enforcing the rules of 1 Corinthians 14 in contexts that Paul didn't envision or in circumstances other than those that evoked his inspired counsel. What I'm saying is this. If a meeting was of a decidedly different nature and purpose from that which Paul assumes in 1 Corinthians 14—a meeting, for example, the overt aim and advertisement of which was *not* the instructional edification of the body, a meeting at which the presence of un-believers was neither encouraged nor expected—the effect of un-interpreted tongues, against which Paul warns in this chapter, *may* well be a moot point (and I emphasize the word *may*). If there was a gathering of Christians exclusively for the purpose of worship and prayer, a gathering in which the circumstances that evoked Paul's prohibition of uninterpreted tongues did not apply, would the pro-hibition stand? Perhaps not.

Chapter 7

PUBLIC EXPRESSION OF TONGUES

IN THIS CHAPTER we will address two important and related questions. They pertain primarily to the place where tongues-speech should occur. Some argue that tongues should only be exercised in the corporate gathering of the local church and always with interpretation. These folks do not believe tongues is meant for private devotions in one's prayer closet. So what does the Word of God have to say in response to these questions?

14. Does Paul always insist on interpretation if tongues is used in the public gathering of the church, and if so, why?

The answer to this question is an unequivocal yes. But a bit more explanation is in order. There can be little doubt that Paul places a high value on the edification or spiritual strengthening of believers in the body of Christ. In fact, he earlier said in 1 Corinthians 12:7 that all spiritual gifts, of whatever sort, are given by the Spirit "for the common good." By "the common good" he means the building up of all Christians in the local church. Gifts are not primarily intended by God to build up the one who is the recipient. Rather, we are each to use our gift or gifts so others will be encouraged and instructed in the truths of Christianity. That does not mean, however, that a person who exercises his or her gift won't or shouldn't be edified by it. It is inevitable, and good, that a believer is built up spiritually when one's gift is being used. It's just not the direct and primary goal. But it is certainly an indirect and secondary effect.

That the edification of others is preeminent in Paul's thinking is clear from a close reading of 1 Corinthians 14. Paul's preference for the gift of prophecy over that of uninterpreted tongues is due to the fact that the former builds up other believers. Tongues, when interpreted, also edifies others (v. 5). Prophecy is especially suited to edify, encourage, and console our brothers and sisters in the body of Christ (v. 3). Indeed, "the one who prophesies builds up the church" (v. 4).

In 1 Corinthians 14:6–12 Paul unpacks this principle in some detail. His point is that in order for a spiritual gift to be a blessing to someone else, there must be intelligibility. Incomprehensible communication in the corporate assembly is of no benefit to anyone. You have to understand and comprehend what is being said in order to profit from it. Uninterpreted tongues in the gathered assembly of God's people, says Paul, amounts to little more than "speaking into the air" (v. 9). Unintelligible speech simply cannot instruct or encourage or rebuke or bless others. So make absolutely certain that if someone speaks in tongues when the church is gathered together, there is an interpretation. Otherwise, keep silent. The bottom line for Paul is this: "when you come together," whatever spiritual gift is put into practice, "let all things be done for building up" (v. 26).

Now, some draw the wrong conclusion from this. They think that since Paul speaks with such energy about the failure of un-interpreted tongues in the gathered assembly to edify others, he must be opposed to the use of uninterpreted tongues anywhere and everywhere. But that is not what he says. I'll take up that issue momentarily, but first let's take a close look at the instruction Paul gives on how tongues is to be used when the whole church is assembled. He writes this:

> If any speak in a tongue, let there be only two or at most three, and each in turn, and let someone interpret. But if there is no one to interpret, let each of them keep silent in church and speak to himself and to God.
> —1 Corinthians 14:27–28

It would appear that some of the Corinthian believers had made two mistakes in their exercise of this gift. First, they had overemphasized its importance, thinking those who exercised a gift so obviously supernatural must themselves be extraordinarily favored of God. Their childish immaturity led them to conclude that tongues-speech was evidence of a transcendent and superior spirituality. Second, they were employing (indeed, flaunting) their tongues-speech in the public assembly without interpretation. Paul's response to such abuse is *not* to ban the gift of tongues from church life. Sinful, selfish abuse does not nullify the reality of a divine gift. His recommendation is not rejection but correction.

Briefly, the apostle's counsel in 1 Corinthians 14:26–40 is this. First, steps must be taken to prevent a simultaneous cacophony of tongues-speech. Try to imagine an entire body of believers all speaking loudly in tongues at the same time. One might think this would be a sign of the Spirit's powerful presence, but Paul forbids it because of the obvious failure of such a scenario to build up others.

Second, only two, or at most three, should speak during the course of a service. This is so the meeting does not become disorderly or unwieldy. Furthermore, he does not want those with the gift of tongues to assume a more prominent place in the body than is justified. Finally, tongues-speakers should never think they cannot control the gift. The Holy Spirit does not compel or overwhelm. If two or three have already spoken, Paul expects the others to keep quiet (implying that they have control or mastery over their gift). No one can ever say, "But I just couldn't help myself. The presence and power and impulse of the Holy Spirit were just too much for me to contain. I would have been quenching the Spirit's work had I kept silent!" No. The Holy Spirit never, ever moves or prompts someone to violate what He has previously said in Scripture.

There is another interpretation of Paul's instruction that should be noted. Some argue that he is not restricting tongues-speech to only two or three in the course of a corporate meeting; rather, he is saying that after two or three have spoken, room should be given for an interpretation of each. It is assumed that once this is done, two or three more may then speak, again to be followed by interpretation. On this view Paul isn't insisting that only two or three can speak in tongues at any one meeting of the church, but only that after two or three have spoken, there should be interpretation. Whether others would then speak in tongues as well is not something he directly addresses.

I'm not inclined to embrace this latter view for the simple fact that it would have played into the hands of those in Corinth who believed tongues was such a superior gift to all others that it should be given extraordinary prominence in the gathering of the church. That is to say, would not this view make it possible for those with the gift of tongues to justify dominating the meeting to such an extent that those with other spiritual gifts never, or rarely, had an opportunity to exercise them?

15. Does Paul teach that tongues may be used in private devotional prayer, or must all tongues-speech take place in the corporate assembly of the church, followed by interpretation?

We have already come across evidence in 1 Corinthians 14 that Paul believed there was spiritual benefit in a person praying in tongues in private without a subsequent interpretation. I argued earlier that when Paul says he wants "all to speak in tongues" (v. 5), he has uninterpreted tongues in view. The reason we know this is because he immediately asserts his preference for prophecy on the basis of the fact that prophecy, unlike uninterpreted tongues, "builds up the church" (v. 4). However, if someone interprets the tongues-speech, "the church may be built up" (v. 5) by it no less so than they are when someone prophesies.

But there is considerably more evidence that Paul not only believed in the great value of prayer in tongues in private but that he himself regularly practiced it.

Let's go back for a moment to a verse briefly noted previously. When the church is gathered together, tongues must be followed by interpretation. In the absence of someone with that gift, Paul tells the person with the gift of tongues to "keep silent in church and" to "speak to himself and to God" (v. 28). But where should this happen? I think it's quite obvious. Given the explicit prohibition of uninterpreted tongues-speech "in church," it seems virtually certain that Paul had in mind prayer in tongues in private, i.e., in a context other than the corporate gathering.

Some insist that Paul is instructing the tongues-speaker to pray silently to himself and to God while yet in the church gathering. But even if this is true (which I doubt), we would then have apostolic endorsement of *private* tongues-speech. If, as many cessationists contend, all tongues-speech is revelatory and is designed only for rational communication, Paul's counsel makes no sense. Why would God impart infallible, revelatory knowledge only for the recipient to speak it to himself and back to God? It seems as if the cessationist must envision the tongues-speaker waiting patiently until an interpreter arrives, at which time he can then speak audibly. But this is reading into the text a scenario conspicuous by its absence. Paul's instruction is for a situation in which there is *no* interpreter. He says nothing about the tongues-speaker waiting until one is present.

Furthermore, is it consistent with Paul's emphasis in 1 Corinthians 14 on all working together for mutual edification that he should recommend that some (perhaps many) focus their spiritual energy inwardly (praying in tongues) while someone else is speaking outwardly, ostensibly to edify the very people who on Paul's advice aren't even paying attention? No, I don't think so. Let me try to clarify that point. It simply makes no sense for Paul to say to the person who has the gift of tongues, "Hey, if there isn't anyone present to interpret your tongue, you can still use your gift in the gathered assembly. Just keep it low and speak quietly enough that no one can hear you except God." But if Paul was opposed to the private use of tongues in which no one but the speaker can be edified, this counsel would make no sense. The cessationist can't have it both ways. He can't argue that tongues is never intended for private use and then argue that private tongues-speech is precisely what Paul commands in 1 Corinthians 14:28.

Before proceeding, let me address one other question that is often asked. Unfortunately it is a question for which no explicit answer is given in the biblical text. Unavoidably then, any answer is going to be somewhat speculative in nature.

The question is this: How would the person with the gift of tongues know whether someone else has been given the interpretation of it? Paul seems to assume that the tongues-speaker would know this. He says it clearly: "But if there is no one to interpret, let each of them [i.e., the ones speaking in tongues] keep silent in church and speak to himself and to God" (1 Cor. 14:28). There are a couple of possible ways to answer this.

First, we should remember that most local churches in the first century were comparatively small. People didn't meet in huge auditoriums or conference centers. They met in homes. I suspect that on average most local churches in the first century rarely exceeded one hundred fifty people. Some homes had open courtyards or ter-races that might conceivably have had space for more. But even in such instances it would be quite the norm for virtually all people to know everyone else who was a member of that particular congrega-tion. I once pastored a church of some two hundred people, and I knew everyone by name and most everyone else did as well. In such a scenario it could be expected that the person speaking in tongues could look around and identify a person whom they knew had the gift of interpretation. In the absence of such an individual, Paul expected them to keep quiet.

Second, in 1 Corinthians 14:13 Paul exhorts the person who speaks in tongues to pray to God that he might also be given the gift of interpretation. Here it is:

> Therefore, one who speaks in a tongue should pray that he
> may interpret.
>
> —1 CORINTHIANS 14:13

There are many things to learn from this passage, not least of which is that not all spiritual gifts are bestowed at the moment of conversion. The person who has the gift of tongues is obviously a born-again believer, and yet Paul urges that individual to pray that the Spirit would be pleased to grant yet another spiritual gift. We also learn from this text that even though it is the Spirit's will to determine who gets what gift (1 Cor. 12:11), He expects us to ask Him for them. The Spirit's sovereignty in the distribution of spiri-tual gifts does not preclude the responsibility of each believer to pray for a particular gift, or perhaps even for several. It may well be the Spirit who has Himself evoked in the heart of a believer a desire for a particular gift because it is the Spirit's will to grant it to him or her.

In any case, what is most important for us here is that the potential absence of a person with the gift of interpretation can be overcome by simply praying that God would grant that ability to the very person who feels led to speak in tongues. Perhaps you are tempted to ask this question: Well, if the Spirit can provide an interpretation, why bother with speaking in tongues in the first place? Why not simply skip the tongue and go straight to the interpretation so everyone else can be edified and instructed by what is said? Paul doesn't answer the question. We can only assume he believed there was something profoundly important and of value to others to hear the word in tongues followed by its interpretation. Perhaps it is the supernatural phenomenon itself that he thinks would be uplifting to others, and he doesn't want them to miss out on the opportunity to witness this gift in operation. Beyond that we can only speculate.

Now, as we return to the original question of how the person with the gift of tongues might know if there was present a person with the gift of interpretation, Paul had a good answer: Pray that God might give you yourself this gift and you can exercise both for the benefit of others! But there is yet another possible answer to our question. Look at the following passage, where Paul gives this word of instruction:

> What then, brothers? When you come together, each one
> has a hymn, a lesson, a revelation, a tongue, or an interpre-
> tation. Let all things be done for building up.
> —1 CORINTHIANS 14:26

It would appear from this that Paul envisioned people coming to the meeting already in possession of a gift and a sense for how it should be utilized. When you come to the meeting, says Paul, some of you might have in your heart a hymn to sing, while others may have prepared a "lesson," or a word of theological instruc-tion. Still others might have already received from God a revela-tion on the basis of which they would then prophesy. Someone else might be strongly inclined to speak in tongues, while yet another would come either with an interpretation already in her heart or at least with the assurance that God would provide it should another choose to speak in tongues.

What this suggests is that at any gathering of a local church someone with the gift of tongues who feels prompted to speak out loud could, as it were, coordinate or connect in advance with those they know have the gift of interpretation to see if they have come to the meeting with an interpretation already in mind. Or those who regularly provide interpretation would enter the meeting already in possession of something God had revealed to them and would communicate this to the person who regularly speaks in tongues. My point is that Paul's language in 1 Corinthians 14:26 ("when you come together, each one *has* a hymn, a lesson, a revelation, a tongue, or an interpretation," emphasis added) indicates that people arrive already prepared to exercise their gift. It would only require the person who "has" a tongue to communicate with the person who "has" an interpretation (or vice versa) in order to make Paul's instructions in 1 Corinthians 14:27–28 more easily obeyed.

But I digress! Our concern here is to find evidence that Paul himself prayed and sang in tongues in his private devotional life. For that we turn our attention to 1 Corinthians 14:14–19. What follows is somewhat repetitive of what I wrote earlier, but it is so critically important that it calls for careful consideration yet again.

Paul says the person who speaks in tongues is truly praying to God (v. 14), praising or worshipping God (v. 15), and thanking God (v. 16). But he also says this can be done all the while his "mind" is "unfruitful" (v. 14). As noted earlier, the word *unfruitful* means either "*I* don't understand what I am saying" or "*other people* don't understand what I'm saying," or perhaps both (with the primary emphasis on the former). I'm inclined to think he has in view his own lack of understanding. After all, he says, "*My* mind is unfruitful," not that the minds of others are unfruitful. In other words, Paul doesn't understand what he is praying or how he is giving thanks or in what manner he is worshipping. But praying, praising, and giving thanks are most certainly taking place! And all this at the same time *he lacks cognitive awareness* of what is happening.

The immediate response of many is to say: "Well, if one's mind is unfruitful, if one doesn't understand what one is saying, then it is worthless. Why would anyone find benefit or blessing in something he doesn't understand? Surely Paul's response to his mind being 'unfruitful' is to stop speaking in tongues altogether. Shut it down. Forbid it."

But that isn't Paul's conclusion! No sooner does he say that his "mind is unfruitful" then he makes known his determined resolve: "I *will* pray with my spirit, but I *will* pray with my mind also; I *will* sing praise with my spirit, but I *will* sing with my mind also" (1 Cor. 14:15, emphasis added). We know Paul is referring to praying and singing in tongues because in the next verse he describes giving thanks with one's spirit as unintelligible to those who may visit the church meeting.

This reading of Paul's intent makes many Christians extremely uncomfortable. They insist that if one's mind is not engaged in such a way that the believer can intellectually and cognitively grasp what is occurring, the experience, whatever its nature may be, is useless, perhaps even dangerous. Worse still, might this sort of practice expose a person to demonic influence? Once the safeguards of intellectual discernment are lowered, are we not exposing ourselves to the potential for theological heresy? Failure to engage the mind, so goes the argument, serves only to diminish the centrality of Scripture in the life of the believing community.

I strongly disagree, and so does Paul. If the apostle had been fearful of transrational experience (which, as noted earlier, is far and away different from being *irrational*), he would have repudiated speaking in tongues and warned others of its inherent dangers. After all, what possible benefit can there be in a spiritual experience that one's mind can't comprehend? At the very least we should expect Paul to say something to diminish its importance or to marginalize its practice. But he does no such thing.

Let's look again closely at Paul's conclusion. He even introduces it by asking the question, in view of what has just been said in 1 Corinthians 14:14, "What is the outcome then?" (1 Cor. 14:15, NASB), or "What am I to do?" (ESV). I know what many of you think he should do: "Put a stop to this ridiculous and useless practice of speaking in tongues. There is only one viable response, only one reasonable conclusion: I'll never speak in tongues again since my understanding is unfruitful." But that isn't what he says.

His response is found in 1 Corinthians 14:15. There we read that he is determined to do both! "I *will* pray with my spirit," i.e., I will pray in tongues, and "I *will* pray with my mind also," i.e., I will pray in Greek or the language of the people so others who speak and understand the language can profit from what I say. Clearly Paul believed a spiritual experience beyond the grasp of his mind, which is what I mean by *transrational*, was yet profoundly profitable. He believed it wasn't absolutely necessary for an experience to be rationally cognitive for it to be spiritually beneficial and glorifying to God.

This isn't in any way to denigrate or impugn the crucial importance of one's intellect in the Christian life. Paul insists that we submit to the renewal of our mind, not its repression (Rom. 12:1–2). All I'm saying, what I believe Paul is saying, is that praying in tongues is profoundly beneficial and glorifying to God even though it exceeds or transcends the capacity of our minds to decipher.

How? I don't know! Paul doesn't say. Nowhere does he make an attempt to explain the spiritual dynamics of what happens when a person prays, praises God, or gives thanks in uninterpreted tongues. We simply don't know how it can be beneficial and edifying. But Paul, writing under the inspiration of the Spirit, says it is. And his personal practice of praying in tongues confirms it. If that isn't enough for you, there isn't much more I can say.

This leads to an important question. If Paul is determined to pray with the Spirit, i.e., pray in uninterpreted tongues, *where and when will he do it?* Since he has ruled out doing it in the public meeting of the church, he must be referring to *his private, devotional prayer life.* Paul's private prayer experience was also characterized by singing in or "with the Spirit" (1 Cor. 14:15, NASB), an obvious reference to singing in tongues, what must have constituted a free and more melodious and musical form of tongues-speech.

What Paul proceeds to say in 1 Corinthians 14:18–19 becomes grist for the mill on both sides in this debate. The Charismatic appeals to verse 18, while the cessationist points a finger at verse 19:

> I thank God that I speak in tongues more than all of you.
> —1 CORINTHIANS 14:18

> Nevertheless, in church I would rather speak five words with my mind in order to instruct others, than ten thousand words in a tongue.
> —1 CORINTHIANS 14:19

In verse 18 it's as if Paul opens the door to his prayer closet and allows us a brief peek into his private devotional life with God. His quiet times with the Lord were anything but quiet, as they featured praying and singing and praising in tongues, an experience for which he is profoundly grateful to God.

"But wait a minute," responds the cessationist. "The crucial issue with Paul isn't whether he speaks in tongues but what is appropriate in the public assembly of the church. Paul is determined only to do what is cognitively rational and thus edifying to others in the meeting of the church."

That's right. So how do we resolve this problem? It's really not that difficult. Paul has said that tongues-speech in the public gathering of the church is prohibited unless there is an interpretation. Since the purpose of such meetings is the edification of other believers, Paul prefers to speak in a language all can understand. Consequently, he rarely speaks in tongues in a public setting and will only do so if assured that an interpretation will follow.

However, if Paul speaks in tongues more frequently and fervently than anyone else, yet in church almost never does (preferring there to speak in a way all can understand), where does he speak in tongues? In what context would the affirmation of verse 18 take shape? The only possible answer is that Paul exercised his remarkable gift *in private, in the context of his personal, devotional intimacy with God.* Again, the only grounds I can see for objecting to this scenario is the reluctance that many cessationists have for spiritual experiences that bypass or transcend the mind.

Let's remember, this is the man who wrote Romans. This is the man whose incomparable mind and power of logical argumentation rendered helpless his theological opponents. This is the man who is known to history as the greatest theologian outside of Jesus Himself. This is the man who took on and took out the philosophers in Athens (Acts 17)! *Yes, logical, reasonable, highly educated Paul prayed in tongues more than anyone!*

My conclusion is that while we must vigorously affirm the critical importance of loving God with our minds and pursuing the edification of others in the church, the Charismatic exegesis of this passage in 1 Corinthians 14 is on the mark. I simply don't see any way around the fact that Paul not only believed in the spiritual value of praying in private in uninterpreted tongues but also himself practiced it. In fact, he happily declares that he prays in private in uninterpreted and therefore unintelligible tongues more than all the tongue-happy Corinthians combined!

RESPONDING TO OBJECTIONS

Thomas Edgar is one cessationist who has devoted considerable energy in an attempt to prove that tongues was never intended for private prayer.[1] British New Testament scholar Max Turner has responded to each of Edgar's arguments in precisely the way I would. So I will take advantage of Turner's excellent response to help us navigate our way to an answer for this question.[2]

Edgar's first argument is to direct our attention to 1 Corinthians 14:22 where Paul says tongues are for a "sign" (he also appeals to verses in the dubious ending of Mark, 16:15–17).[3] If tongues is intended to provide a "sign," they obviously have no role in one's personal and necessarily secretive prayer life. Turner rightly responds by reminding us that this is an example of unwarranted reductionism.[4] The latter term refers to the tendency to reduce the purpose of tongues (or any other gift) to one and only one purpose. But tongues clearly has a multiplicity of functions, one of which is the building up of the believer in private prayer. Edgar also stumbles in how to reconcile his view with what we've already seen in Acts 10 and 19. There is no indication in these texts that tongues served either an evangelistic purpose or as a sign.

Another argument is that a gift used in private could not edify the church as a whole, and that would put tongues in a separate category, different from all other spiritual gifts, each of which is supposed to build up the body of Christ. But Turner is quick to point out that when tongues is exercised in the public gathering of the church, there is always to be an interpretation. When that occurs, people are clearly edified. (See 1 Corinthians 14:5.) And as I've already argued, any time a believer is built up spiritually, the rest of the church stands to benefit. This argument of Edgar also fails to realize that every spiritual gift serves to build up or edify the one who makes use of it. When I teach, I'm built up by the exercise of my gift. That isn't my primary reason for teaching, but it is a wonderful, albeit indirect, product of my teaching gift. The same is true of all other gifts.

But wouldn't the private exercise of a gift like tongues be self-centered? No. When employed in prayer, praise, and thanksgiving, as Paul says of tongues in 1 Corinthians 14, it is profoundly and unmistakably *God*-centered.

Edgar also argues that if tongues can edify the one who uses it, wouldn't God give it to all His children? Again, however, this fails to realize that all spiritual gifts and not just tongues have the capacity to edify the person exercising it. Therefore, "the person who has not received the gift [of tongues] is not thereby necessarily impoverished."[5]

If the purpose of tongues is to aid one in private prayer devotions, why would there be a need for the gift of interpretation? Turner responds to this by pointing out that "on Edgar's view it should be an anomaly that the gift of interpretation is required at all."[6] Yet we see in 1 Corinthians 14 that when tongues is accompanied by interpretation, it edifies both the congregation as a whole and the person who is speaking. Interpretation is thus needed for the corporate expression and edifying fruit of tongues while it is unnecessary when used in private. There is nothing in the least inconsistent with these two assertions.

But tongues don't edify the speaker, says Edgar. Doesn't Paul himself say that his mind is "unfruitful" when he speaks in tongues without interpretation? Yes, he does. But that doesn't mean tongues aren't helpful to the speaker. It simply means they are unintelligible. And that, I suspect, is the stumbling block for Edgar and other like-minded cessationists. They can't fathom how something that is not comprehended can be spiritually beneficial. But Paul clearly believed it was or he would not have resolved to continue to pray in tongues in private.

Edgar also seeks to connect Paul's statement in 1 Corinthians 14:2 that speaking in tongues is speaking only to God and his statement in 1 Corinthians 14:9 that tongues without interpretation is "speaking into the air." In other words, it must therefore be something negative, of no benefit, and thus to be avoided. But Paul's reference to "speaking into the air" is an indictment of making use of the gift in the public assembly without interpretation and has no bearing on whether the gift may be used privately for prayer, praise, and the edification of the speaker. That Paul endorses private prayer in tongues is clear from his expressed desire in 1 Corinthians 14:5 that all speak in tongues. We know this is private prayer because Paul contrasts it with prophecy, which needs no interpretation and thus more readily edifies others. Since Paul says interpreted tongues are the functional equivalent of prophecy and equally capable of edifying others (v. 5), he could only say that he who prophesies is "greater" than the one who speaks in tongues if the tongues in view is uninterpreted. And, of course, as we've just seen in 1 Corinthians 14:14–19, Paul clearly testifies of his own practice of praying in tongues in private. To this we might add his exhortation that if interpretation is not forthcoming, the believer "keep silent in church and speak to himself and to God" (v. 28).

Edgar does not believe praying "with my spirit," referenced in 1 Corinthians 14:14–16, is praying in tongues. Thus he believes Paul is discouraging praying in the Spirit and instead tells us only to pray with the mind. But it is virtually certain that praying and singing with the Spirit is Paul's way of describing tongues. How else could he contrast these with praying and singing "with the mind"? This is clearly confirmed in 1 Corinthians 14:19 where Paul contrasts speaking "with" his "mind" and speaking "in a tongue."

Finally, I've recently encountered yet another attempt by cessationists to deny that either Paul spoke in tongues in private or that he encouraged others to do so. The argument is that when Paul spoke in tongues outside the public gathering of the church, he did so in the same way the early disciples did in Acts 2. In other words, this argument proposes that there are multiple scenarios in which

Paul found himself that were like unto that which occurred on the day of Pentecost. Thus, we are being asked to believe that on countless occasions Paul found himself in a crowd of people gathered from around the inhabited world, all of whom spoke only in their native languages, and that Paul declared to each in their own dialect the "mighty deeds of God" (Acts 2:11, NASB).

There are several insurmountable problems with this view. One is that it would have to ignore all the other evidence I've provided in this chapter that demonstrates the legitimate use of tongues as a private prayer language that also serves to praise and give thanks to God. Another problem is that it fails to account for Paul's language in 1 Corinthians 14:18 where he declares and gives thanks to God for the fact that he speaks in tongues "more than all of you." It seems we are being asked to believe that Paul spoke in tongues in scenarios identical to Acts 2 far more frequently than the Corinthians did in their private devotions or in their corporate church gatherings. I find that highly improbable, if not impossible, to believe.

Furthermore, Paul has just described his tongues-speech as being prayer, praise (singing in tongues), and the giving of thanks. So are we now asked to believe that when Paul found himself in the midst of numerous people who didn't speak his language, he would pray in tongues publicly in front of them, sing praises to God in tongues in front of them, and express his heartfelt personal gratitude to God in tongues in front of them, all with a view to lead them to Christ? I don't think so.

And let's not forget that Paul expressed his desire that all the Corinthians (and all Christians) speak in tongues (1 Cor. 14:5). Are we then being asked to believe that what Paul desired for the people in Corinth (or any other church) is that all of them would likewise find themselves in scenarios similar to Acts 2 so they could then speak in tongues somewhere other than inside the church gathering? Are you beginning to see the multiple weaknesses of this attempt to evade the inescapable fact that Paul prayed in tongues in private and recommends that others do the same?

There is one more fatal flaw in this cessationist argument. There is not one verse nor even a single syllable in the New Testament to suggest that Paul spoke in tongues in public settings or scenarios proposed by this theory. Where in the New Testament, in Acts or anywhere else that describes Paul's public ministry, do we ever get so much as a hint that he spoke in tongues in the presence of people from foreign lands in the way we read in Acts 2? Since Paul himself says he speaks in tongues more than all the tongue-happy Corinthians combined, wouldn't you think we would have at least one (that's all, just one) example of him addressing crowds of foreigners in tongues-speech? For there not to be a single, solitary corroborating example of something Paul says was a regular feature of his spiritual life is simply too much for me (and I hope for you) to believe.

Chapter 8

TONGUES AS A SPIRITUAL GIFT

WE HAVE SEEN repeatedly that the gift of tongues may be exercised in the corporate gathering of the local church only if it is followed by interpretation. Paul based this restriction on his belief that for a word spoken in public to be edifying, it must be intelligible. So we turn now to this somewhat enigmatic spiritual gift referred to as the interpretation of tongues.

16. What is the gift of interpretation of tongues?

As Paul delineates nine of the gifts of the Spirit in 1 Corinthians 12:8–10, the last on his list is "the interpretation of tongues." Later in that chapter he again refers to interpretation in his denial that any one gift is granted to all Christians (v. 30). In his instruction on how believers are to arrive at any particular corporate assembly, he says that whereas one may come with a hymn, another with a word of instruction, another with a revelation from God, another with a tongue, one may also come with "an interpretation" (1 Cor. 14:26).

Paul envisions that in any meeting of God's people "two or at most three" may speak in tongues, "each in turn," which is to say, not simultaneously but one after the other. Once they have concluded, he insists that "someone interpret" (1 Cor. 14:27). Although the apostle doesn't say so explicitly, it may be that he envisions only one person to provide the interpretation of all three utterances in tongues. It is entirely possible, on the other hand, that each utterance in tongues will have its own individual interpreter. If no one is present to interpret at any particular corporate assembly, no one should speak in tongues.

We have previously taken note of Paul's exhortation to the person who wishes to speak in tongues in public, to the effect that he "should pray that he may interpret" (1 Cor. 14:13). There is no indication in what Paul says that this person had ever interpreted an utterance in tongues before. He or she may have, but it is just as likely that this would be their first experience with this spiritual gift. Paul doesn't tell us when the prayer should be uttered, but it seems likely this should occur before the utterance in tongues is given. After all, if there is no interpretation, there should never have been a word in tongues in the first place. It seems only reasonable, then, that the person who is feeling led to speak aloud in tongues should first pray for God to grant him or her the interpretation. If God does not respond to such a prayer by giving the interpretation, the person should then refrain from speaking in tongues altogether.

This procedure appears clear enough, even though the apostle does not give explicit answers to all our questions. What remains for us to do is to determine as best we can precisely how the gift of interpretation functions. What sort of information does it yield? What is the relationship of an interpretation to the utterance in tongues? To those questions we now turn our attention.[1]

WHAT THE GIFT OF INTERPRETATION OF TONGUES IS NOT

We should never confuse this spiritual gift with a person's ability to interpret divine revelation on a broad scale. The person with this gift would not necessarily be extraordinarily capable or skilled in interpreting biblical texts. There are principles of interpretation in the science we call hermeneutics that anyone who has the time and commitment to study them can easily learn. But educating oneself in the rules that govern how to make sense, for example, of John 3:16 is not what Paul had in mind when he spoke of the gift of interpretation. This gift is the Spirit-empowered ability to interpret what is spoken in *tongues*. There is no indication in Scripture that someone who has this *charisma* would be able to interpret dreams, visions, or other revelatory phenomena.

Although not mentioned in the New Testament, there may well be a spiritual gift of *interpretation*, broadly conceived. I say this because of what we see in the experience of both Joseph and Daniel in the Old Testament. When Pharaoh's chief cupbearer was imprisoned with Joseph, both he and the chief baker had a dream "with its own interpretation" (Gen. 41:11). The cupbearer reported this to Pharaoh and said:

> A young Hebrew was there with us, a servant of the captain of the guard. When we told him, he interpreted our dreams to us, giving an interpretation to each man according to his dream.
>
> —GENESIS 41:12

Pharaoh summoned Joseph and told him a dream he had recently experienced. "And Pharaoh said to Joseph, 'I have had a dream, and there is no one who can interpret it. I have heard it said of you that when you hear a dream you can interpret it.' Joseph answered Pharaoh, 'It is not in me; God will give Pharaoh a favorable answer'" (Gen. 41:15–16). We know, of course, that Joseph

125

proceeded to interpret the dream with perfect accuracy, resulting in his promotion in Pharaoh's court. Pharaoh attributed Joseph's skill in dream interpretation to the fact that "the Spirit of God" was in him (Gen. 41:38).

Likewise, Daniel was uniquely enabled by God to interpret revelatory dreams. (See Daniel 2:22–23, 28; 4:4–33; and especially 5:14–16.) However, the gift Paul has in mind functions only in relation to the gift of tongues. This gift of interpretation does not stand alone, as do the other gifts, but is inextricably tied up with tongues.

This gift must also be distinguished from the learned ability to translate a foreign language. I can translate Greek and a good bit of Hebrew and Latin into English, but that is not what Paul has in view. All of us are familiar with scenes at the United Nations or an international political conference where translators are employed to interpret speeches for the representatives of various countries. This is an impressive skill, but it is a natural, learned human ability. The interpreters gained this skill through extensive education and practice. The gift Paul describes, on the other hand, is supernatural, unlearned, and no less a "manifestation" (1 Cor. 12:7) of the Holy Spirit than the gift of miracles or prophecy.

There is a somewhat related phenomenon described in Daniel 5, where a "hand" supernaturally inscribed a message to King Belshazzar that none of his attendants could interpret. He summons Daniel, who proceeds to interpret the meaning. Whereas the inscription was revelatory, the interpretation was not. It was more akin to translation insofar as it was written in Aramaic, a language in which Daniel already had great facility. If the interpretation of tongues were merely the ability to translate a language one previously knew, this would be the only spiritual gift that required no input from or activity of the Holy Spirit.

It would almost appear that theologian Anthony Thiselton's understanding of tongues is a function of his conclusion concerning the nature of interpretation. In an earlier study[2] and again in his commentary on 1 Corinthians, Thiselton argues that the noun *interpretation* in 1 Corinthians 12:10 and the verb *to interpret* in 1 Corinthians 14:5 and 13 refer to the ability to put something otherwise unformed and unspoken into articulate speech. He appeals to the use of these terms in the writings of both Philo and Josephus where they denote "the capacity to express in *words* or articulate speech wonders which had otherwise left a person speechless, or able to react only emotively with awe or joy."[3] Tongues, says Thiselton, are therefore utterances that "well up, in experiences of wonder and praise as the Holy Spirit releases inhibitions and censors, in ways which reflect pre-conscious, pre-cognitive yearnings, sighings, or 'building up' which evade cognitive objectification and formulation."[4] These inarticulate longings and impulses of praise prompted by the Holy Spirit's activity (Rom. 8:26) are "as yet 'raw' and in need of communicative, intelligible, conscious communication."[5] It is the latter that the gift of interpretation purportedly supplies.

This would seem to entail the conclusion that no one has the gift of interpretation alone. Rather, some have tongues while others have *both* tongues *and* interpretation. In other words, claims Thiselton, "this ... is why some have the gift of tongues (which liberate and release innermost sighs to God), and others [in addition to their gift of tongues] have a *further* gift of enabling which allows them to reflect and to put the content of the experience which had generated the inarticulate sign of the Spirit at work into an articulate communicative signal from which all could benefit. Presumably only those who were not content to use tongues only in private were those whom Paul specifically enjoined to pray for this further gift [see 1 Corinthians 14:13], or otherwise to remain self-disciplined in public worship."[6]

It may well be that the model of tongues (and the accompanying gift of interpretation) for which Thiselton argues is, to use his own terminology, one of several *species* or *kinds* of tongues (1 Cor.

12:10) Paul envisioned to be operative in the church. A careful and detailed response to his exegesis is beyond the scope of this book, but at this point I see nothing in his understanding that necessarily precludes the *species* of tongues and interpretation for which I have argued or suggests that tongues was restricted to the apostolic age. In other words, should Thiselton's understanding prove correct, it would have no bearing on the extended question of the perpetuity of either gift.

WHAT THE GIFT OF INTERPRETATION OF TONGUES IS

So if the spiritual gift of interpretation of tongues is not the same thing as interpreting Scripture or making sense of dreams, what is it? I would define it as the Spirit-empowered ability to understand and communicate an otherwise unintelligible public utterance of tongues for the spiritual benefit of the congregation as a whole. I'm hesitant to use the word *translate* to describe this gift, given the fact that this term may lead people to conclude there will always be a one-for-one or word-for-word rendering of the tongues utterance into the vernacular of the people. But there is a spectrum from literal translation at one end to broad summation at the other end whenever the gift of interpretation is exercised. Interpreting a tongues utterance may take any one of several forms.

For example, someone with this gift *may* provide a literal, word-for-word rendering that corresponds in every conceivable way to the content of the tongue. It would be the same in length and emphasis. If the tongue was delivered in what appear to be five sentences that last forty-five seconds, so too would the interpretation.

There may also be a somewhat looser, more fluid rendering that captures the essence of the utterance. Those who engage in the translation of the original text of Scripture into other languages, such as English, often refer to this as "dynamic equivalence." The totality of what was spoken in tongues is brought over into the words of the interpreter, but it may not be in a word-for-word form. At other times something of a commentary is provided in which the interpreter explains (perhaps even exegetes) the tongues utterance. After all, what is said in tongues may be enigmatic, parabolic, or symbolic and thus needs an explanation. This is somewhat similar to what happens in an art museum when a scholar or historian "interprets" a painting. He or she may provide comment on the artist's mood, background, and even his or her perceived intent in crafting the painting or sculpture.

Then, of course, the interpretation may be closer to what we call a paraphrase of what the tongues utterance means. If I may again appeal to the discipline of Bible translation, I here have in mind what the Living Bible provides us as over against the New American Standard Bible. The latter is an essentially wooden and quite literal rendering of each word, as much as is possible, while the former is the translator's own effort to bring the original text into the world of the reader in such a way that the latter can make better sense of what the text is saying.

Finally, I suppose someone may interpret an utterance in tongues by giving us a summation of the gist of what was said. No attempt is made to supply a word in the interpretation that corresponds to a precise word in the tongue. Rather, the interpreter takes the utterance in a tongue and reduces it to a much briefer and summarized statement.

There is nothing in what Paul says about the gift of interpretation to preclude the possibility that the Holy Spirit might enable someone to interpret a tongues utterance anywhere along this spectrum. For example, the person with the gift of tongues might speak for five minutes while the interpreter speaks for only three. There is nothing to prevent a single utterance in tongues from being interpreted by two people whose "translations" differ in terms of length and focus. One person might provide a somewhat lengthy, seemingly word-for-word interpretation while another summarizes its basic content or provides a more practical application of what was spoken in tongues. In any case, the movement is always from the obscurity and unintelligibility of the tongues utterance to clarity and intelligibility of the interpretation, such that everyone in the church can say amen to what was said (1 Cor. 14:16). In this way the entire body is edified.

Think of it this way. If I were to read aloud John 3:16 in the course of a corporate church service and then ask for others to interpret its meaning and apply its truths to our lives, the responses might be noticeably different. One person might lay hold of the word *loved* and unpack the dynamics of God's affection for us that prompted Him to send us His Son. Another may choose to talk about the world and its need for a Savior. One more could be led to talk about what it means to believe in Jesus or perhaps what John meant by *eternal life*. Finally, another may choose to talk about how this verse might be used in sharing the gospel with an unbelieving friend. In each and every case, however, truth is communicated intelligibly based on something in the text of John 3:16. Likewise, when there is an utterance in tongues, differing individuals with the gift of interpretation might conceivably fix their attention on one particular element, word, or phrase while another is led to make practical application to the lives of those in attendance.

Although Paul does not himself say this in 1 Corinthians, it seems reasonable to think an interpretation of a tongue should be subject to judgment by the rest of those present in much the same way a prophetic utterance is to be weighed or evaluated. (See 1 Corinthians 14:29.)

THE CONTENT OF INTERPRETATION

It would seem reasonable to conclude that the content of the interpretation would depend entirely on the content of the tongues utterance. Therefore, we must ask another question first: *What is said when one speaks in tongues?* Earlier we noted that tongues can be

+ prayer (1 Cor. 14:2; whether supplication, petition, intercession, etc.);

+ praise (1 Cor. 14:16; see also Acts 2:11; 10:46); or

+ thanksgiving (1 Cor. 14:16).

If the interpretation must correspond to the utterance, the former will come forth in the form of prayers, praise, and expressions of gratitude to God. The interpretation will be a *Godward* utterance, no less than is the tongues utterance on which it is based.

Earlier, in response to question ten in chapter 6, I addressed the controversial issue of whether there is any such thing as a *message* in tongues, i.e., a message directed *horizontally* to people rather than *vertically* to God. The standard view among most Charismatic believers is that when an utterance in tongues is interpreted, it becomes the equivalent of prophecy. As such, it is horizontal in its orientation, which is to say it is directed to other individuals in the church. But if tongues is always prayer, praise, or thanksgiving, would not its interpretation be the same?

As I said in chapter 6, I may be mistaken in placing this sort of restriction on the content of tongues-speech. Although Paul clearly envisions it as a form of prayer and as a way in which we both praise God and express our gratitude to Him, does this mean tongues can *never* function in any other way? Must we necessarily limit tongues-speech to these three Godward expressions and rule out any and all *manward* utterances? In other words, was Paul in 1 Corinthians 14 providing us with an *exhaustive* portrayal of what might be communicated when one speaks in tongues? Or might it serve other purposes or functions? That question remains to be answered.

17. Why is tongues-speech often so rapid?

People often are bothered by what they hear when someone speaks or prays or praises God in tongues. The sounds that come from a person's mouth are more rapid and quickly spoken than would be the case in ordinary speech in one's native language, and people wonder why. I must say that I have no explicit biblical evidence for the answer I'm going to provide. Paul appears to be utterly unconcerned about how tongues-speech actually sounds to others, unless of course it is spoken in the public gathering of the church, in which case he demands an intelligible interpretation.

That being said, some argue that the rapidity of tongues-speech is due to the fact that it is the Holy Spirit who is praying through us. But this is only partly true. The Holy Spirit does not speak in tongues—you and I do. Of course, when we exercise our gift, it is by virtue of the power and sustaining energy of the Spirit. We must not forget how tongues was portrayed on the day of Pentecost. There Luke says it is the Spirit who "gives utterance" (Acts 2:4; cf. 1 Cor. 14:14–15). This may be the reason prayer in tongues entails a higher level of spiritual energy. In addition, since it is the Holy Spirit who is empowering our prayers, there is no hesitation over which words to speak, no stammering or wondering what to say and how to say it, no uhs punctuating our speech, none of the fear or self-consciousness that characterizes and thus retards normal speaking. When praying in tongues, one need never "wait" until she can think of something to say. There may be other equally valid explanations for the speed of tongues-speech. But I can't think of what they would be.

18. Why do some say speaking in tongues is the least important spiritual gift? Is it?

I had a friend who once pushed back against my teaching on the gift of tongues by pointing out that when Paul enumerated the many spiritual gifts, tongues was near the bottom of the list.

"Surely," he said, "this indicates that tongues is something of a minor gift of the Spirit, a secondary gift, at least in comparison with all the others. That being the case," he concluded, "should we even be talking about it, much less writing a book defending it and urging people to prayerfully pursue it?"

I'm not one to dismiss a question like this. After all, it is true that Paul places both tongues and interpretation last in the listings. In 1 Corinthians 12:8–10 nine gifts are mentioned, tongues and interpretation being the last two. Again in 1 Corinthians 12:28 the apostle lists eight gifts, with tongues coming in last. When he then, in 1 Corinthians 12:29–30, asks his series of rhetorical questions, tongues and interpretation bring up the rear. Now, that last comment may sound prejudicial, but it isn't. If I thought tongues was a second-rate and dispensable gift, I most assuredly would not have devoted my time and energy to writing this book! So what explanation can be given for "ranking" these gifts in this way? Even the word *ranking* is pejorative, for it suggests that some gifts are more important than others.

In the first place, nothing can be made of the fact that in 1 Corinthians 12:8–10 tongues and interpretation are listed last, for the simple fact that Paul doesn't use the adverbs *first, second,* and *third* as he does in 1 Corinthians 12:28–30. Furthermore, in Romans 12 Paul again provides a list of representative spiritual gifts but with no particular emphasis on their comparative importance. There he mentions, in order, prophecy, serving, teaching, exhorting, giving, leading, and showing mercy (vv. 6–8). I doubt if anyone would want to argue that serving is more important than teaching or that exhorting is more valuable than leading and showing mercy. But what about 1 Corinthians 12:28–30, where Paul does employ the adverbs *first, second,* and *third*? What does he mean to suggest by listing the gifts in this way?

Paul labors throughout 1 Corinthians, and especially in chapters 12–14, to make the point that no individual Christian is superior

133

or inferior to any other, especially based on the spiritual gift that he or she may possess. He eloquently pushes back in 1 Corinthians 12:14–26 against any suggestion that because one believer has a particular gift, he does not need or cannot benefit from the contribution of another. No "member" or "part" of the body of Christ is "any less a part of the body" simply because of the person's spiritual gift (1 Cor. 12:22–25). In fact, it is precisely the diversity of the many members and the different ways in which they serve one another that make the body effective in ministry. Equal honor must be given to everyone.

We should also note that only the first three gifts in 1 Corinthians 12:28 are ranked by numbers, and this "could possibly be Paul's way of emphasizing the initial and continuing foundational ministry of the word without which the church could not long survive."[7] It may also be that whereas no distinction is to be made between the value of persons in the church, their spiritual gifts function in differing ways and are not all equally capable of building up others. This, I believe, is what is in Paul's mind when he encourages the Corinthians to "earnestly desire the higher [or, "greater"] gifts" (1 Cor. 12:31). These gifts more readily serve to instruct, encourage, and edify other believers. The one who prophesies, says Paul, "is greater than the one who speaks in tongues," because prophecy doesn't require interpretation (1 Cor. 14:5). Everyone understands instantly what is being said, and thus everyone is more readily built up than if they were to hear uninterpreted tongues. However, as we've noted before, if the tongues-speech is followed by interpretation, it can just as easily and effectively build up others as does prophecy (1 Cor. 14:5).

New Testament scholar Craig Blomberg, on the other hand, believes the enumeration of these first three gifts points to their chronological priority. He explains:

> To establish a local congregation requires a church-planter.
> Then the regular proclamation of God's Word must ensue.
> Next teachers must supplement evangelism with disciple-
> ship and the passing on of the cardinal truths of the faith.
> Only at this point does a viable Christian fellowship exist
> to enable all the other gifts to come into play.[8]

Pushback against this view comes from the observation that the gift of tongues was in point of fact the "first" gift chronologically to be given to the people of God. (See Acts 2.) And yet the tongues described in 1 Corinthians 12–14 is designed for use in private devotional prayer or, when followed by interpretation, in the corporate assembly so others can be built up. Tongues in Acts 2, 10, and 19, on the other hand, functioned in an entirely different way (as previously argued).

Another argument against the idea that Paul is ranking gifts in accordance with their importance or value is the fact that he lists "prophets" ahead of "teachers" (1 Cor. 12:28). This is odd given the fact that teachers who were skilled and well taught in the Word of God were probably expected to be the first to pass judgment on the accuracy of anything a prophet might say. And as helpful as the prophetic gift assuredly is, are we really being asked to believe it is more effective than teaching in building up other believers?

Whatever decision one embraces, it is undeniably the case that no spiritual gift is more important than another and certainly no individual is more valuable than another in the body of Christ based simply on the nature of the gift that God has given. If anything, Paul's relegating of tongues to the bottom of these many gifts may simply have been his not-so-subtle way of rebuking those in the Corinthian church who believed themselves spiritu-ally superior to others based solely on the fact that they spoke in a heavenly language.

**19. Is the fact that tongues is mentioned only in Acts and
1 Corinthians an indication that New Testament authors
regarded it as comparatively unimportant in the Christian life?**

A not uncommon argument among cessationists is that tongues
is not explicitly mentioned in other instances of conversion in Acts
aside from the three we noted in chapter 2. This, they argue, sig-
nifies its lack of importance as an ongoing ministry in the life of
the church. This sort of argument from silence proves little, if anything at all. How many times is it necessary for a gift to be mentioned for it to be a valid expression of spiritual life? Outside of
1 Corinthians the ordinance of the Lord's Supper is never mentioned in Paul's Epistles. Would the cessationist want us to conclude from this that Communion is therefore unimportant? I
suspect that any number of other examples could also be cited.
The simple fact is that tongues is mentioned three times in Acts
and numerous times in 1 Corinthians 12–14. That it is not the
most important gift or ministry is obvious. Who would suggest it
is? But that doesn't give us grounds for ignoring, marginalizing, or
neglecting it altogether.

In a related vein the argument is made that speaking in tongues
was not a major factor in the spread of the gospel or in the practice
of the apostolic church. But as noted previously, in the twenty-two
books of the New Testament that follow Acts, only 1 Corinthians
mentions the Lord's Supper. What are we to conclude from that?
Nothing, aside from the fact that since Paul's instruction on the
Lord's table was so clear and decisive in 1 Corinthians, there was no
need to mention it repeatedly in his other letters. Are we not war-
ranted in concluding from the lack of reference to tongues in his
other Epistles that this gift was not a problem in those churches
and that Paul's guidelines for its exercise as given in 1 Corinthians
were sufficient for the life and ministry of believers in other congre-
gations? I think so.

Others think it is highly significant that Paul did not mention tongues in his list of spiritual gifts in Romans 12 and Ephesians 4. They argue from this that the gift of tongues was either not a matter of importance or that it was not practiced by the Christians in Rome, Ephesus, and elsewhere. But virtually all New Testament scholars acknowledge that no New Testament Epistle contains an exhaustive list of all spiritual gifts. Whether 1 Corinthians 12, Romans 12, Ephesians 4, or 1 Peter 4, what we have are *representative* lists, not comprehensive ones. In Romans 12 Paul only mentions seven spiritual gifts, yet all acknowledge that there is a minimum of nineteen gifts listed in the New Testament. So would the cessationist have us believe these twelve gifts that Paul doesn't mention were unimportant or, worse still, nonexistent in the church at Rome? In Ephesians 4 only five gifts are mentioned (some scholars believe it is only four). So I suppose on the cessationist's logic that fifteen spiritual gifts were absent from the church in Ephesus or were deemed unimportant by the apostle.

I've also heard it said that preoccupation with tongues-speaking is childish (1 Cor. 14:20). Again, this is misleading. Tongues-speaking per se isn't childish. It's a good and glorious gift of God. Nor is a desire to possess this gift a sign of immaturity. What Paul characterizes as childish and immature is (a) the belief that tongues (above and beyond other gifts) was a sign of heightened spirituality and (b) the determination on the part of some in Corinth to dominate the meeting with uninterpreted tongues-speech.

Some also find problematic the argument among Charismatics, such as myself, that one can "develop" the gift of tongues or be taught how to exercise it with greater facility. If what they mean by this is that no one can do anything to induce or persuade God to grant a gift contrary to His sovereign will, of course I agree. But I want to make sure no one means to suggest that once a gift is bestowed, we cannot develop, grow, improve, and be instructed on how to use it more effectively. This would apply to virtually all gifts, such as the gift of teaching, evangelism, leadership, giving, or any and every spiritual gift. If Christians can't be "taught" how to exercise a gift, what are we doing offering courses in homiletics (preaching) in our colleges and seminaries? What are we doing offering seminars on how to more effectively share our faith with non-Christians? And the list could go on.

Along these lines it may prove helpful to take note of what Paul said in Romans 12:6. There he encourages the exercise of prophecy "in proportion to our faith." This translation is slightly misleading, as the possessive pronoun *our* is not in the original text. It more literally reads, "according to the proportion of the faith." Some argue that "the faith" here mentioned refers to the objective truths of Christianity embodied in the gospel tradition. But I think it more likely that Paul is saying that people operate in this particular gift with greater and/or lesser degrees of ability and accuracy, and with greater and/or lesser degrees of confidence or assurance that what they have prophesied is truly from God.

My point is that people who are given the gift of prophecy can and should grow in their facility in its exercise. The same is true of virtually every other spiritual gift. I trust that I am a better and more persuasive teacher today than I was when I started out in pastoral ministry forty-five years ago. I suspect that Billy Graham would have contended that his gift of evangelism increased in power and effectiveness the longer he ministered. And we could go down the line with virtually every other spiritual gift. As we make use of our spiritual gift(s) over time, we learn from our mistakes. We become more discerning. We have increased opportunities to receive feedback from others on ways that we might improve. We observe how the same spiritual gift operates in other believers and thus learn from them how we might make better and more effective use of whatever manifestation of the Spirit that God has granted us.

Chapter 9

TONGUES AND PRAYER

IN THIS CHAPTER I want to address several biblical texts outside of Acts and 1 Corinthians that many have thought are referring to tongues. I'm often asked if tongues are in view in Ephesians 6:18 and Jude 20, where we read of praying "in the Spirit." And what does Romans 8:26–27 mean? And is Mark 16:17 an authentic part of the original text of Scripture? At the close of this chapter I'll also speak to a couple of pastoral questions regarding our use of tongues. So let's begin with those texts.

20. What does it mean to "pray in the Spirit"? Is this a reference to speaking in tongues?

Twice in the New Testament outside 1 Corinthians 14 we read about praying "in the Spirit." The two texts are Ephesians 6:18 and Jude 20–21. Here they are:

...praying at all times in the Spirit, with all prayer and
supplication. To that end, keep alert with all perseverance,
making supplication for all the saints.

—Ephesians 6:18

But you, beloved, building yourselves up in your most holy
faith and praying in the Holy Spirit, keep yourselves in
the love of God, waiting for the mercy of our Lord Jesus
Christ that leads to eternal life.

—Jude 20–21

There are a few other texts that use the same phrase, "in the
Spirit." We are told in Luke 10:21 that Jesus "rejoiced in the Holy
Spirit." Mark refers to King David as declaring "in the Holy Spirit"
the truth of Psalm 110 (Mark 12:36). And Paul reminds the
Corinthians that "no one speaking in the Spirit of God ever says,
'Jesus is accursed!'" (1 Cor. 12:3). And again, in the same verse, "no
one can say 'Jesus is Lord' except in the Holy Spirit."

The reason this issue comes up is that when Paul portrays his
own practice of both praying and singing in tongues, he describes
it as taking place "with my spirit" (1 Cor. 14:15). I want to avoid
getting overly technical here, especially with regard to my appeal
to the original Greek text of Scripture. But you should not be put
off or worried about the fact that most English translations render
the Greek word *pneuma* ("spirit") with a lowercase *s* instead of an
uppercase *S*. Some press this point beyond what Paul intended.
They argue that in 1 Corinthians 14:15 Paul is referring exclusively
to his human spirit but that in Ephesians 6:18 and Jude 20 it is
clearly God the Holy Spirit that is in view. But in 1 Corinthians 14
there is a movement back and forth, as it were, between references
to the Holy Spirit and the human spirit. Often Paul speaks as if
both are in view, which is to say that the human spirit is empowered by the Holy Spirit to give expression to some spiritual gift.

Let's look at several of these. In 1 Corinthians 14:2 Paul says the person who speaks in a tongue "utters mysteries in the Spirit." Is this the Holy Spirit of God or the human spirit? My inclination is to say, "Yes!" A bit farther down, in verse 15, Paul refers to his regular practice of praying in tongues and describes it as praying "with my spirit." This likely points to his human spirit (note his use of the possessive pronoun *my*), but not without the empowering manifestation of the Holy Spirit who is behind and responsible for the exercise of all spiritual gifts, tongues included. The same is true in 1 Corinthians 14:16, where Paul mentions giving thanks in tongues, or giving thanks "with your spirit." One more text to note is 1 Corinthians 14:32, where Paul says that "the spirits of prophets are subject to prophets." (See also Revelation 22:6.) Many take this as referring exclusively to the human spirit of anyone who would prophesy. But I think we should follow the counsel of Pentecostal theologian Gordon Fee, who suggests we translate each of these texts as "S/spirit."[1] His point is that in each case it is the human spirit expressing itself by means of the power and sustaining presence of the Holy Spirit. It is never one to the exclusion of the other.

In every instance we've just cited, the phrase translated either "in" or "with" the Spirit or my spirit is in the dative case (the Greek word *pneumati*). In both Ephesians 6:18 and Jude 20 the preposition *en* ("in" or "with") is included. There is no dispute about the fact that Paul is describing praying and singing in tongues when he uses the word *pneumati* (dative singular of the Greek *pneuma*, which means spirit; see 1 Corinthians 14:15). But what about Ephesians 6:18 and Jude 20? Does their inclusion of the preposition *in* or *with* suggest that something other than tongues is in view? Probably not, but that doesn't necessarily mean they have the same experience in mind that Paul is describing in 1 Corinthians 14.

To write Scripture "in the Holy Spirit" (Mark 12:36) or to rejoice and worship "in the Holy Spirit" (Luke 10:21) or to declare "by the Spirit of God" that "Jesus is Lord" (1 Cor. 12:3, NASB) clearly means to do so under the Spirit's influence or by virtue of the Spirit's empowering presence. It should be taken in contrast with any exercise that is done in the power of one's own human flesh or willpower alone.

Most scholars understand both Ephesians 6:18 and Jude 20 to be using the word *Spirit* in the same way; that is to say, they argue that to "pray in the Spirit" is to bring requests and supplications to God in the power of the Holy Spirit. The Spirit is envisioned as the One who perhaps brings to mind what needs to be said in prayer. Or the Spirit is the One at whose prompting or urging one is to pray. Or the Spirit is the One whom we trust to accurately represent us at the throne of grace. Or the Spirit is the One who supplies the endurance and energy to persevere in prayer rather than so quickly giving up, as we are prone to do.

So I would suggest, first of all, that any and all Christians can pray "in the Spirit" whether or not they have the gift of praying in tongues. Thus praying "in the Spirit" is certainly more than merely praying in tongues. But is it less than praying in tongues? In other words, could it be that both Paul's (Eph. 6:18) and Jude's (Jude 20) exhortation to "pray in the Spirit" can *include* praying in tongues (for those who have the gift) but need not refer exclusively to doing so (as if the exhortation does not apply to those who lack the gift)? I think the answer is yes.

What I'm suggesting, then, is this. For someone like me, every time I pray in tongues, I am praying "with my [human] spirit" by means of or "in the [Holy] Spirit." But for someone else who does not have this spiritual gift, they can pray "in the Spirit" while making use of their native language. My primary reason for saying this is that both Ephesians 6:18 and Jude 20 appear to be exhortations that extend to all Christian men and women. Since we know that not all believers speak in tongues (see 1 Corinthians 12:30; 14:5), aside from the question of whether all could or should do so (to be addressed later), all are responsible to take steps to ensure that their devotion to and practice of prayer is sustained, empowered, and directed by the Holy Spirit of God.

21. Does Romans 8:26–27 refer to the gift of tongues?

There is yet another text that many believe describes praying in tongues, and that is Romans 8:26–27. Paul confesses what all of us have experienced at one time or another, perhaps what some experience on a fairly regular basis: "we do not know what to pray for as we ought" (Rom. 8:26). Instead of this bringing discouragement to our hearts, Paul reminds us that "the Spirit helps us in our weakness" (Rom. 8:26). And how does the Spirit do this? What does He do that overcomes our ignorance and weakness in knowing what to pray for? Says Paul:

> The Spirit himself intercedes for us with groanings too deep for words. And he who searches hearts knows what is the mind of the Spirit, because the Spirit intercedes for the saints according to the will of God.
>
> —Romans 8:26–27

Charismatic Christians are quick to point to this statement in support of their beliefs and practices concerning praying in tongues. But others are less confident that this is what Paul has in mind.

We must first take note of the context in which verses 26–27 occur in Romans 8. Paul has been talking about the suffering we endure while we wait in this life for the final redemption or glorification of our bodies (vv. 18–25). In fact, there is a great deal of "groaning" going on! The material creation, having been subjected to the curse incurred by Adam, "has been groaning together in the pains of childbirth until now" (v. 22). But it doesn't groan alone! Indeed, "we ourselves, who have the firstfruits of the Spirit, groan inwardly as we wait eagerly for adoption as sons, the redemption of our bodies" (v. 23). Again, I don't want to be overly technical, but it's important that you know the precise words Paul uses here.

In verse 22 the material or natural creation has been "groaning together" in the pains of childbirth. The verb is *systenazō*, to groan with. In verse 23 Paul uses the related verb *stenazō*, to groan. The only difference is that the former verb emphasizes that creation does not groan alone but in conjunction with either the rest of creation or in conjunction with us Christians. When Paul comes to verse 26 to describe what the Holy Spirit does in and on behalf of weak Christians, he uses the related noun form of these verbs, *stenagmos*. As I said, there's a whole lot of groaning going on in Romans 8. The material creation groans, we Christians groan, and even the Holy Spirit Himself groans!

But is this groaning of the Holy Spirit literal or physically audible, or could it be metaphorical? The groaning of the material creation is clearly metaphorical. In other words, the natural world is personified and ascribed attributes or actions that are possible only among humans. Trees and rivers and valleys don't audibly groan but are portrayed as laboring under the curse of sin and in a sense longing for the day when the curse is removed. Of course, we humans literally and audibly groan as we wait in anxious expectation to be set free from the perishable and painful bodies in which we now live. But it seems odd to suggest that God the Holy Spirit would audibly groan. More likely this is Paul's way of giving expression to the fact that the Holy Spirit identifies with our deep, profoundly emotional, yet inarticulate yearning for answers to prayers that we feel too weak and ignorant to utter. As our intercessor (Rom. 8:26–27), the One who brings our inexpressible requests to the Father, the Holy Spirit takes up our groaning and in some mysterious way transforms it into meaningful requests that conform to the will of our heavenly Father.

When Paul says that in our present condition we often do not know what to pray for, he is not talking about style or posture or manner but of *content* in prayer. We are ignorant of what we or others may need, ignorant of what God has promised, and unable to put into words the cry of our hearts. But be encouraged, says Paul, because the Holy Spirit takes up where we, because of weakness, leave off. If we do not know what to pray for, the Spirit does. He intercedes for us "with groanings too deep for words." The single Greek word behind the translation "too deep for words" is used only here in the New Testament (*alalētois*). Does it mean ineffable, i.e., incapable of being expressed in human language (cf. 2 Cor. 12:4)? If so, the groans may well be audible, though inarticulate. Or does it mean simply unspoken, never rising to the audible level at all? If the former is correct, the groanings are probably ours that the Holy Spirit inspires and prompts within us. But the latter is probably more likely. The groans are from the Holy Spirit Himself. New Testament scholar Douglas J. Moo explains:

> While we cannot, then, be absolutely sure…it is preferable to understand these "groans" as the Spirit's own "language of prayer," a ministry of intercession that takes place in our hearts (cf. v. 27) in a manner imperceptible to us.…I take it that Paul is saying, then, that our failure to know God's will and consequent inability to petition God specifically and assuredly is met by God's Spirit, who himself expresses to God those intercessory petitions that perfectly match the will of God. When we do not know what to pray for—yes, even when we pray for things that are not best for us—we need not despair, for we can depend on the Spirit's ministry of perfect intercession "on our behalf."…[According to v. 27] God, who sees into the inner being of people, where the indwelling Spirit's ministry of intercession takes place, "knows," "acknowledges," and responds to those "intentions" of the Spirit that are expressed in his prayers on our behalf.[2]

It would appear that Paul is here describing the Spirit Himself praying or interceding "for" us to compensate for our lack of clarity or insight into what most needs to be articulated. In other words, it is the Spirit who prays, not we. As we noted earlier, whereas all spiritual gifts, including tongues, are "manifestations" (1 Cor. 12:7; 14:12) of the Spirit such that we can't and probably shouldn't even try to differentiate between what the Spirit does and what we do in our human spirit, in Romans 8 Paul clearly says it is the Spirit who prays. We don't. In fact, we can't. We are too weak. Therefore, I am not inclined to find in Romans 8 a reference to praying in tongues.[3] Or perhaps I should say that if praying in tongues is included in Paul's thought in Romans 8, it is in no way exclusively concerned with tongues. It would be quite similar to what we saw in regard to praying "in the Spirit." All praying in tongues is praying in the Spirit, but not all praying in the Spirit is praying in tongues. Likewise, it may well be that Paul would include tongues in the reality of the Spirit's "groanings" within and for us, but he would not restrict the latter to praying in tongues. In other words, Romans 8:26–27 is a glorious truth that applies across the board to all Christians, both those who pray in tongues and those who do not.

This latter point is yet one more reason I don't believe Paul is thinking exclusively of prayer in tongues. The contextual argument of Romans 8:18–19 is that all Christians suffer in this present time, all Christians groan under the curse imposed by sin, and all Christians therefore struggle in their weakness to know precisely how and what to bring to God in prayer. The promise of the Spirit's work on our behalf in Romans 8:26–27 thus applies to every believer, every child of God, regardless of what spiritual gift they either have or don't have.

22. Can we learn anything about tongues from Mark 16:17?

The question raised here leads us into the highly complex and technical world of what is known as New Testament textual criticism. I must confess up front that I am not a textual critic. I was taught the basic principles of this discipline while in seminary, and I can follow with some measure of understanding what the experts in this field of study are telling us. But I make no claim to being sufficiently trained in textual criticism that I might speak with authority on the subject of the authenticity of Mark 16:9–20.

That being said, my best judgment is that James Edwards is correct when he concludes: "It is virtually certain that 16:9–20 is a later addition and not the original ending of the Gospel of Mark."[4] The note in the NIV Zondervan Study Bible speaks for most Evangelicals when it says: "Scholars almost universally agree that this section [16:9–20] is a later attempt, perhaps by a second-century scribe, to rectify the perceived problem of v. 8…The earliest and best manuscripts do not have these verses; they are unknown to a number of early church fathers; and the vocabulary and style differ from the rest of Mark."[5]

The ESV Study Bible provides a much longer and more informative explanation for the problem we face here. It is worth reading in full:

> Some ancient manuscripts of Mark's Gospel contain these verses and others do not, which presents a puzzle for scholars who specialize in the history of such manuscripts. This longer ending is missing from various old and reliable Greek manuscripts (esp. Sinaiticus and Vaticanus), as well as numerous early Latin, Syriac, Armenian, and Georgian manuscripts. Early church fathers (e.g., Origen and Clement of Alexandria) did not appear to know of these verses. Eusebius and Jerome state that this section is missing in most manuscripts available at their time. And some manuscripts that contain vv. 9–20 indicate that older manuscripts lack the section. On the other hand, some early and many later manuscripts (such as the

manuscripts known as A, C, and D) contain vv. 9–20, and many church fathers (such as Irenaeus) evidently knew of these verses. As for the verses themselves, they contain various Greek words and expressions uncommon to Mark, and there are stylistic differences as well. Many think this shows vv. 9–20 to be a later addition. In summary, vv. 9–20 should be read with caution. As in many translations, the editors of the ESV have placed the section within brackets, showing their doubts as to whether it was originally part of what Mark wrote, but also recognizing its long history of acceptance by many in the church.[6]

I suspect this is already more information on the textual problem in Mark 16 than most of you ever wanted to know! Let me simply say two things in conclusion. First, from what little I know of textual criticism, I find myself in agreement with those who argue that vv. 9–20 were probably not a part of Mark's original Gospel but were added by a scribe sometime in the second century. Therefore, we should be extremely cautious in trying to derive doctrinal truth based solely on what we read in this "longer ending" of Mark's Gospel. Second, the only possible information that verse 17 might supply when it comes to tongues is the statement that it is a "sign" that accompanies those who believe in Jesus (evidently to confirm that the gospel message they proclaim about Him is true and trustworthy). Here are the two verses in question:

And these signs will accompany those who believe: in my name they will cast out demons; they will speak in new tongues; they will pick up serpents with their hands; and if they drink any deadly poison, it will not hurt them; they will lay their hands on the sick, and they will recover.
—MARK 16:17–18

In any case, I do not believe there is anything in the longer ending of Mark that adds to our understanding of tongues as informed by the remainder of the New Testament. Therefore, I see nothing beneficial in spending any more time and space on this passage.

23. Can a person pray for another person in uninterpreted tongues?

Yet another important question that I regularly hear is whether it is appropriate for one person who has the gift of tongues to pray for another who either may or may not have it. I'm talking about the practice of praying for someone in their presence. I pray for a great many people—friends, family, church members, and staff—in my private devotional experience. And when I do, I often pray in tongues for them. Of course, they cannot hear me. But would it be permissible for me to pray for one of them in tongues as I'm laying hands on them or within close proximity to them? The question assumes the person for whom this prayer is being offered can hear me pray. So the bottom line is this: Must there be present someone to interpret my prayer for another before I am allowed to pray in tongues for them? My answer, though cautious, is no.

Let us remember why Paul insisted on interpretation in the corporate gathering of God's people. When a local church assembles, one of the primary goals is to edify and build up one another. If helpful instruction and encouragement is to take place, what we say to one another must be intelligible. Thus the apostle's demand for interpretation.

But when I'm praying for another person, perhaps in a small group gathering or at the front of our auditorium after the Sunday service or in a one-on-one meeting, my aim isn't to instruct or teach them. My aim is to speak to God on their behalf. They don't need to understand what I'm saying in order to benefit spiritually from what I'm saying to God. Of course, if I am given the interpretation or if someone else with that gift is present to provide it, all the better. But my goal is very specific, namely, to bring this person and his or her needs to the throne of grace.

Two more words of clarification may help. First, you may push back on me and say, "But Sam, how can you pray meaningfully for that person if neither of you understands anything that is being said?" Good question. That is why before I pray aloud in tongues, I ask God silently to craft my language and to shape my requests so they accurately represent at the throne of grace the specific needs this person may have. It basically comes down to whether I trust the Holy Spirit to do that when I pray in tongues. I *do* trust Him. So even if I don't understand what I'm praying (and I never do), I can confidently know that God is hearing precisely what the Spirit knows needs to be said. Don't forget what Paul said in Romans 8:26: the Spirit "himself intercedes for us." Again, "he who searches hearts knows what is the mind of the Spirit, because the Spirit intercedes for the saints according to the will of God" (Rom. 8:27). No, as noted above, this probably isn't a reference to tongues. But it does affirm the truth that God the Father knows what the Spirit is saying to Him on our behalf because the Spirit will always craft prayer requests "according to the will of God [the Father]."

My second word of clarification is one of practical counsel. Unless I know the person for whom I am praying and am aware of his beliefs about praying in tongues, I will always ask permission first. Countless times I have stopped before praying and said something like this: "Joe/Janie, I want to pray for you in English for as many things as God may bring to mind. But oftentimes there comes a point where I run out of words. I simply reach the limit of my understanding and can't think of anything more to pray. But I believe there is a great deal more that God would have me bring to the throne of grace on your behalf. Would it be OK with you if at that time I prayed in tongues? If you're uncomfortable with that, I completely understand. Please don't feel any pressure to say yes." Not once, up until the time of this writing, have I ever had someone say, "No, please don't." That doesn't mean they always agree with me on the practice of praying in tongues, but they typically have enough trust in my love and concern for them that they are happy to have me pray in any language I might choose!

24. How might tongues help us in our spiritual battle with Satan and his demonic forces?

Once again we come across a question for which the New Testament does not provide an explicit answer. At least I don't know of any biblical text that directly or even indirectly addresses this point. But that doesn't mean we can't make some effort at finding an answer.

I'm inclined to believe that praying in tongues is a good way to combat the enemy in our ongoing battle with spiritual forces (Eph. 6:10–17). I say this for two reasons. First, the passage that speaks to the reality of spiritual warfare with more clarity than any other is Ephesians 6. After Paul has delineated and described the various armor of God with which we are to adorn ourselves, he turns to the subject of prayer. We saw previously that Paul urges all Christians to be "praying at all times in the Spirit, with all prayer and supplication" (Eph. 6:18). If praying in tongues is at least included in what it means to pray in the Spirit, this would suggest that one's prayer language would serve to bolster or strengthen us in our standing firm against Satan's tactics. In fact, some even say we should extend Paul's discussion of the armor of God to include prayer. I think it better simply to say the apostle expects all of us to bathe our battle in prayer. Perhaps he intends to say that prayer should be the spiritual framework within which we put on each element of the armor of God. Prayer should precede putting on the armor, should be practiced as we put it on, and should be exercised as we employ the armor to overcome Satan's assault.

My second reason for suggesting that prayer in tongues would be helpful in our battle with the enemy is that I am convinced that although Satan is intelligent, he cannot understand the language the Spirit has crafted for us. One thing needs to be said up front. Satan is not omnipresent! He is a spiritual being whose presence is limited to one place in space. If he is in the presence of a pastor in India, he cannot at the same time be in my presence in Oklahoma City. Of course, there are countless demons who do his bidding. Although they aren't omnipresent, any more than is Satan himself, there are enough of them to warrant the conclusion that anytime we pray or minister to someone who is oppressed, it is likely that a demon is near.

Satan most assuredly has a plan to disrupt and divide the church and to trip up and seduce the individual Christian. Although immeasurably sinful, he is not stupid. He does not act haphazardly or without a goal in view. Paul states clearly in 2 Corinthians 2:10–11 that Satan has "designs," i.e., a strategy, an agenda to undermine unity in the church in that city (and no doubt in every city, yours included!). This is similar to what the apostle says in Ephesians 6:11 concerning the "schemes" (lit., *methodeia*, or method) of the devil. In other words, he is cunning and wily and employs carefully orchestrated stratagems (see Eph. 4:14) in his assault against Christian men and women and the local church. Satan energizes and gives shape to worldly value systems; institutions; organizations; philosophical movements; and political, social, and economic systems. Satan sets his goals and then utilizes and exploits the most effective means, while avoiding all obstacles, to reach his diabolical ends.

We know from several texts that Satan and his demons can plant sinful plans and purposes in the minds of men and women. He "filled" the heart of Ananias "to lie to the Holy Spirit" about the proceeds from the sale of some property (Acts 5:3). And he made use of Peter's impetuous nature to try to deter Jesus from going to the cross (Matt. 16:21–23).

He also sought permission from God to "sift" Peter like wheat (Luke 22:31). He wanted to destroy Peter by inciting him to deny Jesus. But God's intent in permitting Satan to do it was altogether different. God's purposes with Peter were to instruct him, humble him, perhaps discipline him, and certainly to use him as an example to others of both human arrogance and the possibility of forgiveness and restoration. The point is simply that often we cannot easily say that "Satan did it" or "God did it." In cases such as this, both are true (with the understanding that God's will is sovereign, supreme, and overriding), but their respective goals are clearly opposite.

Paul also warns us in 2 Corinthians 2:5–11 that Satan is actively seeking to crush the heart of a repentant sinner who is not lovingly received back into the fellowship of the church. Through this he no doubt aims to sow the seeds of discord and disunity among God's people. We also know that he can exploit our sinful choices by intensifying the course of action we have already chosen. (See Ephesians 4:26–27.)

Much more could be said, but the point is made. However, nowhere in Scripture does it say Satan can read our minds or make sense of our prayer language in tongues. I suspect, but can't prove, that this would be a possibility only if a believer living in unrepentant sin willfully granted Satan access to his or her mind and heart. But short of that, I believe we can confidently trust that when we pray in tongues, Satan cannot decipher what is being said. He therefore has no recourse to thwart our prayers or the efforts that may follow from them.

I once read someone who argued from 1 Corinthians 13:1 that Satan and his demons can understand our prayer in tongues. You will recall that in this passage Paul mentioned speaking "in the tongues of men and angels." Since Satan and all his demons are angels, albeit fallen and rebellious angels, they would surely be able to understand any and all angelic dialects. Whereas that may be true, I also believe most tongues-speech today is a prayer language that is specially crafted, constructed, or fashioned by the Holy Spirit, a language unique to each child of God. And I do not see any reason to think Satan or a demon would be capable of deciphering what the Holy Spirit Himself has directly created.

This conclusion is supported by something we saw earlier in Romans 8. In verse 27 Paul says that "he who searches hearts knows what is the mind of the Spirit." The "he" here is obviously God the Father. Nowhere in Scripture is Satan portrayed as someone who can search our hearts or know our deepest thoughts. This is a power that only the omniscient God of Scripture has. (See 1 Samuel 16:7; 1 Kings 8:39; Psalm 44:21; 139:1–2, 23; Proverbs 15:11; and Jeremiah 17:10.) If Satan can't read our minds or search our hearts, it stands to reason that when we give expression to our thoughts and prayerful desires in tongues, he would be incapable of deciphering or knowing what is said. This ignorance or limitation on his part would then serve to hinder and reduce the effectiveness of his attempts to harm us or intrude into our plans or in some way prevent us from doing what we know God desires.

So although my answer is somewhat speculative, in the sense that I wish I had more explicit evidence from Scripture itself, I can say with a measure of confidence that it is a good strategy to employ prayer in tongues when addressing those who are oppressed by the devil or perhaps even demonized. Of course, this strategy can be used in any and all cases, at any time we pray for any matter or for any individual.

Sadly, far too many Christians are terrified of Satan and have little to no understanding of the authority that has been given to them in the name of Jesus. (See especially Luke 10:17–20.) Should there be a demonic manifestation, they tend to withdraw and quickly look for an "expert" in deliverance ministry. This is where tongues can play a significant role in the believer's response to such situations. I have found this true in my own experience, and others have testified to the same thing. When I pray or sing in tongues, my faith is deepened and my fears are overcome (or at least greatly reduced). Praying in the Spirit in this way has a unique way of strengthening my inner being and awakening in me an expanded awareness of the authority I've been granted because of the life, death, and resurrection of Jesus. My sense of the Spirit's indwelling presence in my heart is intensified, and I feel noticeably more confident in the truth of Luke 10. Others have spoken of renewed commitment and a supernatural boldness in the face of the enemy that simply wasn't present before their time spent praying in tongues.

Now, I wouldn't have anyone conclude from this that tongues is the only way in which a believer can be empowered and made confident in the authority of the risen Christ operating through them. One need not pray in tongues to be filled with the Spirit and to find an uncanny sense of boldness in dealing with demonic spirits. All Christians, not just those who speak in tongues, are assured by Jesus that he has "given [us] authority to tread on serpents and scorpions, and over all the power of the enemy" (Luke 10:19). But if an ordinary believer to whom this authority has been given does not enter into spiritual warfare in a spirit of prayer and conscious dependence on the Holy Spirit, he or she is courting trouble. My point is simply that when a person endowed with tongues makes use of this form of prayerful dependence on God, there is often a sensible, even tangible awareness of the presence of the Spirit and the power given to us to drive out and defeat our demonic oppressors.

When one adds to this what I've already noted, namely, that the demon(s) cannot understand what we are saying to God on behalf of the oppressed or demonized person, we gain a strategic advantage. Of course, this is not to say, much less recommend, that we can or should speak to a demonic spirit in tongues. Rather we speak to God in tongues on behalf of the person who is afflicted and we speak in an intelligible language, in the name of Jesus, to whatever demonic being is harassing them.

Chapter 10

TONGUES AND REVELATION

HERE AND THERE in the previous nine chapters I have touched on the arguments some Christians use to deny that the gift of tongues is valid and operative today. In this chapter I want to address two more objections to tongues that cessationists often voice.

25. Is tongues revelatory?

The first of these two issues pertains to the question of whether tongues is a *revelatory* gift of God. In other words, when people speak in tongues, do they do so as the result of some revelatory activity of God in which the Spirit is imparting information heretofore undisclosed that is then communicated via this gift to the larger body of Christ? Many say yes to this question, which then serves as one reason they believe the gift is no longer valid today. They believe that any and all revelatory gifts such as prophecy, word of knowledge, and tongues have ceased lest the finality and sufficiency of Scripture be compromised.

For one thing, the ongoing validity of the revelatory gifts of prophecy and word of knowledge does not undermine or compromise the finality and sufficiency of the biblical canon. I have argued this point extensively in other places and will not repeat myself here. I simply refer you to my article "Revelatory Gifts of the Spirit and the Sufficiency of Scripture: Are They Compatible?" in the book *Scripture and the People of God*.

My intention here is simply to argue, ever so briefly, that tongues is *not* a revelatory gift. Most cessationists appeal to Paul's use of the word *mysteries* in 1 Corinthians 14:2, a term, they argue, that refers to the redemptive-historical content of revelation. But if this were true, why would Paul proceed to define the content of tongues as simple human prayer, blessing, and gratitude (1 Cor. 14:14–17), terms that have little if any relation to the divine communication of redemptive-historical verities? And why would Paul differentiate between tongues and revelation as he does in 1 Corinthians 14:6, asserting his preference for the latter above the former? (See also 1 Corinthians 14:26.) And why in his description of the exercise of gifts in the local assembly would he restrict the impartation of revelation to those who prophesy and not extend it also to those who minister in tongues (1 Cor. 14:27–30)? There is no indication here that Paul believed speaking in tongues depends upon a spontaneous divine revelation, as is clearly the case with prophecy.

Neither will it do to argue that the Spirit's activity in tongues-speech (as described in 1 Corinthians 14:14) proves the latter's revelatory status. When Paul says, "My spirit prays," he is not claiming direct, verbal inspiration for what is spoken in tongues. The fact that the mind does not understand what the spirit prays hardly proves the latter's inerrancy! It only demonstrates Paul's point of the need for interpretation in a public setting. Cessationists often argue that because the human mind does not function in the production of what is said in tongues, what is said must be infallibly inspired. But contrary to the impression this leaves, *glossolalia* is not an experience in which the Spirit seizes the speech organ, thereby reducing the believer to a passive and robotic instrument through which in an unmediated way the Spirit Himself prays. Rather, the Spirit sovereignly imparts *to* the believer an ability by which the believer prays or praises in a language he cannot of himself interpret. Tongues is a power or capacity imparted by the Spirit that ever remains within the volitional control of the believer. The fact that the Holy Spirit energizes the human spirit to utter words of supplication and thanksgiving in no way implies, far less requires, a revelatory act of God that renders such speech infallible. *All* prayer, according to Ephesians 6:18, is "in the Spirit." Must we conclude by this that *all* prayer is inspired and without error?

This entire line of argumentation assumes that the word *spirit* in 1 Corinthians 14:14 can't be Paul's own human spirit but refers instead to the Holy Spirit or to the gift of tongues as given by the Spirit. This is based on the belief that in Paul's writings *spirit* and *mind* are interchangeable or largely overlap in meaning. For the sake of argument I'll concede the latter point, *except* when the Christian is the recipient of a capacity by which he petitions and praises in an unintelligible language, i.e., in tongues! By his own admission the cessationist believes tongues is unintelligible, something that transcends or bypasses the mind. In other words, the gift of tongues is precisely the Pauline exception to what may be an otherwise valid rule. This is nowhere better seen than in 1 Corinthians 14:14–19, where Paul sustains an unmistakable contrast between, on the one hand, what his ("my") "spirit" speaks (or sings) and does *not* understand, and on the other, what his ("my") "mind" speaks (or sings) and *does* understand.

Let us not forget that all so-called "word" gifts (whether teaching, exhortation, or tongues, for example), indeed, all spiritual gifts of whatever nature, are the work of the Spirit (1 Cor. 12:7–11). In this latter text tongues is in no way differentiated from other gifts in terms of how and to what extent the Spirit is involved in their production and exercise. It is the "same Spirit" and the "same God" who works all these gifts in all persons. Are cessationists prepared to argue on that basis for the infallibility of *all* the charismata? If not, then it seems inconsistent to do so for tongues.

Quite a few cessationists also contend that there is no sustainable biblical basis for the private, devotional use of tongues. It makes sense why they would embrace this view, for if all tongues are revelatory, as they contend, one must explain why God would reveal sacred truths in an unintelligible way to someone who in turn proceeds to speak them back to God in private. But, as noted previously, tongues is not revelatory. Furthermore, the fact that praying in tongues was a staple experience in Paul's private devotional life is evident from at least two texts. First, in 1 Corinthians 14:18–19 (NASB) he declares: "I thank God, I speak in tongues more than you all; however, in the church I desire to speak five words with my mind so that I may instruct others also, rather than ten thousand words in a tongue." As we noted in an earlier chapter, this statement is Paul's somewhat exaggerated way of saying he almost never speaks in tongues in church. In the absence of interpretation, he most definitely won't. Now, if in church Paul virtually never exercises this gift yet speaks in tongues more frequently and fluently and fervently than anyone, even more so than the tongues-happy Corinthians, where does he do it (indeed, if tongues are revelatory, *why* would he do it)? Surely it must be in private. Second, this is confirmed by 1 Corinthians 14:28, where he gives instruction on what to do in the absence of interpretation: "let him [the tongues-speaker] speak to himself and to God" (NASB). Where? Given the explicit prohibition of uninterpreted tongues-speech "in church," it seems likely Paul had in mind prayer in tongues in private—in a context other than the corporate gathering.

Noted cessationist O. Palmer Robertson disagrees and argues that Paul is instructing the tongues-speaker to pray silently to himself and to God while yet in the church gathering. But even if this is true (which I doubt), we then would have apostolic endorsement of *private* tongues-speech. If, as Robertson contends, all tongues-speech is revelatory and is designed only for rational communication, Paul's counsel makes no sense. Why would God impart infallible and *unintelligible* revelatory knowledge (the latter, in itself, strikes me as bizarre) only for the recipient to speak it to himself and back to God? Robertson envisions the tongues-speaker waiting patiently until an interpreter arrives, at which time he can then speak audibly. But this is reading into the text a scenario conspicuous by its absence. Paul's instruction is for a situation in which there is *no* interpreter. He says nothing about the tongues-speaker waiting until one is present.

Furthermore, as noted earlier, it is inconsistent with Paul's emphasis in 1 Corinthians 14 on all working together for mutual edification that he should recommend that some (perhaps many) focus their spiritual energy inwardly (praying in tongues) while someone else is speaking outwardly, ostensibly to edify the very people who, on Paul's advice, aren't even paying attention.

Some cessationists have insisted that Paul's advice to the tongues-speaker in 1 Corinthians 14:28 (NASB) to "speak to himself and God" cannot refer to private exercise of the gift because the context pertains to the church assembly. But if this were the case, it would seem to put them in the position of endorsing the legitimacy of *personal, uninterpreted, non-evangelistic, non-sign* tongues-speech *in the corporate meeting of the church*, a view that I am quite certain they would not want to embrace. It is better to understand the apostle Paul as commending the use of personal, uninterpreted prayer in tongues outside the church assembly in the privacy of one's devotional life.[1]

Robertson refuses to concede that someone can be edified apart from rational understanding. He therefore insists that God not only enables a person to speak in a language not previously learned but also enables him to understand what he is speaking (contrary to 1 Corinthians 14:14). But why then would there be a need for the distinct gift of interpretation? Each person speaking in tongues would already know what he is saying and in turn could communicate such to the congregation. Why forbid a person to speak in tongues in the absence of an interpreter (1 Cor. 14:27–28) if every tongues-speaker is his *own* interpreter? And if the tongues-speaker can understand what he is saying, why encourage him to pray that he might interpret (1 Cor. 14:13)?

It will not do for Robertson to say that the one gifted with interpretation has an exactness that goes "beyond the understanding of the sense of the revelation possessed by the tongues-speaker,"[2] because he believes that anytime God reveals truth to the human mind, there is an a priori guarantee that both the *reception* of what is revealed and its *transmission* are perfectly accurate. In other words, for Robertson *all* revelation comes with a guarantee of perfection and divine exactness in both comprehension and communication.

My conclusion from all this is that the attempt to prove tongues is based on inspired and infallible revelation from God is simply not sustained by a careful reading of what Paul says. Thus, I find no reason to question the contemporary validity of tongues based on the misguided notion that they are revelatory in nature.

26. Is tongues a sign of judgment against unbelieving Jews?

All through my four years in seminary I repeatedly heard this argument. Virtually every book written against the validity of tongues in today's church appealed to the idea that its primary (if not sole) purpose was to declare God's judgment against Jewish people for having rejected Jesus as the Messiah. The passage to which they would look for support is 1 Corinthians 14:20–25. There we read:

> Brothers, do not be children in your thinking. Be infants
> in evil, but in your thinking be mature. In the Law it is

written, "By people of strange tongues and by the lips of
foreigners will I speak to this people, and even then they
will not listen to me, says the Lord." Thus tongues are a
sign not for believers but for unbelievers, while prophecy
is a sign not for unbelievers but for believers. If, therefore,
the whole church comes together and all speak in tongues,
and outsiders or unbelievers enter, will they not say that
you are out of your minds? But if all prophesy, and an
unbeliever or outsider enters, he is convicted by all, he is
called to account by all, the secrets of his heart are disclosed, and so, falling on his face, he will worship God and
declare that God is really among you.

—1 Corinthians 14:20–25

"There it is, Sam," they would say to me. "Paul explicitly declares
that tongues are a sign not for believers but for unbelievers." This
would seem to suggest that the answer to question twenty-six is yes.
But let's look at it more closely.

Paul begins by citing a text from the prophecy of Isaiah. In
Isaiah 28:11 God declares: "For by people of strange lips and with a
foreign tongue the Lord will speak to this people." For us to determine the meaning of this text we must go back a bit farther in the
Old Testament to a warning God gave to Israel in Deuteronomy
28:49. Deuteronomy is the chapter that lists the many curses or
judgments God will bring against His people Israel if they should
fail to "obey the voice" of God and refuse to "do all his command-
ments and his statutes" (Deut. 28:15). If Israel violates the covenant, God will chastise them by sending a foreign enemy, speaking
a foreign tongue: "The Lord will bring a nation against you from
far away, from the end of the earth, swooping down like the eagle,
a nation whose language you do not understand" (Deut. 28:49).
Thus, confusing and confounding speech would serve as a sign of
God's judgment against a rebellious people. This is the judgment

Isaiah says has come upon Israel in the eighth century BC when the Assyrians invaded and conquered the Jews (cf. also what happened in the sixth century BC; see Jeremiah 5:15).

Many cessationists argue that God is judging unbelieving Jews in the first century, the sign of which is language they can't understand (i.e., tongues). The purpose of tongues, therefore, is to signify God's judgment against Israel for rejecting the Messiah and thereby to shock them into repentance and faith. Tongues, so goes the argument, is an evangelistic sign gift. Since tongues ceased to function in this capacity when Israel was dispersed in AD 70, the gift was valid only for the first century.

But there are numerous problems with this view. First, we must be alert to the error of reductionism. What I mean by this is the tendency to take one purpose of a gift, perhaps even the most important and primary purpose of a gift, and *reduce* the gift to *nothing but* that particular purpose. Let's apply that to our text here in 1 Corinthians 14. My point is that even if tongues served as an evangelistic sign gift (a point that I do not believe is true but make only out of concession for the sake of argument), nowhere does the New Testament restrict or reduce that gift to this one purpose. Simply because tongues is said to function in one capacity does not mean it cannot function in others. To say that my primary task at Bridgeway Church is to preach and teach the Word of God does not mean that is all I do. My responsibility cannot be *reduced* to the ministry of the Word. I also counsel people and lead a large staff and evangelize the lost and undertake numerous other tasks. It's important that we understand spiritual gifts in much the same way. We have already noted that tongues also serves the "common good" of the body of Christ (1 Cor. 12:7), and when used appropriately can spiritually edify or build up the person who is speaking or praying. (See 1 Corinthians 14:4.)

Second, if tongues-speech were not a spiritual gift for the church at all, why did Paul ever allow it to be exercised and used in the church? If interpreted, tongues-speech was entirely permissible. But this seems difficult to explain if its only or primary purpose was to declare judgment against unbelieving Jews.

Third, if uninterpreted tongues was designed to pronounce God's judgment against Jewish people and perhaps stir them to repentance, why would God have made available the accompanying gift of interpretation? Interpretation, it seems, would serve only to undermine this alleged purpose of tongues in declaring judgment against those in the Jewish community who had rejected Jesus as Messiah. The spiritual gift of interpretation makes sense only if tongues-speech is profitable and beneficial to Christians in the assembly. Let's be sure we feel the full weight of this point. Consider again what the cessationist is saying. Unintelligible tongues were given by God to serve as a sign of His judgment against the Jewish people, primarily for the sin of having rejected Jesus as Messiah. But if that is the purpose of tongues, there is no reason God would also have given the accompanying gift of interpretation. For tongues to achieve its purpose, it must remain uninterpreted and thus confusing. Simply put, this view of the cessationist simply cannot account for why God bestows the gift of interpretation.

Fourth, if God intended tongues-speech to serve as a sign for unbelieving Jews, Paul would not have counseled *against* its use when unbelievers are present (1 Cor. 14:23). And yet that is precisely what he does. To speak in uninterpreted tongues when unbelievers are present simply exposes you to the charge of being "out of your minds" (1 Cor. 14:23). This is why Paul recommends that prophecy, not tongues, be employed when outsiders attend your meeting.

Finally, the contrasts in this context are between believer and nonbeliever, not Jew and Gentile. Indeed, most commentators concur that the nonbeliever in 1 Corinthians 14:23–24 is probably a Gentile, not a Jew.

For all these reasons, we conclude that the view that tongues is

only (or merely primarily) a sign of judgment on first-century unbelieving Jews is unconvincing. What then is the principle Paul finds
in Isaiah 28:11 that applies to Corinth (and to us)? It is this: one
way in which God brings punishment on people for their unbelief is by speaking to them in an unintelligible language. Speech
that cannot be understood is one way God displays His anger.
Incomprehensible language will not guide or instruct or lead to
faith and repentance but only confuse and destroy.

Now let's apply this to the situation envisioned in first-century
Corinth. If outsiders or unbelievers visit your corporate church
gathering and you speak in a language they cannot understand, you
will simply drive them away. You will be giving a negative "sign" to
unbelievers that is entirely wrong, because their hardness of heart
has not reached the point where they deserve that severe sign of
judgment. So when you come together (1 Cor. 14:26), if anyone
speaks in a tongue, be sure there is an interpretation (1 Cor. 14:27).
Otherwise the tongues-speaker should be quiet in the church
(1 Cor. 14:28). Prophecy, on the other hand, is a sign of God's presence with believers (1 Cor. 14:22), and so Paul encourages its use
when unbelievers are present in order that they may see this sign
and thereby come to Christian faith (1 Cor. 14:24–25).

Therefore, in 1 Corinthians 14:20–25 Paul is *not* talking about
the function of the gift of tongues in general but only about the
negative result of one particular *abuse* of tongues-speech (namely,
its use without interpretation in the public assembly). So do not
permit uninterpreted tongues-speech in church, for in doing so,
you run the risk of communicating a negative sign to people that
will only drive them away.[3]

Chapter 11

TONGUES AND THE BELIEVER

M ANY CHRISTIANS, THOUGH curious about tongues, are also afraid of it. They fear that to desire and pray for this gift or to open themselves to the Spirit will cause them to risk exposing themselves to a demonic influence. Why do people think this way?

First of all, Christians who were raised and nurtured in strong, Bible-based churches are extraordinarily fearful of the slightest artificiality in their Christian experience. They demand a virtual guarantee, in advance, that what they do be genuine. Often this caution is borne of a fear that inevitably paralyzes faith, as well as the willingness to try and to risk. After first speaking in what they hope is tongues, the slightest doubt of its authenticity prompts them never to try again. I'm not suggesting that we not be passionate for what is genuine. But we must not let fear control our lives.

Another factor is that often after first speaking in tongues, people conclude that it doesn't "feel" sufficiently supernatural. It doesn't seem significantly different from what it takes to pray in English. So either it isn't real or it isn't worth the effort.

One's initial experience with tongues can be disconcerting when it doesn't "sound" like a language. It seems like irrational and incoherent gibberish, unlike any speech they've heard before. "How could something so trite and repetitive be of any spiritual value?" Such disillusionment leads to their abandoning the practice altogether.

Finally, many shy away from tongues for fear of "sounding silly." Appearing foolish in the presence of people whose respect and love you cherish can often paralyze one's passion for this spiritual gift. These concerns lead us to the next in our list of thirty crucial questions about speaking in tongues.

27. If I don't have the gift of tongues but want it, what should I do?

Let's get one thing clear right from the start. There isn't the slightest evidence whatsoever that any New Testament author believed a desire for tongues or the exercise of it might expose a person to demonic influence. The church at Corinth was filled with recently converted men and women whose background was characterized by pagan and demonic rituals. It was to these very people that Paul said, "I want you all to speak in tongues" (1 Cor. 14:5)! Nowhere does Paul say or suggest, "I want you all to be *afraid* of tongues." Neither Paul nor anyone else ever says, "Be careful! Tongues are dangerous. When you open your heart and make yourself vulnerable in the pursuit of this gift, Satan could easily step in and exert his power in your life." No! Nowhere do we see this in the New Testament. When Paul turns to the issue of tongues, he says the same thing about this gift as he does about all others: they are expressions of "the same Spirit" and "the same Lord" and "the same God" who "empowers them all in everyone"

(1 Cor. 12:4–6). Tongues is no less a "manifestation of the Spirit" given for the "common good" than any other gift.

In addition, when he begins his detailed description of the gift, he tells us that the one who speaks "in a tongue builds up himself" (1 Cor. 14:4). He doesn't say he or she opens a door to a demon. And when he concludes his argument with a final exhortation, it is specifically that no one should ever "forbid speaking in tongues" (1 Cor. 14:39). Does that sound like the advice of someone who wanted his disciples to be afraid of tongues and to put up their guard lest they be invaded by a demonic spirit? Along these same lines we should remember the words of Jesus Himself:

> What father among you, if his son asks for a fish, will instead of a fish give him a serpent; or if he asks for an egg, will give him a scorpion? If you then, who are evil, know how to give good gifts to your children, how much more will the heavenly Father give the Holy Spirit to those who ask him!
>
> —Luke 11:11–13

If you, one of God's beloved children, come to your immeasurably good heavenly Father and ask Him for this gift of the Holy Spirit, He's not going to give you a demon!

Now that we have dismissed that absurd argument, let me suggest several practical steps you might wish to take.

First, don't let anyone quench your zeal by telling you that if God wanted you to have the gift of tongues, He would already have given it to you. This bad advice is based on an equally bad and unbiblical belief about how many spiritual gifts God may choose to bestow on His children and when He might choose to do it. Some believe every Christian gets every spiritual gift God intends for them at the moment of their conversion, when they are baptized in the Spirit. This is false. It is true, of course, that "to each"

Christian the Spirit gives at least one spiritual gift (1 Cor. 12:7). The apostle Peter confirms this when he says:

> *As each has received a gift,* use it to serve one another, as good stewards of God's varied grace: whoever speaks, as one who speaks oracles of God; whoever serves, as one who serves by the strength that God supplies—in order that in everything God may be glorified through Jesus Christ.
>
> —1 PETER 4:10–11, EMPHASIS ADDED

But nowhere does any New Testament author say or even imply that once you have received a gift at conversion, you shouldn't expect, much less pray for, additional gifts.

There are several texts that actually prove the opposite. No one can say with confidence that there is a limit to how many gifts the Spirit might bestow. The apostle Paul probably had the gifts of evangelism, apostleship, prophecy, miracles, healing, tongues, and teaching, just to mention a few. So what biblical evidence is there that we can and should pray for God to bestow gifts beyond what we already have? Here are several texts.

We should begin with Paul's exhortation in 1 Corinthians 12:31 that we should "earnestly desire the higher gifts." By "higher" Paul means more effective at building up the body of Christ. But if the Corinthians had already received at conversion the only gifts they would ever have, how could Paul have exhorted them to "earnestly desire" to obtain more? A similar point is made in 1 Corinthians 14:1, where he again exhorts the Corinthians (and us) to "earnestly desire the spiritual gifts, especially that you may prophesy." Those to whom this exhortation was given were born-again believers! Paul obviously believed it was possible, and quite desirable, for God to continue to grant more gifts than any person might already have.

That especially applies to prophecy because of its superior capacity to build up others.

In 1 Corinthians 14:5 Paul expresses his wish that "all" the Corinthians would speak in tongues. Why would he do this if he knew the Spirit doesn't grant gifts beyond the time of conversion? Later in that chapter Paul says of the Corinthians, "So with yourselves, since you are eager for manifestations of the Spirit, strive to excel in building up the church" (1 Cor. 14:12). If we only receive spiritual gifts at conversion, Paul should have said something along the lines of "Stop being eager for manifestations or gifts of the Spirit, because He's not going to give you anything beyond what you already have." But of course, that's not what he says!

In the immediately following verse Paul issues this exhortation: "Therefore, one who speaks in a tongue should pray that he may interpret" (1 Cor. 14:13). The one who already speaks in tongues is obviously a Christian, yet Paul exhorts that person to pray that God would grant him yet another gift, the ability to interpret the tongue.

One more text will confirm my point. Paul writes 1 Timothy to his young protégé and spiritual son. He tells him: "Do not neglect the gift you have, which was given you by prophecy when the council of elders laid their hands on you" (1 Tim. 4:14). So here is Paul reminding the born-again Timothy of how he received a spiritual gift when the elders prayed for him. Paul probably had much the same thing in mind when he wrote later to Timothy, telling him "to fan into flame the gift of God, which is in you through the laying on of my hands" (2 Tim. 1:6). If Timothy had received at the time of his conversion all the spiritual gifts that it was possible for him to have, these exhortations by Paul make no sense. Clearly Timothy was granted additional gifts when he was prayerfully ministered to by the elders at Ephesus as well as on that occasion when Paul himself laid hands on Timothy and prayed for him.

So I trust by now that you know it is perfectly legitimate for you or any other Christian to desire and earnestly pursue and pray for additional gifts of the Spirit, including the gift of tongues. It's important, of course, that you keep in mind two things. First, you can't twist the Spirit's arm (as if He had one!). You can't force Him to give you something that is contrary to His will. Paul said it clearly in 1 Corinthians 12:11 that all spiritual gifts are "empowered by one and the same Spirit, who apportions to each one individually as he wills." The obtaining of any spiritual gift isn't ultimately up to what we will or want but is based on what the Spirit wills. So why would Paul still tell us to "earnestly desire" and "pray" for spiritual gifts? The answer isn't that difficult to discern. One of the ways the Spirit's will for us is achieved is when He Himself stirs up a desire for a particular gift in our hearts. Oftentimes we find ourselves hungry or desperate or yearning for some spiritual reality precisely because the Spirit is already at work, antecedently to our desire, awakening in us a recognition of our need for it.

There is one more thing to keep in mind, especially if you are among those who think that because the will of the Holy Spirit determines who gets what gift, we should never pray for or earnestly pursue a gift we don't yet have. Paul tells us in Ephesians 1:11 that God "works all things according to the counsel of his will." But I seriously doubt you will respond to that by saying, "Well, I guess I don't have to pray for God to do anything at all since His will is the ultimate and determinative factor in everything that happens." Or I doubt you will say, "It isn't necessary or even helpful to preach the gospel to lost souls or to pray for people to be healed because God's will determines all such matters." In other words, we know that God's will is ultimate and decisive, but we also know that one way (perhaps the primary way) in which God accomplishes His will is by stirring and motivating us to preach and pray as the means by which He brings that will into being.

I've spoken with some who are reluctant to pray for tongues because they fear that if God were to bestow the gift, they would lose control of themselves and do something foolish or irreverent and perhaps spiral off into some weird physical gyration. But when Paul describes the exercise of tongues, he never portrays people as losing control of their senses or falling under the influence of an alien power. We see this also in Acts. On all three occasions when people spoke in tongues in Acts, they are seen as calm, cool, and collected! The fact that some unbelievers on the day of Pentecost accused them of being drunk isn't because these believers were staggering around and slurring their speech. Their charge was either one of hard-hearted disdain for the exuberant zeal of these disciples or due to the fact that they didn't understand any of the languages that were being spoken. So remember, God's purpose in bestowing the gift of tongues isn't to overwhelm or humiliate you but to empower you to bless God, bless others, and edify your own soul. I can't think of any place or posture that is any safer than being under the influence of the Holy Spirit of God. So again: there is no reason for you to be afraid!

A woman once asked me if God would make her leave her church and join a Charismatic congregation if she received the gift of tongues. She was devoted to her church and had no desire to leave it. I can't predict what God may ask of you with regard to church attendance, but I seriously doubt it would have anything to do with the particular spiritual gift He has granted to you. Of course, it may be that your church is staunchly opposed to tongues and perhaps even accuses those who exercise the gift as being psychologically imbalanced or even demonized. In such a case I suspect that common sense would indicate a change in churches is in order. But even then God may want you to remain in your church as a witness and source of encouragement to others who hold to an unbiblical view of tongues.

If you do choose to remain in a church that denies the validity of tongues today, honor their wishes not to exercise the gift anywhere outside your own private prayer life. God didn't grant us these gifts to be divisive. Neither does He want you to be defensive or argumentative. Be patient and loving with them and allow time for the fruit of this gift to grow. It may prove helpful to seek support and encouragement in a small Bible-study group or home prayer fellowship sponsored by another church that is attended by believers who embrace the gifts of the Spirit.

You may also encounter the charge, "Oh, I guess this means you think you're better than we are. You're the 'have' and we're the 'have-nots.'" This is a tragic misunderstanding not only of the gift of tongues but of our relationship to the work of the Spirit in general. Simply reassure them as gently but firmly as possible that the gift of tongues has *not* made you a better Christian than they. Perhaps the best way to respond is by saying: "I don't believe that I am now a better Christian than you. I simply believe I am now on my way to becoming a better Christian than *I* was before I received this gift." God forbids us to compare ourselves with others, as if we, because of a particular gift, are better than they. (See 1 Corinthians 4:7.) But it is an essential part of the Christian life that we grow up in our faith and deepen in our devotion to Jesus through the increase and expansion of the Spirit's work in our lives.[1]

Also, as I argued in an earlier chapter, speaking in tongues is not an exercise in anti-intellectualism where you have to put your brain on ice. Tongues is often an extremely exhilarating and emotionally charged spiritual experience. But it is just as often quite mundane, and when I pray in tongues, it doesn't feel substantially any different from how I feel when I pray in English. And my love for Scripture and the deep things of God has only grown since I received this gift. So don't live in fear that once you begin to speak in tongues, your gray matter will turn to mush! Don't you think that if there were a cause-and-effect connection between tongues and disdain for doctrine that Paul would have informed us of it and warned us against it? And let us never forget that it was the apostle Paul, author of the Epistle to the Romans and other doctrinal treatises, who said, "I thank God I speak in tongues more than you all!"

So what are we to do when it comes to helping and supporting those who long for this gift? Many think they should "prime the pump" by encouraging the individual to repeatedly say "banana" backward! This is rarely helpful and lacks any biblical support. Neither am I supportive of those who would suggest that the individual simply begin speaking meaningless syllables or made-up words, waiting, as it were, for the Spirit to, in a sense, co-opt or take hold of your vocal capacities. And yet I don't want to be overly dogmatic on this point, as I've heard from a few people that this is in fact the way in which the Spirit then imparted tongues to them.

The simple fact is that there is no prescribed method or procedure in the Bible for how the Spirit imparts the gift of tongues to men and women. I wasn't trying to speak in tongues when it happened. I didn't start out at will uttering strange syllables and words with the hope that the Spirit would take hold of my speech pattern and transform it into genuine tongues. I was praying in plain English when suddenly and without warning I was praying in words that I had never heard or learned before. But that happened only once, at the beginning.

We read in Acts 2:4 that "they were all filled with the Holy Spirit and began to speak in other tongues *as the Spirit gave them utterance*" (emphasis added). That sounds much like what happened to me the first time I spoke in tongues. But in 1 Corinthians 14 Paul clearly envisions a scenario in which people have control over whether to speak in tongues, when to speak in tongues, and for how long. They can start and stop at will.

Some of you will have an experience like mine. Others may simply step out in faith and begin speaking whatever words come into your heart, trusting that the Spirit is the source of your speech and will sustain it within you. You may feel something profoundly emotional and exhilarating. But some may feel nothing at all. Don't draw any conclusion about the legitimacy of your speech based on your feelings. Some of you will be hesitant to speak, fearing that what comes out of your mouth sounds silly or artificial, or worse still, fleshly or demonic. Do not be afraid! For all of you it comes down to whether you believe what Jesus said in Luke 11:11–13, quoted previously.

Quite a few have shared with me how they first spoke in what they had hoped was the gift of tongues only then to abandon the practice because it didn't "feel" supernatural. But it doesn't have to *feel* supernatural to *be* supernatural! Paul says in 1 Corinthians 12:6 that God empowers all spiritual gifts: all! Not just those that appear or feel to be more overtly miraculous, but all of them: service, mercy, teaching, etc. Never conclude that it isn't genuine tongues if you speak and it doesn't feel out of the ordinary, special, or super spiritual. Every gift is a manifestation of the Spirit. In that sense every spiritual gift is supernatural.

This is a high hill to climb for those of us who were raised in intensely cerebral or deeply intellectual churches where theological precision and doctrinal authenticity were prized above all else. Don't take that to mean we shouldn't be rigorously biblical in all we believe and do. But there is something of a built-in defense mechanism in many Christians that makes them extraordinarily sensitive and resistant to the slightest hint of artificiality. So at the first onset of tongues, if it doesn't come with a self-attesting witness of absolute authenticity, we tend to shut down or withdraw. This can be a good thing at times, especially among those in the Charismatic world who are on occasion slightly more gullible and naïve about claims to the miraculous than are others. Discernment is always proper for every believer. But discernment can also easily degenerate into cynicism that views virtually all subjective or experiential phenomena with deep suspicion.

Regardless of the path you walk in your pursuit of tongues, be certain that you persevere in prayer. The apostle Paul doesn't give us any details about what it means to "earnestly desire" spiritual gifts. But at minimum I think we'd all agree that he means for us to relentlessly and ceaselessly press into the heart of God in prayer. (See 1 Corinthians 14:13.) You should never be ashamed or embarrassed by your desire for tongues. Neither should you give in to discouragement if your requests for it are not immediately answered.

There is yet one more practical step that you can take that many have found helpful in their prayerful pursuit of tongues. It has to do with worship. Make every effort to find a time and the proper place to wait in solitude with the Lord. We are an inordinately prideful people who are easily intimidated by others and worry about their opinions of us. So find a moment when no one else is around and you needn't worry that your behavior might provoke their disdain or laughter. Begin to sing your praises as the worship leader sings his or hers as you listen to your favorite song list. You need to do all you can to devote considerable time, perhaps even a few hours, to be alone with the Lord in uninterrupted meditation on His Word and heartfelt singing to Him. I've personally found it especially helpful to combine this with a period of fasting. Devote yourself in single-minded and whole-hearted adoration of the beauty of Christ and the joy of being enjoyed by Him (Zeph. 3:17). Open your heart, open your mouth, and sing forth the love songs He has put within. What happens next is between you and God.

Whatever else you do, be patient. Persevere. Press in. Be relentless. Never cease to ask until God says, "Shut up." (Although I'm not convinced He ever would!) Or never cease to ask until you lose the "earnest desire" for this gift. If in the final analysis God doesn't grant you this gift, don't ever, ever, ever conclude that it is because He loves you less than He does the person to whom He grants tongues. If you faithfully, fervently, and frequently ask God for the gift of tongues, one of two things will happen. Either God will say no, in which case you should thank Him for the spiritual gifts you already have. Or God will say yes, and in some manner, at some point in time, the Spirit will impart to you the ability to pray, praise, and give thanks in words you don't understand but that perfectly express your deepest desires and hopes. There isn't a third option.

28. Can or should all Christians speak in tongues? Is tongues a gift God intends to supply to every believer, or is it only given to some?[2]

This question will often provoke equally heated and dogmatic answers, both yes and no. Most non-Charismatic, Evangelical believers think it hardly worth the time even to ask the question. The simple fact that so many millions of born-again believers do not speak in tongues strikes them as experiential confirmation that the answer is decidedly no. In other words, how can it be that God's will is always that everyone speak in tongues when so many millions of Bible-believing, born-again followers of Jesus throughout the course of two thousand years of church history never have? Must we account for this by arguing that they are all living in disobedience to something God so clearly requires and commands in His Word? On the other hand, few cessationists are even familiar with the depth of argumentation that has been put forth by those who would answer yes. So let's take a minute and try to gain some biblical clarity on this issue.

Recent developments within the Southern Baptist Convention are illustrative of the ongoing controversy about tongues. Many of you may have heard or read that the International Mission Board (known as the IMB) of the Southern Baptist Convention has reversed itself on the question of whether they would appoint Southern Baptist missionaries who employ a "private prayer language," their way of referring to the practice of praying in tongues.

The initial decision of the IMB to ban tongues-speech among its missionaries was announced in 2005. According to an article on the website of the Texas *Baptist Standard*, "The Southern Baptist Convention agency already excludes people who speak in tongues in public worship from serving as missionaries. But the mission board's trustees voted Nov. 15 to amend its list of missionary qualifications to exclude those who use a 'prayer language' in private."[3] The article goes on to say that "the restriction of 'prayer language'—a private version of the charismatic worship practice of tongues-speaking—was approved by a vote of 25-18....Some trustees did not vote on the issue during their Huntsville, Ala., meeting, the agency reported."[4] But when David Platt was appointed to the presidency of the IMB, he soon secured a reversal of this policy.[5] No one can easily predict in what direction the IMB will go now that Platt has resigned as president to return to the local church pastorate.

I cite this ever-changing scenario only to point out that the controversy over the spiritual gift of speaking in tongues shows no signs of going away. As long as there are Christians who believe the gift is valid today while others insist it is not, this issue will be discussed and debated. And no issue related to the gift of tongues is as potentially divisive as the question of whether this gift is intended by God to be received by every born-again believer.

Those Charismatics who would answer yes to our question are dumbfounded that anyone would disagree. As far as they are concerned, Paul's statement in 1 Corinthians 14:5 settles the debate once and for all. There the apostle says, "Now I want you all to speak in tongues." Is Paul's expressed "wish" a reflection of his understanding that God's "will" is the same?

No

Those who insist that tongues is not designed by God for all believers appeal to several texts in 1 Corinthians. For example, they direct our attention to 1 Corinthians 7:7, where Paul uses language identical to what is found in 1 Corinthians 14:5. Paul says this about his own celibacy: "I wish that all were as I myself am. But each has his own gift from God, one of one kind and one of another" (1 Cor. 7:7). Few, if any, would contend that Paul is insisting that all Christians remain single as he is. His wish, therefore, should not be taken as the expression of an unqualified and universal desire. The same understanding, so they argue, should be applied to Paul's expressed wish in 1 Corinthians 14:5 that all Christians speak in tongues.

Yet another argument by those who believe tongues is a gift bestowed on only some Christians is the language Paul employs in 1 Corinthians 12:7–11. There he says tongues, like the other eight gifts mentioned, is bestowed to individuals as the Holy Spirit wills. If Paul meant that all believers were to experience this gift, why did he employ the terminology of "to one is given...and to another...to another," etc.? In other words, Paul seems to suggest that the Spirit sovereignly differentiates among Christians and distributes one or more gifts to this person and yet another different gift to this person and yet another gift to that one, and so on.

Those who answer no to our question are insistent that there is no escaping what Paul says in 1 Corinthians 12:28–30. In this text the apostle argues that all do not speak in tongues any more than all have gifts of healings or all are teachers or apostles. Let's look closely at how Paul frames his question:

> Are all apostles? Are all prophets? Are all teachers? Do
> all work miracles? Do all possess gifts of healing? Do all

speak with tongues? Do all interpret? But earnestly desire the higher gifts. And I will show you a still more excellent way.

—1 Corinthians 12:29–31

It's difficult, if not impossible, to escape the conclusion that Paul expects us to respond by saying no. This is reinforced when we take note of how such questions were posed in Greek. But first consider how we ask questions in English when we already know the answer. English speakers have a way of emphasizing certain words, of elevating our voice, and even utilizing certain facial expressions when we intend for the person listening to know that the answer to our question is decidedly no. For example:

+ "You're not going to jump off that ledge to your death, are you?"
+ "Not everyone is a fan of the Dallas Cowboys, are they?"

In each of these cases we anticipate a negative response: no.

But in Greek there is a specific grammatical structure that is designed to elicit a negative response to the question being asked. Such is precisely what Paul employs here in 1 Corinthians 12. The translation provided by the New American Standard Bible makes this slightly more explicit than does the English Standard Version.

All are not apostles, are they? All are not prophets, are they? All are not teachers, are they? All are not workers of miracles, are they? All do not have gifts of healings, do they? All do not speak with tongues, do they? All do not interpret, do they?

—1 Corinthians 12:29–30, nasb

181

You can clearly see from the way the questions are phrased that the author wants you to respond by saying, "No, of course not."

YES

Many think this forever settles the argument. But those who insist on answering yes to our question are quick to remind us that 1 Corinthians 7:7 isn't the only place where Paul uses the "I want" or "I wish" terminology. One must also address passages such as the following:

> For I do not want you to be unaware, brothers, that our fathers were all under the cloud, and all passed through the sea [actually, a more literal translation would be something along the lines of, "For I do not wish you to be ignorant, brothers…"].
>
> —1 CORINTHIANS 10:1

> But I want you to understand that the head of every man is Christ, the head of a wife is her husband, and the head of Christ is God.
>
> —1 CORINTHIANS 11:3

> Now concerning spiritual gifts, brothers, I do not want you to be uninformed.
>
> —1 CORINTHIANS 12:1

In each of these three texts the same Greek verb (*thelō*) is used that we find in 1 Corinthians 14:5 ("I want" or "I wish"), and in all of them what the apostle wants applies equally and universally to every believer. Furthermore, in 1 Corinthians 7 Paul goes on to tell us explicitly why his wish for universal celibacy cannot and should not be fulfilled. It is because "each has his own gift from God" (1 Cor. 7:7). But in 1 Corinthians 14 no such contextual clues are found that suggest Paul's wish or desire for all to speak in tongues cannot be fulfilled. Then again, Paul's use of *thelō* in 1 Corinthians 14:5 may suggest only that this is Paul's *desire* without telling us whether he (or we) might consider the desire within the realm of possibility. At minimum we may conclude that Paul would be pleased if everyone spoke in tongues. But that doesn't necessarily mean they all should.

Those who believe the answer to our question is yes pose yet another question. "Why," they ask, "would God *not* want each believer to operate in this particular gift?" In other words, they ask: "Why would God withhold from any of His children a gift that enables them to pray and to praise Him so effectively, a gift that also functions to edify them in their faith?" But could not the same question be asked of virtually every other spiritual gift? Why would God not want all His people to be able to teach or to show mercy or to serve or to give generously or to pray for healing with great success or to evangelize? In any case I think we should avoid speculating on what we think God may or may not want for all of us unless we have explicit biblical instruction to that effect.

Paul's statement in 1 Corinthians 14:23 also factors into the debate. There he says: "If, therefore, the whole church comes together and all speak in tongues, and outsiders or unbelievers enter, will they not say that you are out of your minds?" Paul's question reveals a scenario in the church at Corinth that the apostle finds quite problematic. Those who had the gift of tongues were all speaking aloud without the benefit of interpretation. Whether they did this simultaneously or in succession, we don't know. But the problem this posed for unregenerate visitors was obvious. The latter would have no idea of what was being said and would likely conclude that those speaking were mad or deranged or in some sense out of their minds, a scenario hardly conducive to effective evangelism! This most likely accounts for Paul's subsequent demand that only two or three speak in tongues and that there always be an interpretation to follow. But aside from that issue, the argument is that Paul at least envisions the *hypothetical possibility* that every Christian in Corinth could speak in tongues, even if he advises against it in the corporate meeting of the church. Or could it simply be that he is speaking in deliberately exaggerated language when he says that "all speak in tongues"?

A view that many Charismatics are now supporting is that 1 Corinthians 12:7–11 and 12:28–30 refer to the gift of tongues in *public ministry*, that is to say, ministry exercised during the corporate gathering of the entire church, whereas 1 Corinthians 14:5 is describing the gift in *private devotion*. In 1 Corinthians 12:28 Paul specifically says he is describing what happens "in the church" or "in the assembly" (cf. 1 Cor. 11:18; 14:19, 23, 28, 33, 35). Not everyone is gifted by the Spirit to speak in tongues during the gathered assembly of God's people. But the potential does exist for every believer to pray in tongues in private. These are not two different gifts, however, but two different contexts in which the one gift might be employed. A person who ministers to the entire church in tongues is someone who already uses tongues in his or her prayer life.

Well-known Pentecostal pastor Jack Hayford argues in much the same way, using different terms. He suggests that the *gift* of tongues is (1) limited in distribution (1 Cor. 12:11, 30), and (2) its public exercise is to be closely governed (1 Cor. 14:27–28) while the *grace* of tongues is so broadly available that Paul wishes that all enjoyed its blessing (1 Cor. 14:5), which includes (1) distinctive communication with God (1 Cor. 14:2); (2) edifying of the believer's private life (1 Cor. 14:4); and (3) worship and thanksgiving with beauty and propriety (1 Cor. 14:15–17).[6] The difference between these operations of the Holy Spirit is that *not every* Christian has reason to expect he or she will necessarily exercise the public *gift*, while *any* Christian may expect and welcome the private *grace* of spiritual language in his or her personal time of prayer fellowship *with* God

(1 Cor. 14:2), praiseful worship *before* God (1 Cor. 14:15–17), and intercessory prayer *to* God (Rom. 8:26–27).

Paul's point at the end of 1 Corinthians 12 is that not every believer will contribute to the body in precisely the same way. Not everyone will minister a prophetic word, not everyone will teach, and so on. But whether everyone might pray privately in tongues is another matter not in Paul's purview until 1 Corinthians 14.

It must be noted, however, that nowhere does Paul or any other New Testament author differentiate explicitly between tongues as a "gift" and tongues as a "grace." All "gifts" are expressions of God's "grace" to us through the Holy Spirit. Indeed, as most of you are undoubtedly aware, the Greek word for a spiritual *gift* (*charisma*) is clearly related to the Greek word for *grace* (*charis*). All spiritual gifts, not just tongues, are expressions of divine grace. I must confess a discomfort on my part in establishing a distinction between two expressions of tongues based on a supposed difference in words that nowhere is found in the New Testament.

Those who embrace this view find what they believe is a parallel in Paul's perspective on who may prophesy. "All are not prophets, are they?" (1 Cor. 12:29, NASB). No, of course not. But Paul is quick to say that the potential exists for "all" to prophesy (1 Cor. 14:1, 31). Why could not the same be true for tongues? Couldn't Paul be saying that whereas all do not speak in tongues as an expression of corporate, public ministry, it is possible that all may speak in tongues as an expression of private praise and prayer? Just as Paul's rhetorical question in 1 Corinthians 12:29 is not designed to rule out the possibility that all may utter a prophetic word, so also his rhetorical question in 1 Corinthians 12:30 is not designed to exclude anyone from exercising tongues in their private devotional experience.

One problem with the view that Hayford defends is that when Paul says, "God has appointed *in the church* first apostles, second prophets, third teachers" (1 Cor. 12:28, emphasis added), and so on, he isn't referring to what happens "in the church" gathering or corporate assembly. The phrase "in the church" means in the body of Christ at large (whether that be in Corinth or Thessalonica or Rome or any other place where God's people may be found). However, in several other texts Paul quite clearly has in view the public meeting of God's people. (See 1 Corinthians 11:18; 14:19, 23, 28, 33, and 35.) But in the one passage where Paul denies that all have been given the gift of tongues, he is referring to "the body of Christ" (1 Cor. 12:27), of which we are "individually members." New Testament scholar Max Turner also points out that

> the other functions signified in 12:28–30 are surely not restricted to what happens when the Corinthian believers formally assemble. We must assume that prophecy, teaching, healings, miracles, leading and administration, were all both inside and outside the formal 'assembly'. But all this in turn means that the question of 12:30, 'Not all speak in tongues, do they? (No!)', cannot be restricted to mean 'Not all have a special gift to speak tongues "in the assembly", do they?' It must mean only *some* speak in tongues *at all*, whether privately or in the assembly.[7]

My sense, then, is that Paul is not making a distinction between tongues that are exercised in public and tongues that remain a staple of private devotional prayer. Although there is certainly a variety of "kinds" or "species" of tongues, the difference is not one between private tongues and public tongues.

As you can see, good arguments exist on both sides of the fence when it comes to answering this question. I must confess it seems unlikely that God would withhold the gift of tongues from one of His children if they passionately and sincerely desire it. My suspicion is that, all things being equal, if you deeply desire this gift, it is probably (but not certainly) because the Holy Spirit has stirred your heart to seek for it. And He has stirred your heart to seek for it because it is His will to bestow it. So if you long for the gift of tongues, persevere in your prayers. My sense (with no guarantee) is that God will answer you in His time with a satisfying yes.

On the other hand, it is important to remember that as far as we can tell, there is no other spiritual gift that is ever described, defined, or portrayed in the New Testament as one that God bestows, or wants to bestow, on every single Christian. In other words, as I pointed out earlier, few if any would argue that God wants all to have the gift of teaching, or the gift of mercy, or the gift of leadership, or the gift of evangelism. Why, then, would tongues be unique, the only one among the many *charismata* that God intends for all believers to exercise?

In the final analysis, I am inclined to conclude that it is not necessarily God's will that all Christians speak in tongues. But I'm open to being persuaded otherwise![8]

Chapter 12

TONGUES IN EARLY CHRISTIANITY, PART I

THE QUESTION WE will address in this chapter is part of a much larger debate among Evangelical Christians. Those whom I have referred to as cessationists argue that certain spiritual gifts of a more overtly miraculous or supernatural nature (in particular, those of 1 Corinthians 12:8–10) ceased sometime following the death of the last apostle or perhaps immediately after the Book of Revelation was written. We who are continuationists, on the other hand, find no evidence in Scripture to suggest that those gifts or any others were designed to operate only within a short time frame of some fifty to sixty years in the first century. All of God's gifts are intended for all of God's people throughout the entire course of church history.

I have devoted considerable energy to addressing this debate in other books and articles, and I see no need to repeat myself here.[1] Our only concern in this chapter is whether we have good reason to believe tongues is a gift of the Spirit that was designed not only for the first-century church but for the church of our day as well. In the next chapter we also will briefly explore the presence of tongues-speech throughout the intervening nineteen centuries of church history.

29. Do we have good biblical reasons to believe the gift of tongues is still valid for today?

The question before us is whether we have solid biblical reasons for believing that tongues is a gift God intends to be present and operative in the lives of His people today, both individually and in the corporate experience of the local church. My initial response to this query is to say, "What possible evidence is there in the New Testament that such a question should ever have been raised in the first place?" Our examination of the purpose of tongues-speech and response to cessationist misunderstandings of what tongues is and how it functioned all lead to the simple conclusion that the New Testament is devoid of any text or argument that would cause us to doubt whether God intends for tongues to be operative in the Christian world today. Simply put, there are no good or persuasive reasons anyone should relegate tongues to the first century of church history.

To this we add several other points. For example, as we carefully examined every text in which tongues-speech is mentioned, we discovered that it consistently served a positive and spiritually beneficial role in the life of God's people. Although the Corinthians had obviously elevated tongues inordinately and had likely pointed to it as a sign of heightened spirituality, Paul's counsel is never to forbid the gift but instead to regulate it so others might be blessed. As long as tongues in the corporate assembly is followed by interpretation, it should never, ever be forbidden. Paul couldn't have been any clearer when he said, "Do not forbid speaking in tongues" (1 Cor. 14:39). Whatever abuses may have been present in Corinth, the apostle did not believe this was grounds for banning the gift or suppressing its exercise.

We also saw that tongues serves to edify and strengthen the one who makes use of it in his or her private devotional life. If no less than the apostle himself regularly prayed to God, praised God, and expressed his gratitude to God in uninterpreted tongues in the isolation of his own prayer closet, it stands to reason that we today should embrace this precious gift of the Spirit and make good use of it to the same end.

This line of reasoning applies equally to all other gifts of the Spirit. Some have tried to argue that since certain miraculous gifts functioned to authenticate the apostolic message, we should not expect them to be operative in today's church. But there is no reason whatsoever to think these gifts in the twenty-first-century church couldn't, wouldn't, or shouldn't function in the same way when we proclaim the gospel. To say this work of authentication or attestation is no longer needed since we now have the completed canon of inspired Scripture is an argument altogether absent from the New Testament. Nowhere in the Bible are we told that because we now have the Bible, we no longer need or might profit from what miraculous gifts of the Spirit can achieve. Nowhere.

We must also resist the tendency toward reductionism. What I mean by this is thinking that simply because spiritual gift A serves us well in one particular capacity, it cannot serve us well in yet another. I'm always happy to grant that miraculous gifts of the Spirit served to attest to the authenticity of the apostolic message. But why is that a reason such gifts can no longer function in a multitude of other capacities beyond the time of the first century and even into the twenty-first? In fact, Paul makes it quite clear that the primary task of all spiritual gifts, both the so-called more miraculous as well as the so-called more mundane gifts is to build up and strengthen the body of Christ. This is especially clear from 1 Corinthians 12:7–10, where we find what are typically called "miraculous" or "supernatural" gifts of the Spirit. There Paul explicitly declares that the Spirit gives these gifts "for the common good" (v. 7). Should it be proven (and it can't) that God designed supernatural gifts to authenticate the apostolic message only in the first century, we still have other purposes to which these gifts might be applied.

There is also the argument from the sufficiency of Scripture. Although most cessationists think this doctrine is a good reason to reject the validity of miraculous and revelatory gifts of the Spirit today, precisely the opposite is true. I believe it is the cessationist denial of the ongoing validity of miraculous gifts like tongues and prophecy that compromises the sufficiency of Scripture. Let me explain.

The sufficiency of Scripture can mean many things, but at the heart of the doctrine is our belief that the Bible contains every theological truth and every ethical norm that is required for living a Christ-exalting and God-glorifying life. What the Bible contains and teaches is "enough" to enable us to lead godly lives in this present age.

This then raises the question, "What precisely does the Bible say God has done or provided to enable us to be edified, built up, and thoroughly equipped for every good work?" Among the plethora of things is the blessing of the many spiritual gifts, those in 1 Corinthians 12:7–10 in particular. The all-sufficient Word of God explicitly commands us to earnestly desire "the higher gifts" (1 Cor. 12:31), which Paul goes on to identify primarily as prophecy. He again commands us to "earnestly desire the spiritual gifts, especially that you may prophesy" (1 Cor. 14:1). Again, "Now I want you all to speak in tongues, but even more to prophesy" (1 Cor. 14:5). And if there is any doubt about Paul's meaning, he closes this chapter with the exhortation, "So, my brothers, earnestly desire to prophesy, and do not forbid speaking in tongues" (1 Cor. 14:39).

Note well: It is in the all-sufficient Scriptures that we find these exhortations. It is the Bible, which we believe tells us everything we need for Christian growth and godliness, in which we find these commands. Do we believe the Bible tells us what to embrace and what to avoid? Yes. Do we believe the Bible is altogether sufficient to give us every command we need to obey and every warning we need to heed? Yes. Do we believe the Bible warns us about those misguided beliefs and practices that may well threaten its own sufficiency? Yes.

Well, what then does the Bible say about both miraculous and more mundane gifts of the Spirit? It says we need them because they serve "the common good" (1 Cor. 12:7). It says prophecy is given to God's people "for their upbuilding and encouragement and consolation" (1 Cor. 14:3). It says that when we come into the corporate gathering of God's people, "each one has a hymn, a lesson [or teaching], a revelation, a tongue, or an interpretation," and that all things should "be done for building up" (1 Cor. 14:26). And yet nowhere does it ever remotely suggest, much less explicitly assert, that the ongoing validity of the very gifts it endorses is a dangerous threat to the reality of Scripture's own sufficiency.

So let me address myself to my cessationist friends who have had the courage to read through this book all the way to the end. Where do you think we continuationists derive our belief in the ongoing validity of miraculous gifts of the Spirit? We didn't concoct the idea on our own. We get our view from Scripture! It is the Scriptures, the all-sufficient Scriptures, that teach us to earnestly desire spiritual gifts, especially that we might prophesy (1 Cor. 14:1). It is the Scriptures, the all-sufficient Scriptures, that teach us such gifts are not merely given to authenticate the apostolic message but also to build up God's people (1 Cor. 12:7 and all of 1 Cor. 14). It is the Scriptures, the all-sufficient Scriptures, that tell us to "earnestly desire to prophesy, and" not to "forbid speaking in tongues" (1 Cor. 14:39). It is the Scriptures, the all-sufficient Scriptures, that tell us that in the new covenant age inaugurated at Pentecost,

God's people, young and old, male and female, will experience reve-latory dreams and visions and will prophesy (Acts 2). And it is the Scriptures, the all-sufficient Scriptures, that nowhere tell us these gifts will only last for about fifty or sixty years and then disappear.

My point here is that to believe in the sufficiency of Scripture means we believe what it says and obey its commands. But the ces-sationist would appear to appeal to the notion of the Bible's suf-ficiency in order to deny the Bible's functional authority. That is the irony. They say they believe the Bible is inerrant and sufficient to tell us all we need to know to live godly lives, but then they deny the Bible's teaching concerning the operation of spiritual gifts to build up and edify God's people. If they truly believe in the Bible's sufficiency, then tell me where in the Bible it teaches that the miraculous gifts of the Spirit were designed only for the few decades of the first century.

I have heard more than a few cessationists say something to the effect that God gave the church gifts such as tongues and prophecy until the apostolic message reached its final maturity and so ceased. With the completion of the message the need for such gifts was also complete. May I ask: *Where in the New Testament does any author ever say that?* What text or texts might you cite to support that assertion?

If, as cessationists undoubtedly believe, the Bible is sufficient for all instruction and sufficient to provide inerrant guidance for what-ever we might need to grow in godliness, why does the all-sufficient Bible not say what they continually assert? Wouldn't it have been prudent for the apostles to have told us that God intended their teaching on miraculous spiritual gifts to operate only for a mere fifty or sixty years of church life?

What continues to baffle me is that cessationists who affirm the sufficiency of the Bible cannot admit this very Bible fails to pro-vide us with a single text in which we are told that the many gifts it encourages us to pursue and practice were temporary or were characterized by some inherent obsolescence. I must repeat myself here: if the Bible is sufficient to give us all we need to live godly lives, and I certainly believe it is, then why does it not give us a single, solitary text in which it tells us to ignore the exhortations to earnestly desire spiritual gifts, especially prophecy, or a single, solitary text in which it tells us that we should in fact forbid speaking in tongues, or a single, solitary text that tells us the gifts given to edify and encourage the people of God were not meant for any generation of Christians beyond those of the first century? Why does the written Word only tell us to make good use of such gifts for the edification of the body and not tell us that such was meant only for the early church? I simply don't know how my cessationist friends can affirm biblical sufficiency when they disregard without textual support the many examples and exhortations concerning the use of these gifts. So, in summary, I contend that if you believe in the sufficiency and the functional authority of Scripture, you *must necessarily* believe in the ongoing validity and edifying power of miraculous gifts of the Spirit.

I have another question closely related to the previous one. I'm going to assume we all believe the New Testament was given to provide us with instruction and guidelines designed to shape and govern the life of the local church in the age of the new covenant. If that is the case, what are we to do with the consistently positive portrayal of gifts of the Spirit that we see in the inspired Word of God? In other words, when we look to the many New Testament Epistles and their description of life as believers in the local church, what do we find? We read about spiritual gifts operating in Thessalonica (1 Thess. 5:19–22), in Antioch (Acts 13:1–2), in Caesarea (Acts 10:44–48; 21:8–9), in Rome (Rom. 12:3–8), in Samaria (Acts 8:4–8), in Ephesus (Acts 19:1–7; 1 Tim. 1:18; 4:14), in Galatia (Gal. 3:1–5), and of course in Corinth (1 Cor. 12–14). Given this consistently positive portrayal of how the gifts should operate, someone must mount up an overwhelming case for why we should not pray for, pursue, and practice such gifts in the church today.[2]

In my interaction with my cessationist friends (and yes, they *are* friends) I often hear it said that the miraculous gifts of the Spirit were somehow uniquely tied or tethered to the original apostles. In the absence of those men we should not expect the gifts to be found. But again, when I read the New Testament, I discover numerous non-apostolic Christians—ordinary believing folk like you and me—exercising with great success and spiritual benefit to others the many gifts we are supposed to believe no longer exist in the church.

As I wrote in my book *Practicing the Power*,[3] others aside from the apostles who exercised miraculous gifts include the 70 who were commissioned in Luke 10:9, 19–20; at least 108 people among the 120 who were gathered in the Upper Room on the day of Pentecost (Acts 1:15; 2); Stephen (Acts 6–7); Phillip (Acts 8); Ananias (Acts 9); church members in Antioch (Acts 13:1); new converts in Ephesus (Acts 19:6); women at Caesarea (Acts 21:8–9); the unnamed brethren of Galatians 3:5; believers in Rome (Rom. 12:6–8); believers in Corinth (1 Cor. 12–14); and Christians in Thessalonica (1 Thess. 5:19–20).

Another argument by some cessationists is that the experience of the early church as recorded in Acts must be viewed as a distinct and unique period that cannot be reproduced or copied today. After all, the early church had the presence of the apostles, and we obviously don't. But I would argue instead for the fundamental continuity or spiritually organic relationship between the church in Acts and the church in subsequent centuries. As I wrote in *Practicing the Power*:

> No one denies that there was an era or period in the early church that we might call "apostolic." We must acknowl-edge the significance of the personal physical presence of the apostles and their unique role in laying the foundation

for the early church. But nowhere does the NT ever suggest that certain spiritual gifts were uniquely and exclusively tied to them or that with their passing the gifts passed as well. The universal church or body of Christ that was established and gifted through the ministry of the apostles is the same universal church and body of Christ that exists today (something that only the most extreme of hyper-Dispensationalists would deny). We are together with Paul and Peter and Silas and Lydia and Priscilla and Luke members of the same body of Christ.[4]

TEXTS THAT PROVE THE GIFTS ARE STILL FOR THE CHURCH

Cessationists often ask me to provide them with a text in which the gifts are explicitly said to be for the church until the second coming of Christ. I'm happy to comply with this request.

Ephesians 4:11–13
The first one that comes to mind is in the Book of Ephesians. Here is what Paul said:

> And he gave the apostles, the prophets, the evangelists, the shepherds and teachers, to equip the saints for the work of ministry, for building up the body of Christ, until we all attain to the unity of the faith and of the knowledge of the Son of God, to mature manhood, to the measure of the stature of the fullness of Christ.
> —EPHESIANS 4:11–13

I'm not sure how Paul could have been any more explicit concerning the duration of these gifts. He speaks of the operation of spiritual gifts (together with the office of apostle), and in particular the gifts of the prophet, evangelist, pastor, and teacher, as functioning in the building up of the church "until we all attain to the unity of the faith and of the knowledge of the Son of God, to

197

mature manhood, to the measure of the stature of the fullness of Christ" (v. 13). That word *until* is crucial. Until *what* time or when will we no longer need the operation of these gifts? Not "until" the body of Christ attains to mature manhood and measures up to the stature of the fullness of Christ. Since the church most assuredly has not yet attained the latter, and won't until Jesus comes back, we can confidently anticipate the presence and power of such gifts until that day arrives.

1 Corinthians 13:8–12

I have already addressed on several occasions in this book the arguments for the cessation of tongues and found them wanting. We have seen repeatedly that tongues is a gift of God imparted by the Holy Spirit "for the common good" (1 Cor. 12:7). When used in the corporate assembly of God's people, accompanied by interpretation, tongues builds up other believers. When used in private devotion, it also serves to edify the speaker (1 Cor. 14:4). Tongues is simply one form of prayer (1 Cor. 14:2, 14) as well as a way in which the believer can sing praise to God (1 Cor. 14:15) and give expression to heartfelt gratitude for all that God has done (1 Cor. 14:16–17). These activities are not uniquely tied to the first century of Christian history. They are appropriate at any and all times in the life of a believer.

Furthermore, we've seen that tongues did not serve as an evangelistic tool, nor was it especially intended by God to be a sign of judgment against unbelieving Jews. And the primary argument of the cessationist, namely that all tongues-speech was in a human language not previously studied or learned by the speaker, simply doesn't hold up under a close consideration of how tongues is described in 1 Corinthians 12–14.

It seems reasonable to conclude, therefore, that whatever argument can be made for the continuation of all other spiritual gifts applies with equal force to the gift of tongues. There is one passage of Scripture in particular that seems to identify the duration of tongues with unmistakable clarity. The ironic thing about this text is that cessationists have often used it to argue for precisely the opposite! I'm talking about 1 Corinthians 13:8–12.

As stated, one of the great ironies in the ongoing dialogue between continuationists such as myself and cessationists is that the biblical passage most often cited in defense of the idea that miraculous gifts of the Spirit have ceased turns out on closer inspection to be one of the more explicit affirmations that such gifts continue until the time of Christ's second coming. Here is the text in question:

> Love never ends. As for prophecies, they will pass away; as for tongues, they will cease; as for knowledge, it will pass away. For we know in part and we prophesy in part, but when the perfect comes, the partial will pass away. When I was a child, I spoke like a child, I thought like a child, I reasoned like a child. When I became a man, I gave up childish ways. For now we see in a mirror dimly, but then face to face. Now I know in part; then I shall know fully, even as I have been fully known.
>
> —1 CORINTHIANS 13:8–12

People who embrace cessationism point out that whereas Paul says in verses 8 and 10 that "when the perfect comes," prophecy and knowledge will "pass away" or "be done away with"; tongues, on the other hand, simply "cease." They take this to mean the spiritual gift of speaking in tongues simply dies out of its own accord. There is something intrinsic to the character of tongues-speech, so they say, that alone accounts for why it will cease. No one has to take any action against tongues to cause them to cease. They just stop. This is often based on the fact that the verb *cease* is in the middle voice. But as theologian D. A. Carson points out, the verb *pauō* regularly appears in the middle voice and "never unambiguously bears the meaning 'to cease of itself' (i.e., because of something intrinsic in the nature of the subject)."[5] Simply put, most New Testament scholars are in agreement that no theological conclusions can be drawn about the duration or cessation of any of these gifts based on the verbs that are used.[6]

Neither is it popular even among cessationists to argue that the "perfect" is anything less than the state of spiritual consummation that is introduced at the time of the second coming of Christ. One of the more articulate cessationists in our day is New Testament professor and scholar Richard Gaffin. He is certainly correct when he says:

> To argue, as some cessationists do, that "the perfect" has
> in view the completion of the New Testament canon
> or some other state of affairs prior to the Parousia [the
> second coming of Christ] is just not credible exegetically.[7]

Gaffin rightly links up the "perfect" of 1 Corinthians 13:10 with the "unity" or "fullness" of Ephesians 4:13 and concludes that Paul has in view "the situation brought by Christ's return."[8]

What is of greatest importance is that Paul clearly declares that spiritual gifts such as prophecy and word of knowledge will pass away when the perfect comes. I would also include tongues in this; in fact, I would include all spiritual gifts. Spiritual gifts are wonderful, and we need them. But even when they operate at the highest and most effective level, they can only bring us knowledge that is partial. As Paul says, "We know in part and we prophesy in part" (1 Cor. 13:9). Spiritual gifts, for all their value and power, cannot bring us into the experience of knowing God as God knows us. For that we must await the arrival of the "perfect" (1 Cor. 13:10).

So what is the "perfect"? Cessationists typically embrace one of two interpretations, both of which are clearly wrong.

Some argue that the "perfect" refers to *the completed canon of Scripture*. Tongues, prophecy, and knowledge, among other miraculous gifts, ceased when the Book of Revelation was written. Few serious New Testament scholars hold this view today. Its weaknesses are obvious.

First, there is no evidence that even Paul anticipated the formation of a canon of Scripture following the death of the apostles. In fact, Paul seems to have expected that he himself might survive until the coming of the Lord (1 Thess. 4:15–16; 1 Cor. 15:51). Second, there is no reason to think Paul could have expected the Corinthians to figure out that he meant the canon when he used the term *to teleion*.[9] Third, as Max Turner points out, "The completed canon of Scripture would hardly signify for the Corinthians the *passing away of merely 'partial' knowledge* (and prophecy and tongues with it), and the arrival of 'full knowledge', for the Corinthians already had the Old Testament, the gospel tradition (presumably), and (almost certainly) more Pauline teaching than finally got into the canon."[10]

A fourth reason the cessationist argument fails is that in 1 Corinthians 13:12 Paul says in effect that with the coming of the perfect, our partial knowledge will give way to a depth of knowledge that is only matched by the way we are known by God. That is to say, when the perfect comes, we will *then* see "face to face" and will know even as we are now known by God. Few people any longer dispute that this is language descriptive of our experience in the eternal state, subsequent to the return of Christ. As Turner says, "However much we respect the New Testament canon, Paul can only be accused of the wildest exaggeration in verse 12 if that is what he was talking about."[11]

Fifth, the cessationist view rests on the assumption that prophecy was a form of divine revelation designed to serve the church in the interim, until such time as the canon was formed. But a careful examination of the New Testament reveals that prophecy had a much broader purpose that would not in the least be affected by the completion of the canon.

Others argue that the "perfect" refers to *the maturity of the church.* When the church has advanced beyond its infancy and is fully established, the need for spiritual gifts like prophecy and tongues will have ended. But in 1 Corinthians 13:11–12 Paul isn't talking about relative degrees of maturity but of absolute perfection.

Thus, it seems clear to me that by "perfect" Paul is referring to that *state of affairs brought about by the second coming of Jesus Christ at the end of human history.* The "perfect" is not itself the coming of Christ but rather that experience or condition of perfection that we will enjoy in the new heavens and new earth. Paul's point, in my opinion, is really rather simple: spiritual gifts like prophecy, word of knowledge, tongues, and all the others will pass away at some time future to Paul's writing, referred to by him as perfection. This state of perfection again clearly points to the eternal state following Christ's return. We know this from two things that he says in 1 Corinthians 13:12.

First, Paul says, "Now I know in part; then [When? When the perfect comes.] I shall know fully, even as I have been fully known." Paul doesn't mean we will be omniscient in the eternal state, as if to say we will know absolutely everything in exhaustive detail. It does mean that we will be free from the misconceptions and distortions associated with this life in a fallen world. Our knowledge in the age to come will in some ways be comparable to the way God knows us now. God's knowledge of us is immediate and complete. Our knowledge of God will be the same when we enter His presence in the new heavens and new earth. Thus, Paul's distinctions "are between 'now' and 'then,' between what is incomplete (though perfectly appropriate to the church's present existence) and what is complete (when its final destiny in Christ has been reached and 'we see face to face' and 'know as we are fully known')."[12]

Second, in 1 Corinthians 13:12 Paul says, "For now [during

the present church age, before the arrival of the perfect] we see in a mirror dimly, but then [when the perfect comes, we will see] face to face." The term *face to face* is standard biblical language for the appearance of a human in the immediate presence of God, beholding Him in an unmediated way. (See Genesis 32:30; Exodus 33:11; Numbers 14:14; Deuteronomy 5:4; 34:10; Judges 6:22; and Revelation 22:4). Paul has in mind direct personal communication such that awaits us in the age to come. In this life we suffer from the limitation of seeing in a mirror dimly, whereas when the perfect comes, we will behold God directly without any intermediary or obscuring of His glory. Thus, to try to make the "perfect" refer to a time in the present age before the coming of Christ and the eternal state when all sin will be abolished is to trivialize and minimize the language of 1 Corinthians 13:12.

To use the language of 1 Corinthians 13:11, living now in the present church age is like being a child; we are limited, and our knowledge is imperfect. But when the perfect comes, we will have advanced into adulthood. Sin will be abolished; evil and corruption and the limitations of this life will have passed away. We will see God face to face, and we will then know even as we have been fully known. There is a massive qualitative and quantitative difference between what we know now by means of the gifts of the Spirit and what we will know in the consummation. In the consummation brought about by the return of Christ, and not until then, will spiritual gifts cease to operate. No one has explained this better than David Garland:

> The "perfect" is shorthand for the consummation of all things, the intended goal of creation; and its arrival will naturally displace the partial that we experience in the present age. Human gifts shine gloriously in this world but will fade to nothing in the presence of what is perfect. But they also will have served their purpose of helping to

build up the church during the wait and to take it to the threshold of the end. When the anticipated end arrives, they will no longer be necessary.[13]

To sum up, the point Paul is making is the difference between what is true and appropriate for us now in this present age and what will be our experience later in the age to come. Life in the present church age yields only knowledge that is partial. It is never altogether free from error. But life in the age to come, which is to say, life in the state of perfection, will be characterized by an un-mediated relationship to God that is devoid of error or mistake or misconception. The perfection or completeness that is to come is not an experience of ours in the present age but has to do with life, joy, and knowledge in the new heaven and new earth (Rev. 21–22). "At the coming of Christ the final purpose of God's saving work in Christ will have been reached; at that point those gifts now neces-sary for the building up of the church in the present age will dis-appear, because 'completeness' will have come."[14]

Chapter 13

TONGUES IN EARLY
CHRISTIANITY, PART II

Our final question concerns the presence (or absence) of tongues and other miraculous gifts of the Spirit during the course of the last two thousand years of church history:

30. Did tongues and other miraculous gifts of the Spirit disappear in church history following the death of the apostles only to reappear in the twentieth century?

After studying the documentation for claims to the presence of these gifts, D. A. Carson concludes that "there is enough evidence that some form of 'charismatic' gifts continued sporadically across the centuries of church history that it is futile to insist on doctrinaire grounds that every report is spurious or the fruit of demonic activity or psychological aberration."[1]

It may surprise some to discover that we have extensive knowledge of but a small fraction of what happened in the history of the church. It is terribly presumptuous to conclude that the gifts of the Spirit were absent from the lives of people about whom we know virtually nothing. In other words, as someone once said, the absence of evidence is not necessarily the evidence of absence!

We simply don't know what was happening in the thousands upon thousands of churches and home meetings of Christians in centuries past. I cannot say with confidence that believers regularly prayed for the sick and saw them healed any more than you can say they didn't. You cannot say they never prophesied to the comfort, exhortation, and consolation (1 Cor. 14:3) of the church any more than I can say they did. Neither of us can say with any confidence whether countless thousands of Christians throughout the inhabited earth prayed in tongues in their private devotions. That is hardly the sort of thing for which we could expect extensive documentation. We must remember that printing with movable type did not exist until the work of Johannes Gutenberg (c. AD 1390–1468). The absence of documented evidence for spiritual gifts in a time when documented evidence for most of church life was, at best, sparse is hardly good grounds for concluding that such gifts did not exist.

If the gifts were sporadic (and I'm not persuaded they were), there may be an explanation other than the theory that they were restricted to the first century. We must remember that before the Protestant Reformation in the sixteenth century the average Christian did not have access to the Bible in his own language. Biblical ignorance was rampant. That is hardly the sort of atmosphere in which people would be aware of spiritual gifts (their name, nature, function, and the believer's responsibility to pursue them) and thus hardly the sort of atmosphere in which we would expect Christians to seek and pray for such phenomena or to recognize them were they to be manifest. If the gifts were sparse, and this again is highly debatable, it was as likely due as much to ignorance and the spiritual lethargy it breeds as to any theological principle that limits the gifts to the lifetime of the apostles.

Especially important in this regard is the concentration of spiritual authority and ministry in the office of bishop and priest in the emerging Church of Rome. By the early fourth century (much earlier, according to some) there was already a move to limit to the ordained clergy opportunity to speak, serve, and minister in the life of the church. Lay folk were silenced and marginalized and left almost entirely dependent on the contribution of the local priest or monarchical bishop.

Although Cyprian (bishop of Carthage from AD 248 to 258) spoke and wrote often of the gift of prophecy and receiving visions from the Spirit,[2] he was also responsible for the gradual disappearance of such *charismata* from the life of the church. He, among others, insisted that only the bishop and priest of the church should be permitted to exercise these revelatory gifts. In the words of James Ash, "The charisma of prophecy was captured by the monarchical episcopate, used in its defense, and left to die an unnoticed death when true episcopal stability rendered it a superfluous tool."[3]

If we concede for the sake of argument that certain spiritual gifts were less prevalent than others in certain seasons of the church, their absence may well be due to unbelief, apostasy, and other sins that serve only to quench and grieve the Holy Spirit. If Israel experienced the loss of power because of repeated rebellion, if Jesus Himself "could do no mighty work there, except that he laid his hands on a few sick people and healed them," all because of their "unbelief" (Mark 6:5–6), we should hardly be surprised at the infrequency of the miraculous in periods of church history marked by theological ignorance and both personal and clerical immorality.

We must also remember that God mercifully blesses us both with what we don't deserve and what we refuse or are unable to recognize. I am persuaded that numerous churches today that advocate cessationism experience these gifts but dismiss them as something less than the miraculous manifestation of the Holy Spirit.

For example, someone with the gift of discerning spirits may be described as possessing remarkable sensitivity and insight. Someone with the gift of word of knowledge is rather said to have deep understanding of spiritual truths. Someone who prophesies is said to have spoken with timely encouragement to the needs of the congregation. Someone who lays hands on the sick and prays successfully for healing is told that God still answers prayer but that gifts of healing are no longer operative. These churches wouldn't be caught dead labeling such phenomena by the names given them in 1 Corinthians 12:7–10 because they are committed to the theory that such phenomena don't exist.

If this occurs today (and it does, as it did in a church in which I ministered for several years), there is every reason to think it has occurred repeatedly throughout the course of history subsequent to the first century.

Consider this hypothetical example. Let us suppose that a man had been assigned to write a descriptive history of church life in what is now southern France in, say, AD 845. How might he label what he saw and heard? If he were ignorant of spiritual gifts, being untaught, or perhaps a well-educated cessationist, his record would make no reference to prophecy, healing, tongues, miracles, word of knowledge, etc. Such phenomena might well exist, perhaps even flourish, but would be identified and explained in other terms by our hypothetical historian.

Centuries later we discover his manuscript. Would it be fair to conclude from his observations that certain spiritual gifts had ceased subsequent to the apostolic age? Of course not! My point in this is simply that in both the distant past and the present the Holy Spirit can empower God's people with gifts for ministry that they either do not recognize or, for whatever reason, explain in terms other than those of 1 Corinthians 12:7–10. The absence of explicit reference to certain *charismata* is therefore a weak basis on which to argue for their permanent withdrawal from church life.

The question we are considering is this: If the Holy Spirit wanted the church to experience the miraculous *charismata*, would they not have been more visible and prevalent in church history (and I'm only conceding for the sake of argument that they were not)? Let's take the principle underlying that argument and apply it to several other issues.

We all believe the Holy Spirit is the *teacher* of the church. We all believe the New Testament describes His ministry of *enlightening* our hearts and *illuminating* our minds to understand the truths of Scripture. (See, for instance, Ephesians 1:15–19; 1 John 2:20, 27; and 2 Timothy 2:7.) Yet within the first generation after the death of the apostles the doctrine of justification by faith was compromised. Salvation by faith plus works soon became standard doctrine and was not successfully challenged (with a few notable exceptions) until Martin Luther's courageous stand in the sixteenth century.

My question, then, is this: If God intended for the Holy Spirit to continue to teach and enlighten Christians concerning vital biblical truths beyond the death of the apostles, why did the church languish in ignorance of this most fundamental truth for more than 1,300 years? Why did Christians suffer from the absence of those experiential blessings this vital truth might otherwise have brought to their church life?

If God intended for the Holy Spirit to illumine the minds of His people concerning biblical truths after the death of the apostles, why did the church languish in ignorance of the doctrine of the priesthood of all believers for almost one thousand years? Those of you who believe in a pretribulational rapture of the church must also explain the absence of this "truth" from the collective knowledge of the church for almost 1,900 years!

Undoubtedly the response will be that none of this proves the

Holy Spirit ceased His ministry of teaching and illumination. None of this proves God ceased to want His people to understand such vital doctrinal principles. And the alleged relative infrequency or absence of certain spiritual gifts during the same period of church history does not prove that God was opposed to their use or had negated their validity for the remainder of the present age.

Both theological ignorance of certain biblical truths and a loss of experiential blessings provided by spiritual gifts can be, and should be, attributed to factors other than the suggestion that God intended such knowledge and power only for believers in the early church.

Finally, and most important of all, is the fact that what has or has not occurred in church history is ultimately irrelevant to what *we* should pursue, pray for, and expect in the life of our churches today. The final criterion for deciding whether God wants to bestow certain spiritual gifts on His people today is the Word of God. I'm disappointed to often hear people cite the alleged absence of a particular experience in the life of an admired saint from the church's past as reason for doubting its present validity. As much as I respect the giants of the Reformation and of other periods in church history, I intend to emulate the giants of the New Testament who wrote under the inspiration of the Holy Spirit. I admire John Calvin, but I obey the apostle Paul.

In sum, neither the failure nor success of Christians in days past is the ultimate standard by which we determine what God wants for us today. We can learn from their mistakes as well as their achievements. But the only question of ultimate relevance for us and for this issue is, "What saith the Scripture?"

MIRACULOUS SPIRITUAL GIFTS IN CHURCH HISTORY[4]

We are now ready for a brief survey of church history (from the apostolic fathers to Augustine). The representative examples cited will demonstrate that the miraculous gifts of the Spirit were, and are, still very much in operation. Indeed, before Chrysostom in the east (AD 347–407) and Augustine in the west (AD 354–430) no church father ever suggested that any or all of the charismata had ceased in the first century. And even Augustine later retracted his earlier cessationism (see below). So let's conduct a quick overview.[5]

The Epistle of Barnabas, written sometime between AD 70 and 132, says this of the Holy Spirit: "He personally prophesies in us and personally dwells in us."[6] The author of *The Shepherd of Hermas* claims to have received numerous revelatory insights through visions and dreams. This document has been dated as early as AD 90 and as late as AD 140–155. Justin Martyr (c. AD 100–165), perhaps the most important second-century apologist, is especially clear about the operation of gifts in his day:

> Therefore, just as God did not inflict His anger on account of those seven thousand men, even so He has now neither yet inflicted judgment, nor does inflict it, knowing that daily some [of you] are becoming disciples in the name of Christ, and quitting the path of error; who are also receiving gifts, each as he is worthy, illumined through the name of this Christ. For one receives the spirit of understanding, another of counsel, another of strength, another of healing, another of foreknowledge, another of teaching, and another of the fear of God.[7]
>
> For the prophetical gifts remain with us, even to the present time. And hence you ought to understand that [the gifts] formerly among your nation have been transferred to us. And just as there were false prophets contemporaneous with your holy prophets, so are there now

many false teachers amongst us, of whom our Lord fore-warned us to beware; so that in no respect are we deficient, since we know that He foreknew all that would happen to us after His resurrection from the dead and ascension to heaven.[8]

For numberless demoniacs throughout the whole world, and in your city, many of our Christian men exor-cising them in the name of Jesus Christ, who was crucified under Pontius Pilate, have healed and do heal, rendering helpless and driving the possessing devils out of the men, though they could not be cured by all the other exorcists, and those used incantations and drugs.[9]

Irenaeus (c. AD 120/140–200/203), certainly the most impor-tant and influential theologian of the late second century, writes:

Wherefore, also, those who are in truth His disciples, receiving grace from Him, do in His name perform [mira-cles], so as to promote the welfare of other men, according to the gift which each one has received from Him. For some do certainly and truly drive out devils, so that those who have thus been cleansed from evil spirits fre-quently both believe [in Christ], and join themselves to the Church. Others have foreknowledge of things to come: they see visions, and utter prophetic expressions. Others still, heal the sick by laying their hands upon them, and they are made whole. Yea, moreover, as I have said, the dead even have been raised up, and remained among us for many years. And what shall I more say? It is not pos-sible to name the number of the gifts which the Church, [scattered] throughout the whole world, has received from God, in the name of Jesus Christ, who was crucified under Pontius Pilate, and which she exerts day by day for the benefit of the Gentiles, neither practising deception upon any, nor taking any reward from them [on account of such miraculous interpositions]. For as she has received freely from God, freely also does she minister [to others].[10]

Nor does she [the church] perform anything by means of angelic invocations, or by incantations, or by any other wicked curious art; but, directing her prayers to the Lord, who made all things, in a pure, sincere, and straight-forward spirit, and calling upon the name of our Lord Jesus Christ, she has been accustomed to work miracles for the advantage of mankind, and not to lead them into error.[11]

In like manner we do also hear many brethren in the church, who possess prophetic gifts, and who through the Spirit speak all kinds of languages [i.e., tongues], and bring to light for the general benefit the hidden things of men, and declare the mysteries of God, whom also the apostle terms "spiritual," they being spiritual because they partake of the Spirit.[12]

Tertullian (d. 225; he first coined the term *Trinity*) spoke and wrote on countless occasions of the operation of the gifts of the Spirit, particularly those of a revelatory nature such as prophecy and word of knowledge.

But from God—who has promised, indeed, "to pour out the grace of the Holy Spirit upon all flesh, and has ordained that His servants and His handmaids should see visions as well as utter prophecies"—must all those visions be regarded as emanating.[13]

He described the ministry of one particular lady as follows:

For, seeing that we acknowledge spiritual charismata, or gifts, we too have merited the attainment of the prophetic

THE LANGUAGE OF HEAVEN

gift, although coming after John (the Baptist). We have now amongst us a sister whose lot it has been to be favoured with sundry gifts of revelation, which she experiences in the Spirit by ecstatic vision amidst the sacred rites of the Lord's day in the church: she converses with angels, and sometimes even with the Lord; she both sees and hears mysterious communications; some men's hearts she understands, and to them who are in need she distributes remedies....After the people are dismissed at the conclusion of the sacred services, she is in the regular habit of reporting to us whatever things she may have seen in vision (for all her communications are examined with the most scrupulous care, in order that their truth may be probed)....Now, can you refuse to believe this, even if indubitable evidence on every point is forthcoming for your conviction?[14]

Tertullian contrasts what he has witnessed with the claims of the heretic Marcion:

Let Marcion then exhibit, as gifts of his god, some prophets, such as have not spoken by human sense, but with the Spirit of God, such as have both predicted things to come, and have made manifest the secrets of the heart....Now all these signs (of spiritual gifts) are forthcoming from my side without any difficulty, and they agree, too, with the rules, and the dispensations, and the instructions of the Creator.[15]

We also have extensive evidence of revelatory visions in operation in the life of the martyrs Perpetua, who died in AD 202, and her handmaiden Felicitas. I encourage everyone to read Perpetua's moving testimony of perseverance in faith despite the most horrific of deaths.[16]

It's also important that we briefly take note of the movement known as Montanism (of which Tertullian was a part in his later years). Montanism, named after its founder Montanus, arose in Phrygia in about AD 155, although early Christian historians Eusebius and Jerome both date the movement to AD 173. What did the Montanists believe and teach that had such a significant impact on the ancient church and its view of spiritual gifts?[17] Several items are worthy of mention.

First, at its heart Montanism was an effort to shape the entire life of the church in keeping with the expectation of the immediate return of Christ. Thus they opposed any developments in church life that appeared institutional or would contribute to a settled pattern of worship. Needless to say, those who held official positions of authority within the *organized* church would be suspicious of the movement.

Second, Montanus himself allegedly spoke in terms that asserted his identity with the Paraclete of John 14:16. The prophetic utterance in question is as follows:

> For Montanus spoke, saying, "I am the father, and the son and the paraclete."[18]

However, many have questioned whether Montanus is claiming what his critics suggest. More likely he, as well as others in the movement who prophesied, is saying that one or another or perhaps all of the members of the Trinity are speaking through them. For example, in yet another of his prophetic utterances, Montanus said:

> You shall not hear from me, but you have heard from Christ.[19]

Third, Montanus and his followers (principally, two women named Priscilla and Maximilla) held to a view of the prophetic

gift that was a departure from the apostle Paul's teaching in
1 Corinthians 14, insofar as they practiced what can only be called
"ecstatic" prophecy in which the speaker either lost consciousness or
fell into a trancelike state, or perhaps was but a passive instrument
through which the Spirit might speak. One of the prophetic utterances that survived (there are only sixteen) found in the writings of
Epiphanius, a bishop of Cyprus at the close of the fourth century,
confirms this view:

> Behold, a man is like a lyre and I pluck his strings like
> a pick; the man sleeps, but I am awake. Behold, it is the
> Lord, who is changing the hearts of men and giving new
> hearts to them.[20]

If this is what Montanus taught, he would be asserting that
when a person prophesied, God was in complete control. The individual is little more than an instrument, such as the strings of a lyre,
on which God plucks His song or message. The man or woman is
asleep, in a manner of speaking, and thus *passive* during the prophetic utterance.

This concept of prophecy is contrary to what we read in
1 Corinthians 14:29–32, where Paul asserts that "the spirits of
prophets are subject to prophets." The Montanists cannot be
charged with having originated this view, for it is found among
the Greek apologists of this period. Justin Martyr and Theophilus
both claimed the Spirit spoke through the Old Testament prophets
in such a way as to possess them. Ante-Nicene Christian apologist Athenagoras says Moses, Isaiah, Jeremiah, and other Old
Testament prophets were

> lifted in ecstasy above the natural operations of their
> minds by the impulses of the Divine Spirit, [and that
> they] uttered the things with which they were inspired,

the Spirit making use of them as a flute-player breathes into a flute.[21]

The point is that at least on this one point the Montanists were not espousing a view of prophecy that was significantly different from what others in the mainstream of the church of that day were saying.

Fourth, the gift of tongues was also prominent among the Montanists, as was the experience of receiving revelatory visions. Eusebius preserved a refutation of Montanism written by Apollinarius in which the latter accused these "prophets" of speaking in unusual ways. For example, "He [Montanus] began to be ecstatic and to speak and to talk strangely."[22] Again, Maximilla and Priscilla are said to have spoken "madly and improperly and strangely, like Montanus."[23] Finally, he refers to the Montanists as "chattering prophets."[24] We cannot be certain, but the word translated "chattering," found nowhere else in all of Greek literature, may refer to speaking at great length in what sound like languages, i.e., speaking in tongues.

Fifth, Montanus did assert that this outpouring of the Spirit, of which he and his followers were the principal recipients, was a sign of the end of the age. The heavenly Jerusalem, said Montanus, will soon descend near Pepuza in Phrygia.[25] The Montanists also stressed monogamy and insisted on chastity between husband and wife. They were quite ascetic in their approach to the Christian life (which is what attracted Tertullian into their ranks). They strongly emphasized self-discipline and repentance.

Finally, although Montanism was often treated as heresy, numerous authors in the early church insisted on the overall orthodoxy of the movement. Hippolytus spoke of their affirmation of the doctrines of Christ and creation,[26] and the "heresy hunter" Epiphanius (c. AD 315–403), bishop of Salamis, conceded that the

Montanists agreed with the church at large on the issues of orthodoxy, especially the doctrine of the Trinity.[27]

Epiphanius wrote that the Montanists were still found in Cappadocia, Galatia, Phrygia, Cilicia, and Constantinople in the late fourth century.[28] This assessment was confirmed by Eusebius, who devoted four chapters of his monumental *Ecclesiastical History* to the Montanists. Didymus the Blind (AD 313–98) wrote of them, and the great church father Jerome (AD 342–419/420) personally encountered Montanist communities in Ancyra when he was travelling through Galatia in AD 373.[29] The point being that Montanism was alive and influential as late as the close of the fourth century.

Ironically, and tragically, one of the principal reasons the church became suspect of the gifts of the Spirit and eventually excluded them from the life of the church is because of their association with Montanism. The Montanist view of prophecy, in which the prophet entered a state of passive ecstasy in order that God might speak directly, was perceived as a threat to the church's belief in the finality of the canon of Scripture. Other unappealing aspects of the Montanist lifestyle, as noted above, provoked opposition to the movement and hence to the *charismata* as well. In sum, it was largely the Montanist view of the prophetic gift, in which a virtual "Thus saith the Lord" perspective was adopted, that contributed to the increasing absence in church life of the *charismata*.

We now return to other important figures in the life of the early church. The work of Theodotus in the late second century is preserved for us in Clement of Alexandria's *Excerpta ex Theodoto*. In 24:1 we read: "The Valentinians say that the excellent Spirit which each of the prophets had for his ministry was poured out upon all those of the church. Therefore the signs of the Spirit, healings and prophecies, are being performed by the church."[30]

Clement of Alexandria (born c. AD 150 and died between AD 211 and 215) spoke explicitly of the operation in his day of the spiritual gifts Paul listed in 1 Corinthians 12:7–10.[31] Early Christian theologian Origen (c. AD 185–254) acknowledged that the operation of the gifts in his day was not as extensive as was true in the New Testament, but they were still present and powerful: "And there are still preserved among Christians traces of that Holy Spirit which appeared in the form of a dove. They expel evil spirits, and perform many cures, and foresee certain events, according to the will of the Logos."[32]

The pagan Celsus sought to discredit the gifts of the Spirit exercised in churches in Origen's day, yet the latter pointed to the "demonstration" of the validity of the gospel, "more divine than any established by Grecian dialectics," namely that which is called by the apostle the "manifestations of the Spirit and of power."[33] Not only were signs and wonders performed in the days of Jesus, but "traces of them are still preserved among those who regulate their lives by the precepts of the gospel."[34] Many believe Celsus is referring to prophecy and tongues in the Christian community when he derisively describes certain believers "who pretend to be moved as if giving some oracular utterance" and who add to these oracles "incomprehensible, incoherent, and utterly obscure utterances the meaning of which no intelligible person could discover."[35] This, of course, is precisely what one would expect a pagan skeptic to say about prophecy and tongues.

Hippolytus (c. AD 170–c. 235) sets forth guidelines for the exercise of healing gifts, insisting that "if anyone says, 'I have received the gift of healing,' hands shall not be laid upon him: the deed shall make manifest if he speaks the truth."[36]

Early Christian theologian Novatian writes in *Treatise Concerning the Trinity*:

> Indeed this is he who appoints prophets in the church, instructs teachers, directs tongues, brings into being powers and conditions of health, carries on extraordinary

works, furnishes discernment of spirits, incorporates administrations in the church, establishes plans, brings together and arranges all other gifts there are of the charismata and by reason of this makes the Church of God everywhere perfect in everything and complete.[37]

I earlier mentioned Cyprian, bishop of Carthage, who spoke and wrote often of the gift of prophecy and the receiving of visions from the Spirit.[38] Many report that third-century bishop Gregory Thaumaturgus (AD 213–270) ministered in the power of numerous miraculous gifts and performed signs and wonders. Eusebius of Caesarea (AD 260–339), theologian and church historian in the court of Constantine, opposed the Montanists' abuse of the gift of prophecy but not its reality. He affirmed repeatedly the legitimacy of spiritual gifts but resisted the Montanists who operated outside the mainstream church and thus contributed, said Eusebius, to its disunity.

Cyril of Jerusalem (died c. AD 386) wrote often of the gifts in his day: "For He [the Holy Spirit] employs the tongue of one man for wisdom; the soul of another He enlightens by Prophecy; to another He gives power to drive away devils; to another He gives to interpret the divine Scriptures."[39]

Although Athanasius nowhere explicitly addressed the issue of Charismatic gifts, many believe he is the anonymous author of *Vita S. Antoni*, or "The Life of St. Anthony." Anthony was a monk who embraced an ascetic lifestyle in AD 285 and remained in the desert for some twenty years. The author of *Vita S. Antoni* describes numerous supernatural healings, visions, prophetic utterances, and other signs and wonders. Even if one rejects Athanasius as its author, the document does portray an approach to the Charismatic gifts that many, evidently, embraced in the church of the late third and early fourth centuries. Another famous and influential monk,

Pachomius (c. AD 292–346), was known to perform miracles and empowered to converse "in languages he did not know."[40]

The influential and highly regarded Cappadocian Fathers (who led in the mid to late fourth century) must also be considered. Basil of Caesarea (born AD 329 or 330) spoke often of the operation in his day of prophecy and healing. He appeals to Paul's description in 1 Corinthians 12 of "word of wisdom" and "gifts of healing" as representative of those gifts that are necessary for the common good of the church.[41]

> Is it not plain and incontestable that the ordering of the Church is effected through the Spirit? For He gave, it is said, "in the church, first Apostles, secondarily prophets, thirdly teachers, after that miracles, then gifts of healing, helps, governments, diversities of tongues," for this order is ordained in accordance with the division of the gifts that are of the Spirit.[42]

Spiritual leaders in the church, such as bishops or presbyters, says Basil, possess the gift of discernment of spirits, healing, and foreseeing the future (one expression of prophecy).[43]

Basil's younger brother Gregory of Nyssa (born c. AD 336) speaks on Paul's words in 1 Corinthians 13:

> Even if someone receives the other gifts which the Spirit furnishes (I mean the tongues of angels and prophecy and knowledge and the grace of healing), but has never been entirely cleansed of the troubling passions within him through the charity of the Spirit,...he is still in danger of failing.[44]

The final Cappadocian, Gregory of Nazianzen (born AD 330), provides extensive descriptions of the physical healing that both his father and mother experienced as well as several visions that accompanied them.[45]

Hilary of Poitiers speaks of "the gift of healings" and "the working of miracles" that "what we do may be understood to be the power of God" as well as "prophecy" and the "discerning of spirits." He also refers to the importance of "speaking in tongues" as a "sign of the gift of the Holy Spirit" together with "the interpretation of tongues," so "that the faith of those that hear may not be imperiled through ignorance, since the interpreter of a tongue explains the tongue to those who are ignorant of it."[46]

By the late fourth century the gifts of the Spirit were increasingly found among ascetics and those involved in the monastic movements. The various compromises and accommodations to the wider culture that infiltrated the church subsequent to the formal legalization of Christianity under Constantine drove many of the more spiritually minded leaders into the desert.

Something must be said about Augustine (AD 354–430), who early in his ministry espoused cessationism, especially with regard to the gift of tongues.[47] However, in his later writings he retracted his denial of the ongoing reality of the miraculous and carefully documented no fewer than seventy instances of divine healing in his own diocese during a two-year span. (See his *City of God*, Book XXII, chapters 8–10.) After describing numerous miracles of healing and even resurrections from the dead, Augustine writes:

> What am I to do? I am so pressed by the promise of finishing this work, that I cannot record all the miracles I know; and doubtless several of our adherents, when they read what I have narrated, will regret that I have omitted so many which they, as well as I, certainly know. Even now I beg these persons to excuse me, and to consider how long it would take me to relate all those miracles, which the

necessity of finishing the work I have undertaken forces me to omit.[48]

Again, writing his *Retractions* around AD 426–27, near the close of life and ministry, he concedes that tongues and the more spectacular miracles such as people being healed "by the mere shadow of Christ's preachers as they pass by" have ceased. He then says, "But what I said should not be understood as though no miracles should be believed to be performed nowadays in Christ's name. For I myself, when I was writing this very book, knew a blind man who had been given his sight in the same city near the bodies of the martyrs of Milan. I knew of some other miracles as well; so many of them occur even in these times that we would be unable either to be aware of all of them or to number those of which we are aware."[49]

Augustine also made reference to a phenomenon in his day called *jubilation*. Some believe he is describing singing in tongues. He writes:

Words cannot express the things that are sung by the heart. Take the case of people singing while harvesting in the fields or in the vineyards or when any other strenuous work is in progress. Although they begin by giving expression to their happiness in sung words, yet shortly there is a change. As if so happy that words can no longer express what they feel, they discard the restricting syllables. They burst into a simple sound of joy; of jubilation. Such a cry of joy is a sound signifying that the heart is bringing to birth what it cannot utter in words. Now who is more worthy of such a cry of jubilation than God himself, whom all words fail to describe? If words will not serve, and yet you must not remain silent, what else can you do but cry out for joy? Your heart must rejoice beyond words, that your unbounded joy may be unrestrained by syllabic bonds.[50]

MIRACULOUS SPIRITUAL GIFTS IN THE MIDDLE AGES

Although there is less evidence as we enter the period of the Middle Ages (the reasons for which I've already noted), at no time did the gifts disappear altogether. Due to limitations of space I will only be able to list the names of those in whose ministries are numerous documented instances of the revelatory gifts of prophecy, healing, discerning of spirits, miracles, tongues, together with vivid accounts of dreams and visions.[51] They include the following:

> John of Egypt (d. 394); Leo the Great (400–461; he served as bishop of Rome from 440 until 461); Genevieve of Paris (422–500); Benedict of Nursia (480–547); Gregory the Great (540–604); Gregory of Tours (538–594); the Venerable Bede (673–735; his *Ecclesiastical History of the English People*, written in 731, contains numerous accounts of miraculous gifts in operation); Aidan, bishop of Lindisfarne (d. 651), and his successor, Cuthbert (d. 687), both of whom served as missionaries in Britain; Ansgar (801–865), one of the first missionaries to Scandinavia; Bernard of Clairvaux (1090–1153); Bernard's treatise on the *Life and Death of Saint Malachy the Irishman* (1094–1148); Richard of St. Victor (d. 1173); Dominic, founder of the Dominicans (1170–1221); Anthony of Padua (1195–1231); Bonaventure (1217–1274); Francis of Assisi (1182–1226; documented in Bonaventure's *The Life of St. Francis*); Thomas Aquinas (1225–1274); Peter Waldo, founder of the Waldenses (d. 1217); together with virtually all of the medieval mystics, among whom are several women: Hildegard of Bingen (1098–1179), Gertrude of Helfta (1256–1301), Birgit of Sweden (1302–1373), St. Clare of Montefalco (d. 1308), Catherine of Siena (1347–1380), Julian of Norwich (1342–1416), Margery Kempe (1373–c. 1440); and Teresa of Avila (1515–1582); as well

as Dominican preacher Vincent Ferrer (1350–1419); and
John of the Cross (1542–1591).[52]

If one should object that these are exclusively Roman Catholics,
we must not forget that during this period in history there was
hardly anyone else. Aside from a few splinter sects there was little
to no expression of Christianity outside the Church of Rome. (The
formal split with what became known as Eastern Orthodoxy did
not occur until AD 1054.)

Although beyond the Middle Ages and more in the era of the
Reformation we should also remember Ignatius of Loyola (1491–
1556), founder of the Jesuits and author of the *Spiritual Exercises*.
Spiritual gifts, especially tongues, are reported to have been
common among the Mennonites and the Moravians, the latter
especially under the leadership of Count von Zinzendorf (1700–
1760), as well as among the French Huguenots in the late seventeenth century and the Jansenists of the first half of the eighteenth
century. John Wesley (1703–1791) defended the ongoing operation
of tongues beyond the time of the apostles.[53] One could also cite
George Fox (1624–1691), who founded the Quaker church and was
known to believe in and practice the gift of tongues.[54]

MIRACULOUS SPIRITUAL GIFTS
IN THE SCOTTISH REFORMATION

Those who insist that revelatory spiritual gifts such as prophecy,
discerning of spirits, and word of knowledge ceased to function
beyond the first century also have a difficult time accounting
for the operation of these gifts in the lives of many who were
involved in the Scottish Reformation, as well as several who ministered in its aftermath. Jack Deere, in his book *Surprised by the
Voice of God*,[55] has provided extensive documentation of the gift
of prophecy at work in and through such Scottish reformers as
George Wishart (1513–1546, a mentor of John Knox), John Knox

himself (1514–1572), John Welsh (1570–1622), Robert Bruce (1554–1631), and Alexander Peden (1626–1686).[56]

I strongly encourage you to obtain Deere's book and read the account of their supernatural ministries, not only in prophecy but often in gifts of healings. Deere also draws our attention to one of the historians of the seventeenth century, Robert Fleming (1630–1694), as well as one of the major architects of the Westminster Confession of Faith, Samuel Rutherford (1600–1661), both of whom acknowledged the operation of the gifts in their day.[57]

THE CASE OF CHARLES SPURGEON

As noted earlier, I don't think it at all unlikely that numerous churches that advocated cessationism experienced these gifts but dismissed them as something less than the miraculous manifestation of the Holy Spirit. One illustration of this comes from the ministry of Charles Spurgeon (1834–1892), who tells of an incident in the middle of his sermon when he paused and pointed at a man whom he accused of taking an unjust profit on Sunday of all days! The culprit later described the event to a friend:

> Mr. Spurgeon looked at me as if he knew me, and in his sermon he pointed to me, and told the congregation that I was a shoemaker, and that I kept my shop open on Sundays; and I did, sir. I should not have minded that; but he also said that I took ninepence the Sunday before, and that there was fourpence profit out of it. I did take ninepence that day, and fourpence was just the profit; but how he should know that, I could not tell. Then it struck me that it was God who had spoken to my soul through him, so I shut up my shop the next Sunday. At first, I was afraid to go again to hear him, lest he should tell the people more about me; but afterwards I went, and the Lord met with me, and saved my soul.[58]

Spurgeon then adds this comment:

> I could tell as many as a dozen similar cases in which
> I pointed at somebody in the hall without having the
> slightest knowledge of the person, or any idea that what I
> said was right, except that I believed I was moved by the
> Spirit to say it; and so striking has been my description,
> that the persons have gone away, and said to their friends,
> "Come, see a man that told me all things that ever I did;
> beyond a doubt, he must have been sent of God to my soul,
> or else he could not have described me so exactly." And
> not only so, but I have known many instances in which
> the thoughts of men have been revealed from the pulpit. I
> have sometimes seen persons nudge their neighbours with
> their elbow, because they had got a smart hit, and they
> have been heard to say, when they were going out, "The
> preacher told us just what we said to one another when we
> went in at the door."[59]

On another occasion Spurgeon broke off his sermon and
pointed at a young man, declaring: "Young man, those gloves you
are wearing have not been paid for: you have stolen them from
your employer."[60] After the service the man brought the gloves
to Spurgeon and asked that he not tell his mother, who would be
heartbroken to discover that her son was a thief!

My opinion is that this is a not uncommon example of what the
apostle Paul described in 1 Corinthians 14:24–25. Spurgeon exercised the gift of *prophecy* (or some might say the *word of knowledge*,
1 Cor. 12:8). He did not label it as such, but that does not alter
the reality of what the Holy Spirit accomplished through him. If
one were to examine Spurgeon's theology and ministry, as well as
recorded accounts of it by his contemporaries and subsequent biog-
raphers, most would conclude from the absence of explicit reference to miraculous charismata such as prophecy and the word of

knowledge that such gifts had been withdrawn from church life. But Spurgeon's own testimony inadvertently says otherwise!

Finally, of course, one would have to point to the last 115 or more years of contemporary church history and the emergence of the Pentecostal/Charismatic/Third Wave movements, together with the more than 650 million adherents worldwide, many of whom personally testify to having experienced or witnessed in others the miraculous charismata.

I can only hope and pray that many will now see that it is both unwarranted and unwise to argue for cessationism based on the testimony of God's people in the last two thousand years of church history.

Chapter 14

ENCOURAGING TESTIMONIES OF
OTHERS WHO SPEAK IN TONGUES

I CAN'T THINK OF a better way to conclude this book than by giving you a handful of fascinating and encouraging testimonies of how the gift of tongues has been a blessing to other Christians and how God has used this gift to make a powerful impact on the body of Christ. Although we should base our beliefs only on Scripture, these stories can serve to confirm what we've already determined on biblical grounds to be the truth concerning speaking in tongues.

JACKIE PULLINGER AND CHASING THE DRAGON[1]

I met Jackie Pullinger for the first time in January 1991. I was in Anaheim, California, at the invitation of my friend Jack Deere, attending a national Vineyard conference. The first night there Jack took me to dinner and said he had a few friends he'd like me to meet. One was Mike Bickle, with whom I would later serve for seven years in Kansas City on the staff of Metro Christian Fellowship. The other was Jackie Pullinger. Jack had not prepared me for what was to come. I don't think I've been the same since.

"So, Jackie, tell me about yourself," I said somewhat nonchalantly. For the next two hours I listened as she told me the story of her life and her ministry in the Walled City of Hong Kong. I distinctly remember calling my wife later that night and telling her, "Honey, I think I just met a Christian!" I know that sounds odd, but until I met Jackie, I don't believe I really knew what being a Christian was all about. I had never encountered such humility and power, such self-sacrifice and joy, such unbridled love for Jesus and for the lost and broken of the world. We returned to the Anaheim Convention Center in preparation to hear Jackie speak at the evening plenary session. As we prepared to walk in, we opened the door for Jackie only to discover that she had disappeared. We panicked. The three of us fanned out to find her. It didn't take long. There she was, kneeling over a homeless man who had been digging through the garbage in one of the huge dumpsters looking for food. Jackie was praying for him.

"Jackie, come on! They're waiting for you inside."

"Let them wait," she replied, somewhat dismissively. "It's only a conference."

As we finally rushed her in to get prepared to speak, I'll never forget what she said. "You're responsible for what you see. You can't change the world, Sam. You can't help everyone. But you are responsible for what you see. I saw him and did what I could." It was a lasting lesson I learned that night. We had the privilege in Kansas City of hosting Jackie on two more occasions. Only those who have heard her speak and watched her minister can understand the impact she has on spoiled, wealthy Western Christians. But I digress.

Now, let me back up and tell you how Jackie arrived at where she is today.

Jackie, born and raised in England (with an identical twin sister), was only five years old when she first sensed the call of God on her life. As she grew to adulthood, the message became even clearer: "Go."

"Where, Lord?"

"Go. Trust me, and I will lead you. I will instruct you and teach you in the way which you shall go. I will guide you with my eye."[2] Rebuffed and turned down by every missionary organization she contacted (no one wanted a twenty-year-old who had studied at the Royal College of Music in London and lacked proper "missiological" training), Jackie sought the advice of a pastor. His counsel was short and straight to the point: "Well, if you've tried all the conventional ways and missionary societies and God is still telling you to go, you had better get on the move.... If I were you I would go out and buy a ticket for a boat going on the longest journey you can find and pray to know where to get off."[3]

She did. Jackie Pullinger quite literally took the proverbial "slow boat to China" and has been ministering in Hong Kong for more than fifty years. The infamous Walled City, where Jackie set up shop, sat on only six-and-one-half acres of land but was home for upwards of 50,000 people! It was quite literally a world unto itself, with neither China nor Britain exercising proper jurisdiction. It was a haven for thieves, murderers, extortionists, drug lords, pornographers, illegal immigrants and refugees, the homeless, runaways, pimps, and prostitutes (many of whom were twelve- and thirteen-year-old girls sold into the trade by neighbors, boyfriends, and even parents). Pornographic theaters as well as opium and heroin dens lined the narrow walkways and alleys. The city was ruled by the Triads, Chinese secret societies that had degenerated into ruthless criminal gangs.

The filth was beyond belief. Open sewers, human refuse flowing freely in the streets, rats that no longer reacted to the shrill screams of frightened visitors. Bodies of addicts who overdosed the night before were piled outside the city.

Into this nightmare walked a twenty-year-old girl from England who had no money, no job, and couldn't speak a word of Mandarin.[4] But she managed to learn enough to tell the heroin addicts about Jesus. Much to her disappointment, she saw very little fruit in the first two years of her ministry. Things began to change when she met a young Chinese couple who bluntly told her: "You haven't got the Holy Spirit." Jackie was offended. "Of course I have the Spirit," she thought to herself. "I couldn't believe in Jesus if I didn't."[5]

Jackie soon discovered they were talking about the gift of tongues. The couple laid their hands on her, prayed, and encouraged her to begin speaking. Nothing happened. The couple persisted, but so did Jackie! Finally, when she could stand it no longer, Jackie opened her mouth and said, "Help me, God." I'll let Jackie tell you what happened:

> As soon as I made the conscious effort to open my mouth, I found that I could speak freely in a language I had never learned. It was a beautiful articulate tongue, soft and coherent in that there was a clear speech pattern with modulated rise and fall. I was never in any doubt that I had received the sign that I had asked for. But there was no accompanying exultation. I had imagined being lifted up into praise and glory, but it was a most unemotional experience.[6]

The absence of an emotional high was frustrating and confusing to Jackie. For the next several months she largely neglected any exercise of her new gift. Her ministry in the Walled City continued, but with very few lasting results.

Then she met an American couple. It had been two years since she first arrived in Hong Kong and one year since she supposedly received the gift of tongues. "Do you pray in tongues, Jackie?" they asked. "No, not anymore. I haven't found it that useful." The American lady responded:

> That's very rude of you.... It's not a gift of emotion—it's a gift of the Spirit. You shouldn't despise the gifts God has given you. The Bible says that he who prays in tongues will be built up spiritually, so never mind what you feel—do it.[7]

Jackie promised the couple that she would devote fifteen minutes every day to praying in tongues. After about six weeks Jackie noticed something remarkably different in her ministry. People with whom she shared the gospel began to believe in Jesus! But that isn't where the story ends. It was only the beginning.

The single greatest obstacle to deliverance from drugs was the indescribable and unbearable pain of withdrawal. The agony of going cold turkey had driven the vast majority of addicts back to their habit. But Jackie made a startling discovery. She herself has no explanation for why God chose to do it this way, but she is happy He did. It was her custom to pray for her new converts to be filled with the Holy Spirit and to receive a prayer language. They always did.

But then she observed that when the pain of withdrawal would begin, it would just as quickly end if the individual would begin praying in tongues! It took a while to convince a few of the converts, but the horrors of withdrawal made them desperate. As Jackie and others would pray for them in tongues, they too would cry out to God in their new language. Miraculously, and virtually without exception, each one came off drugs without the wrenching pain associated with this experience.

Most of these addicts had been on heroin or opium for years and had quite literally run out of space on their bodies in which to inject themselves with the drug. Their lives were controlled by their addiction, and few would hesitate to steal or even kill to support their habit. Many had sold friends and family members into prostitution to keep the flow of drugs coming. Yet when they converted to faith in Jesus and prayed in tongues, the power of addiction was defeated.

I have no explanation for this. I don't have a biblical text that I can cite in support of how God has used tongues in Jackie's ministry. All I can do is state the facts as I know them and let you draw your own conclusion. But the simple truth is that every single person, numbering in the hundreds, who prayed to receive Christ under Jackie's ministry also received the gift of tongues. And every single heroin addict who prayed in tongues at the onset of withdrawal pains came through the experience without the slightest discomfort.

Whether God will make use of tongues in a similar way through the ministry of others is something neither I nor Jackie nor anyone else can predict. Our responsibility is to obey God's Word and trust Him for the results.

WHEN A PROMINENT SCHOLAR SPEAKS IN TONGUES

Let me share another story that may be an encouragement to you in this regard. What follows is a letter I received from a nationally known and widely respected scholar concerning her own experience with tongues. She is an accomplished author and a brilliant theologian. Here is what she said:

> For what it's worth, let me quickly relate my own tongues experience. Twenty years ago, in high school, my wild and crazy Pentecostal boyfriend and his Pentecostal cohorts tried every which way to get me—a conservative Baptist girl—to speak in tongues. I wasn't opposed to the idea, but try as they did (prayer, moaning, speaking in tongues over me...everything short of slashing themselves with

knives), nothing happened. They came to the conclusion that I was horribly unspiritual and resistant to God's work in my life. I can't say that I was deeply marred by the experience, but it did leave me feeling somewhat wary of the validity of the gift.

In June of this year [1995], the Spirit put on my heart the desire to enter an extended fast. On the fourth day (a really, really difficult day of battling against the physical and mental desire to eat) while I was pouring my heart out to God, foreign and strange words welled up from deep within and came spilling out of my mouth. It was quite a few moments before it dawned on me that I was speaking in tongues. Over the next days and weeks of the fast, I was able to use this gift to battle against severe temptation. I doubt whether I would have had the physical, mental, and spiritual strength to complete the fast without it. I felt as though the Spirit of God within was interceding to the Father on my behalf. The gift remains with me. I feel most moved to use it during times of deep intercession or deep praise. "Deep" is the best adjective I can think of—it is kind of hard to describe, but I think you know what I mean.[8]

The interesting thing about this woman's experience is that she was not seeking the gift of tongues. She was simply seeking God with all her heart, soul, mind, and strength. I'm not suggesting that you must follow her example nor that you will necessarily receive a new prayer language simply because you fast and pray. But you might!

THE EXPERIENCE OF A MOTHER AND HER CHILDREN

The following is the testimony of one mother, Kendra, and her ten-year-old twin children, Nate and Natalie, all of whom (together with Kendra's husband, Jimmy) are active in Bridgeway Church where I serve as lead pastor. I have their permission to use their names and tell you what happened.

Nate's story

On March 14, 2018, I was sitting on the floor in my living room in front of my mom, playing video games on the computer. Mom had worship music playing on the television. We were talking about different spiritual gifts like prophecy. I asked Mom to pray for me to receive the gift of tongues because I really wanted more spiritual gifts and sometimes I didn't know what to say to God. She said yes and asked my sister, Natalie, to pray with her over me. Mom asked me if it was OK if she and Natalie prayed out loud in tongues over me. They prayed for a little while, and then Mom asked me if I felt anything, but I didn't.

They prayed a little more, and again Mom asked me if I felt anything, but I didn't. She asked if Holy Spirit had given me syllables that I was thinking about, and I said yes. Mom asked me to say it out loud. As I said it, I started speaking in tongues just like they were. Then I stopped to ask my mom if she was sure I wasn't going to bite my tongue because my tongue was moving so fast and weird. I continued to pray in tongues for a little while. Then I started playing video games on my computer again.

Speaking in tongues wasn't as exciting as I thought it might be, but I am still glad that I have this gift. I usually pray in tongues every day right before I go to sleep and every morning when I am waking up. Now, even when I don't know what to say, I can still pray to God.

Natalie's story

On July 23, 2017, when I was nine-and-a-half, I was lying with my mom on her bed. She was playing with my hair while talking to me. She asked what I wanted her to pray for me. I wanted courage and boldness to pray out loud for other people like she does. When she prayed for me, I got a picture in my mind of me being a piece of dough that Jesus was making into a loaf of bread. Then my mom asked if I had ever wanted to speak in tongues. I said, "Yes!" I thought it would be cool to talk to God my own way and to remember how amazing He is. Sometimes I don't know what to pray, so praying in tongues would be awesome.

She asked Holy Spirit to give me the gift and started to pray for me in tongues. My tongue started to curl up without me doing it. It was a strange feeling. I was thinking of syllables in my mind. I told my mom about my tongue curling and the syllables in my mind. She told me to say them out loud. When I said them, more syllables came out of my mouth without me trying. I told her I thought it would be easier to sing them than to say them. So I started to sing in tongues. It made me feel sleepy and peaceful. Then I went to bed and prayed in tongues until I fell asleep.

I still pray in tongues a lot, especially at night when I am alone. I love to talk to Jesus by praying in tongues until I fall asleep.

Kendra's story

One day I felt the need to meet with my pastor, Sam, without any pressing agenda. I wasn't certain why, but I scheduled a meeting. I recently had encountered some new experiences with Holy Spirit that I was still processing through. I was definitely skeptical of any miraculous gifts, but these new experiences had opened my mind to the possibility that there was more of God than I knew about. During this meeting Sam started talking to me about the gift of tongues. I wasn't sure how we came to this subject, but I was very intrigued. He recommended a book for me to read and prayed that I might receive tongues. Nothing happened immediately.

One evening, about a week after the meeting, Holy Spirit brought up a memory in my past. I was journaling about the memory when I felt like Jesus wanted me to lie flat on the ground.

Once on the ground I heard in my mind very clearly, "Just rest." As I lay there, my face started contorting involuntarily in so many different directions all at once. Being a medical professional, I started compiling my list of differential diagnoses in my head and deciding if I should wake up my husband. But there was such a peace in my entire body that I decided this *could* be spiritual.

After several minutes of facial contortions everything stopped again. I heard for the second time, "Just rest." I felt as if my body was completely weightless and relaxed. Suddenly from deep in my throat this voice came out, moving my jaw faster than this Southern girl had ever moved it. There was no voluntary movement on my part. I was in awe, yet logically trying to figure out what was going on. I thought, "This must be speaking in tongues. This has to be what others have told me about." I rationalized with myself that if God was God, then of course He could do anything with my body that He wanted to. This must be God. All the time I was thinking this, my mouth was under the full control of Holy Spirit.

Later that night, I asked Holy Spirit to "do it again." Again my mouth moved so fast and my voice was saying things I didn't understand. I rushed to find a mirror. In amazement and giggles I was in awe at realizing who God really was and the power He had over my life. Such feelings of divine love filled my heart. He was in total control, and I felt so safe in His care. I'll never be the same!

CONCLUSION

I trust you are greatly encouraged to hear of what the Holy Spirit has done in my life as well as in the lives of these I've mentioned in this final chapter. No, I can't guarantee that you will receive the gift of tongues should you ask for it. But I'm almost certain that you will not receive it if you don't ask. Speaking in tongues is not the most important of all the spiritual gifts. But neither is it the least significant among them. It is merely one of the many tools with which God has blessed His church for the building up of the body of Christ. My prayer is that you will have been both instructed and challenged from what you've read in *The Language of Heaven*. May God direct your heart into a deeper experience of His love and a Spirit-empowered capacity to pray and praise Him with greater zeal and passion.

ABOUT THE AUTHOR

Sam Storms, PhD, is lead pastor of preaching and vision at Bridgeway Church in Oklahoma City. He is also the founder and president of Enjoying God Ministries (www.samstorms.com) and serves on the council of the Gospel Coalition. Sam earned his BA in history from the University of Oklahoma in 1973, a ThM in historical theology from Dallas Theological Seminary in 1977, and a PhD in intellectual history from the University of Texas at Dallas in 1984. Before joining the staff of Bridgeway Church, Sam served as visiting associate professor of theology at Wheaton College in Wheaton, Illinois, and is a past president of the Evangelical Theological Society.

Sam and his wife of forty-seven years, Ann, are the parents of two daughters and grandparents of four. Sam is the author or editor of twenty-seven books, among which are *Practicing the Power: Welcoming the Gifts of the Holy Spirit in Your Life* (Zondervan), *Kingdom Come: The Amillennial Alternative* (Christian Focus), *The Singing God* (Passio), and *The Beginner's Guide to Spiritual Gifts* (Bethany House). Sam is also the general editor of the *ESV Men's Devotional Bible* (Crossway).

If there is a central and all-consuming passion in Sam's heart, it is for the convergence of Word and Spirit in the lives of God's people and the ministries of the local church. He has devoted his life to equipping followers of Jesus to eagerly embrace both the functional authority of God's written Word and the full range of miraculous gifts of the Spirit, all to the glory of God in Christ. Sam longs to see Christian men and women who are intellectually exhilarated by complex biblical truths yet unafraid to give public expression to deep emotional delight and heartfelt affection for Jesus.

Sam believes the urgent need of the church today is for theologically sophisticated followers of Christ who are hungry for the revelatory gifts of the Spirit while always subject to the final authority of the written text of Scripture. You can gain access, free of charge, to Sam's written work by visiting his website and blog at www.samstorms.com.

NOTES

CHAPTER 1:
MY FIRST EXPERIENCE OF SPEAKING IN TONGUES

1. The few brave souls who displayed any interest in Charismatic phenomena might have sneaked away to attend the local gathering of the Full Gospel Business Men's Fellowship. But aside from that, very few would have been caught dead attending a Pentecostal or Charismatic church service.

2. The best portrayal of the Jesus people movement and CWLF is Larry Eskridge's *God's Forever Family: The Jesus People Movement in America* (New York: Oxford University Press, 2013).

3. This is the doctrine known as cessationism. Although there are differing expressions of theological cessationism, some more strict than others, the fundamental notion is that those spiritual gifts of a more overtly miraculous or supernatural nature, such as the nine listed in 1 Corinthians 12:8–10, were designed by God only for the early church until such time as either the last apostle died or the final book of the biblical canon had been written. Cessationists are quick to point out that they do not deny the reality of miracles in our day. What they deny is that God supplies believers in the present day with these miraculous gifts.

4. See my book *Convergence: Spiritual Journeys of a Charismatic Calvinist* (Kansas City, MO: Enjoying God Ministries, 2005).

5. Some would argue that the word translated "fan into flame" (ESV) simply means to kindle, without any suggestion of a prior diminishing operation.

CHAPTER 2:
TONGUES IN SCRIPTURE

1. See Exodus 23:16; 34:22; Leviticus 23:15–16; Deuteronomy 16:9–10, 16; and 2 Chronicles 8:13.

2. Eckhard J. Schnabel, *Acts*, Zondervan Exegetical Commentary on the New Testament (Grand Rapids, MI: Zondervan, 2012), 116.

3. Schnabel, *Acts*, 120.

4. Schnabel, *Acts*, 121.

5. In his magisterial, four-volume commentary on Acts, Craig Keener cites some two dozen verified cases of individuals speaking in a human language for which they had received no prior training or education. See Craig S. Keener, *Acts: An Exegetical Commentary*, vol. 1 (Grand Rapids, MI: Baker Academic, 2012), 829, n. 419 and n. 420.

6. Schnabel, *Acts*, 115.

7. J. Rodman Williams, *Renewal Theology: Salvation, the Holy Spirit, and Christian Living*, vol. 2 (Grand Rapids, MI: Zondervan Publishing House, 1990), 215.

8. Williams, *Renewal Theology*, 215. Others who find in Acts 2 a miracle of "hearing" include Luke T. Johnson, s.v. "Tongues, Gift of," in *The Anchor Bible Dictionary* (New York: Doubleday, 1992), VI:597, and more recently Anthony C. Thiselton, *The First Epistle to the Corinthians* (Grand Rapids, MI: Eerdmans, 2000), 977.

9. D. A. Carson, *Showing the Spirit: A Theological Exposition of 1 Corinthians 12–14* (Grand Rapids, MI: Baker Book House, 1987), 138.

10. Max Turner, *The Holy Spirit and Spiritual Gifts*, rev. ed. (Peabody, MA: Hendrickson, 2009), 218, https://www.amazon.com/Holy-Spirit-Spiritual-Gifts-Testament/dp/0801047927.

11. Keener, *Acts*, 1:823.

12. For those wishing to dig more deeply into this question, I highly recommend the short essay by D. A. Carson, "When Did the Church Begin?," *Themelios* 41, no. 1 (2016): 1–4, also available at http://themelios.thegospelcoalition.org/article/carson-when-did-the-church-begin.

13. John R. W. Stott, *The Spirit, the Church, and the World: The Message of Acts* (Downers Grove, IL: InterVarsity Press, 1990), 68.

14. In using this language, I wouldn't want you to think in quantitative terms. The Holy Spirit can't be parceled out in pieces or greater or lesser quantities. In speaking of "more" of the Spirit, I simply mean a greater manifestation of His presence and power.

15. Some argue that tongues-speech was present in Acts 8 because Simon was able to "see" (v. 18) their reception of the Holy Spirit. But it could just as easily have been their boldness, their joy, their praise, or any number of other manifestations of the Spirit's presence. We are better off not trying to prove anything from what Luke does not explicitly record.

16.   This means that there may well be occasions when speaking in tongues is in fact the initial physical evidence of having been baptized in the Spirit. But that is not the same as saying that tongues must necessarily follow Spirit baptism in every case. More on this in the next chapter.

17.   Schnabel, *Acts*, 505.

18.   David G. Peterson, *The Acts of the Apostles* (Grand Rapids, MI: Eerdmans, 2009), 340.

19.   Peterson, *The Acts of the Apostles*, 340.

20.   James D. G. Dunn, *Baptism in the Holy Spirit: A Re-Examination of the New Testament Teaching on the Gift of the Spirit in Relation to Pentecostalism Today* (Philadelphia: Westminster Press, 1970), 86.

21.   G. R. Beasley-Murray, *Baptism in the New Testament* (Eugene, OR: Wipf & Stock, 1972, 2006), 109, 111.

22.   Keener, *Acts*, 3:2822–2823.

CHAPTER 3:
TONGUES AND SPIRIT BAPTISM

1.   "Assemblies of God 16 Fundamental Truths," The General Council of the Assemblies of God, accessed February 7, 2019, https://ag.org/Beliefs/Statement-of-Fundamental-Truths, brackets in the original.

2.   I should point out that not all "classical Pentecostals" affirm the doctrine of initial evidence. Well-known New Testament scholar Gordon Fee has rejected all three of these doctrines relating to Spirit baptism while remaining within the Assemblies of God denomination. See Gordon Fee, "Baptism in the Holy Spirit: The Issue of Separability and Subsequence," *Pneuma* 7, no. 1 (Fall 1985): 87–99.

3.   For a more detailed response to this question see my book *Tough Topics: Biblical Answers to 25 Challenging Questions* (Wheaton, IL: Crossway, 2013), 252–275.

4.   The most exhaustive treatment of these issues is found in H. I. Lederle, *Treasures Old and New: Interpretations of "Spirit-Baptism" in the Charismatic Renewal Movement* (Peabody, MA: Hendrickson Publishers, 1988).

5.   See Martyn Lloyd-Jones, *Joy Unspeakable: Power and Renewal in the Holy Spirit* (Wheaton, IL: Harold Shaw Publishers, 1984).

6.   See C. Peter Wagner, *The Third Wave of the Holy Spirit* (Ann Arbor, MI: Servant Publications, 1988).

7.   See my comments in *Are Miraculous Gifts for Today? Four Views*, ed. Wayne A Grudem (Grand Rapids, MI: Zondervan, 1996), especially pages 176–85. Among the texts that should encourage us to expect post-conversion encounters with and experiences of the Holy Spirit are Luke 11:13; Romans 5:5; 8:15–17; Galatians 3:1–5; Ephesians 1:15–23; 3:16–19; 5:18; Philippians 1:19; 1 Thessalonians 4:8; and 1 Peter 1:8; as well as the many passages in Acts that speak of believers being "filled" with the Spirit for ministry and life. These texts would appear to dispel the concept of a singular, once-for-all deposit of the Spirit that would supposedly render superfluous the need for subsequent, post-conversion anointing. The Spirit who was once given and now indwells each believer is continually given to enhance and intensify our relationship with Christ and to empower our efforts in ministry. But we need not label any one such experience as Spirit baptism.

8.   It should be noted that in the New Testament to be baptized "by" someone is always expressed by the preposition *hupo* followed by a genitive noun. People were baptized "by" John the Baptist in the Jordan River (Matt. 3:6; Mark 1:5; Luke 3:7). Jesus was baptized "by" John (Matt. 3:13; Mark 1:9). The Pharisees had not been baptized "by" John (Luke 7:30), etc. Most likely, then, if Paul had wanted to say the Corinthians had all been baptized "by" the Holy Spirit, he would have used *hupo* with the genitive, not *en* with the dative.

9.   Gordon D. Fee, *God's Empowering Presence: The Holy Spirit in the Letters of Paul* (Peabody, MA: Hendrickson, 1994), 181.

10.   Some Pentecostals respond by arguing that the tongues Paul has in mind in 1 Corinthians 14:5 is the "gift" of tongues or a private prayer language that must be differentiated from the "sign" of tongues that constitutes the initial physical evidence of Spirit baptism. I must confess that this theory strikes me as a case of special pleading. In other words, why would anyone create this distinction between two different expressions of tongues or employ this argument unless motivated to find biblical support for the idea that Spirit baptism is always followed by tongues-speech? For the latter doctrine to be true, we need clear evidence from other biblical texts, something I have found to be lacking.

11.   I've constructed this explanation based on material from Fee, "Baptism in the Holy Spirit."

12. Lederle, *Treasures Old and New*, 60.

13. Wayne Grudem, *Systematic Theology* (Grand Rapids, MI: Zondervan, 1994), 772–773, emphasis in the original.

14. Dunn, *Baptism in the Holy Spirit*, 68–70.

15. This event is spoken of in numerous sources. One is in Colin G. Kruse, *The Gospel According to John: An Introduction and Commentary* (Downers Grove, IL: IVP Academic, 2007), 137. Kruse says it happened sometime between AD 6 and 9.

16. Frederick Dale Bruner, *A Theology of the Holy Spirit: The Pentecostal Experience and the New Testament Witness* (Grand Rapids, MI: Eerdmans, 1970), 176.

17. John Piper, *Let the Nations Be Glad: The Supremacy of God in Missions* (Grand Rapids, MI: Baker, 1993), 146, 148, emphasis in the original.

CHAPTER 4:
TONGUES AND FOREIGN LANGUAGES

1. I will address each of these misunderstandings of tongues in subsequent chapters.

2. David E. Garland, *1 Corinthians*, Baker Exegetical Commentary on the New Testament (Grand Rapids, MI: Baker Academic, 2003), 584.

3. Thiselton, *The First Epistle to the Corinthians*, 1085.

4. Thiselton, *The First Epistle to the Corinthians*, 1085.

5. Paul Gardner, *1 Corinthians*, Zondervan Exegetical Commentary on the New Testament (Grand Rapids, MI: Zondervan, 2018), 591.

6. This estimate is based on figures from 2017. See Conrad Hackett and David McClendon, "Christians Remain World's Largest Religious Group, but They Are Declining in Europe," Pew Research Center, April 5, 2017, http://www.pewresearch.org /fact-tank/2017/04/05/christians-remain-worlds-largest-religious-group -but-they-are-declining-in-europe/.

7. For evidence of this, see my chapter "What Can We Know About Angels?" in *Tough Topics*, 120–136.

8. Gordon D. Fee, *The First Epistle to the Corinthians*, rev. ed. (Grand Rapids, MI: Eerdmans, 2014), 69. See also Richard B. Hays, *First Corinthians* (Louisville, KY: Westminster John Knox Press, 1997), 223.

9.   Christopher Forbes, *Prophecy and Inspired Speech: In Early Christianity and Its Hellenistic Environment* (Peabody, MA: Hendrickson, 1997), 185–186, emphasis in the original.

10.   Thiselton, *The First Epistle to the Corinthians*, 973, 1061–1062.

11.   Keener, *Acts*, 1:808.

12.   Grudem, *Systematic Theology*, 1072.

13.   Robert W. Graves, *Praying in the Spirit* (Tulsa, OK: Empowered Life Academic, 2016), 122.

14.   Garland, *1 Corinthians*, 584. Mark J. Cartledge provides an extremely helpful survey of the status of scholarly research on the nature of tongues in his article, "The Nature and Function of New Testament Glossolalia," *The Evangelical Quarterly* 72, no. 2 (2000), 135–150. His conclusion, with which I generally concur, is that "Luke considered glossolalia to be real unlearned human languages (xenolalia), while Paul understood glossolalia to be either real unlearned human languages (xenolalia) or a mysterious kind of heavenly language which he called the 'language of angels'" (149). See also Mark J. Cartledge, *Charismatic Glossolalia: An Empirical-Theological Study*, Ashgate New Critical Thinking in Theology and Biblical Studies (Aldershot, UK: Ashgate Publishing Company, 2002).

CHAPTER 5:
THE PURPOSE OF TONGUES, PART I

1.   If you do not read New Testament Greek, feel free to ignore this endnote. Those who do understand Greek may object to my use of the word *command* by pointing out that "building yourselves up" is a participle, not an imperative. The command in this passage is that we keep ourselves in the love of God. However, I would remind everyone of the "so-called imperatival use of the participle" (Peter H. Davids, *The Letters of 2 Peter and Jude* [Grand Rapids, MI: Eerdmans, 2006], 92). Virtually every commentator on Jude concurs with this interpretation. See, for example, Gene L. Green, *Jude and 2 Peter*, Baker Exegetical Commentary on the New Testament (Grand Rapids, MI: Baker Academic, 2008), 120; and Richard J. Bauckham, *Jude, 2 Peter*, Word Biblical Commentary, vol. 50 (Waco, TX: Word Books, 1983), 111–112. For additional insight I encourage you to consult Andreas J. Köstenberger, Benjamin L. Merkle, and Robert L. Plummer, *Going Deeper With New Testament Greek: An Intermediate Study of*

the Grammar and Syntax of the New Testament (Nashville: B & H Academic, 2016), 338–339.

2.   Gardner, *1 Corinthians*, 594.

3.   D. A. Carson, *A Call to Spiritual Reformation* (Grand Rapids, MI: Baker Academic, 1992), 191.

4.   Andrew T. Lincoln, *Ephesians*, Word Biblical Commentary, vol. 42 (Dallas: Word Books, 1990), 213.

5.   See my discussion of this passage in question 21 in chapter 9.

6.   Thomas R. Schreiner, *Spiritual Gifts: What They Are and Why They Matter* (Nashville: B & H Publishing Group, 2018), 123–146.

7.   *Concise Oxford English Dictionary*, 12th ed. (2011), s.v. "ecstasy." See also *Oxford English Dictionary*, s.v. "ecstasy," accessed February 7, 2019, https://en.oxforddictionaries.com/definition/ecstasy.

8.   *Concise Oxford English Dictionary*, s.v. "ecstatic."

9.   *Merriam-Webster*, s.v "ecstasy," accessed February 7, 2019, https://www.merriam-webster.com/dictionary/ecstasy; *Merriam-Webster*, s.v. "ecstatic," accessed February 7, 2019, https://www.merriam-webster.com/dictionary/ecstatic.

10.   Paul Gardner (*1 Corinthians*) finds little to object in the use of the word *ecstatic*. He says: "Using the word in this sense is not to speak of something even remotely similar to a drug-induced haze or a trance-like state induced in some religious act more akin to voodoo than to biblical Christianity. Rather, it is to speak about the gracious activity of God among his people in which, for the grace fully to be appreciated by the church, the communication must have its code broken and an intelligible translation or 'articulation' given" (600).

11.   *Merriam-Webster*, s.v "ecstasy."

12.   Graves, *Praying in the Spirit*, 56.

CHAPTER 6:
THE PURPOSE OF TONGUES, PART II

1.   Blue Letter Bible, s.v. *"psallō,"* accessed February 8, 2019, https://www.blueletterbible.org/lang/Lexicon/Lexicon.cfm?strongs=G5567&t=KJV.

2.   Mark J. Cartledge, *Charismatic Glossolalia: An Empirical-Theological Study* (Burlington, VT: Ashgate Publishing, 2002), 211.

Chapter 7:
Public Expression of Tongues

1.   See Thomas Edgar, *Miraculous Gifts: Are They for Today?* (Neptune, NJ: Loiseaux Brothers, 1983).

2.   Turner, *The Holy Spirit and Spiritual Gifts*, 232–235.

3.   See question 22 in chapter 9 for a discussion of the validity of Mark 16:9–20.

4.   Max Turner, "Spiritual Gifts Then and Now," *Vox Evangelica* 15 (1985): 7–63.

5.   Turner, *The Holy Spirit and Spiritual Gifts*, 233.

6.   Turner, *The Holy Spirit and Spiritual Gifts*, 233.

Chapter 8:
Tongues as a Spiritual Gift

1.   What follows is a revised and expanded version of what may be found in my book *The Beginner's Guide to Spiritual Gifts* (Ventura, CA: Regal, 2012), 193–197.

2.   Anthony Thiselton, "The 'Interpretation' of Tongues: A New Suggestion in the Light of Greek Usage in Philo and Josephus," *Journal of Theological Studies* 30, no. 1 (April 1979), 15–36, https://doi.org/10.1093/jts/XXX.1.15.

3.   Thiselton, *The First Epistle to the Corinthians*, 976.

4.   Thiselton, *The First Epistle to the Corinthians*, 1108. For this view see also the work by Gerd Theissen, *Psychological Aspects of Pauline Theology* (Edinburgh, UK: T. & T. Clark, 1987), 74–114; 292–341.

5.   Thiselton, *The First Epistle to the Corinthians*, 1061.

6.   Thiselton, *The First Epistle to the Corinthians*, 1110.

7.   Gardner, *1 Corinthians*, 548.

8.   Craig L. Blomberg, *1 Corinthians*, The NIV Application Commentary (Grand Rapids, MI: Zondervan, 1994), 247.

Chapter 9:
Tongues and Prayer

1.   Gordon D. Fee, *Listening to the Spirit in the Text* (Grand Rapids, MI: Eerdmans, 2000), 45.

2.   Douglas J. Moo, *The Epistle to the Romans* (Grand Rapids, MI: Eerdmans, 1996), 526–527.

3.   I come to this conclusion rather tentatively, open to being persuaded otherwise. I am especially intrigued by the arguments of

Gordon Fee, who contends that Paul has tongues in view in Romans 8:26–27. See his arguments in *God's Empowering Presence*, 575–586.

4. James R. Edwards, *The Gospel According to Mark* (Grand Rapids, MI: Eerdmans, 2002), 497.

5. *NIV Zondervan Study Bible*, ed. D. A. Carson (Grand Rapids, MI: Zondervan, 2015), 2059.

6. *ESV Study Bible* (Wheaton, IL: Crossway Bibles, 2008), 1933.

CHAPTER 10:
TONGUES AND REVELATION

1. As Gordon Fee notes, "Speaking 'by himself' (= privately) stands in contrast to 'in the assembly' in verse 28, meaning he or she should pray 'to God' in this way in private" (*God's Empowering Presence*, 251).

2. O. Palmer Robertson, *The Final Word: A Biblical Response to the Case for Tongues and Prophecy Today* (Carlisle, PA: The Banner of Truth Trust, 1993), 33.

3. I was greatly helped in my understanding of this text by the comments of Wayne Grudem in his *The Gift of Prophecy in the New Testament and Today*, rev. ed. (Wheaton, IL: Crossway Books, 2000), 145–154. See also my treatment of this text in *The Beginner's Guide to Spiritual Gifts* (Bloomington, MN: Bethany House, 2012), 167–170.

CHAPTER 11:
TONGUES AND THE BELIEVER

1. I've been dependent in the previous few paragraphs on what I wrote in my book *The Beginner's Guide to Spiritual Gifts*, 189–193. Used with permission.

2. Much of what follows is a substantially revised and expanded adaptation of the chapter, "Should All Christians Speak in Tongues?" in my book *Tough Topics*, 276–282.

3. Robert Marus, "International Mission Board Seeks to Tie Tongues," *Baptist Standard*, December 2, 2005, https://www.baptiststandard.com/archives/2005-archives/international-mission-board-seeks-to-tie-tongues/.

4. Marus, "International Mission Board Seeks to Tie Tongues."

5. Bob Smietana, "International Mission Board Drops Ban on Speaking in Tongues," *Christianity Today*, May 14, 2015, https://www

.christianitytoday.com/ct/2015/may-web-only/imb-ban-speaking-in
-tongues-baptism-baptist-missionary.html.

6. Jack Hayford, *The Beauty of Spiritual Language* (Dallas: Word Publishing, 1992), 102–106.

7. Max Turner, "Early Christian Experience and Theology of 'Tongues': A New Testament Perspective," in *Speaking in Tongues: Multi-Disciplinary Perspectives*, ed. Mark J. Cartledge (Waynesboro, GA: Paternoster Press, 2006), 27.

8. For those who wish to go deeper, a recent scholarly and quite helpful discussion of this issue may be found in the *Asian Journal of Pentecostal Studies*. See Max Turner, "Tongues: An Experience for All in the Pauline Churches?" *Asian Journal of Pentecostal Studies* 1, no. 2 (1998): 231–253; Simon K. H. Chan, "A Response to Max Turner," *Asian Journal of Pentecostal Studies* 2, no. 2 (1999): 279–281; Robert P. Menzies, "Paul and the Universality of Tongues: A Response to Max Turner," *Asian Journal of Pentecostal Studies* 2, no. 2 (1999): 283–295; and Max Turner, "A Response to the Responses of Menzies and Chan," *Asian Journal of Pentecostal Studies* 2, no. 2 (1999): 297–308.

CHAPTER 12:
TONGUES IN EARLY CHRISTIANITY, PART I

1. If you have a desire to dig more deeply into this issue, I suggest you read my chapter, "A Third Wave View," in the book *Are Miraculous Gifts for Today? Four Views*, ed. Wayne A. Grudem (Grand Rapids, MI: Zondervan, 1996), 175–223; as well as "Are Miraculous Gifts for Today?" in my book *Tough Topics*, 232–251; and finally, Appendix 2, "Are Miraculous Gifts for Today?" in my book *Practicing the Power: Welcoming the Gifts of the Holy Spirit in Your Life* (Grand Rapids, MI: Zondervan, 2017), 244–269.

2. Let's be sure not to forget that the problem in Corinth wasn't with spiritual gifts but with "unspiritual" or immature people. One cannot indict spiritual gifts or lay a charge at their feet without simultaneously indicting God. He is, after all, the One who thought up the idea of spiritual gifts and the One who bestowed them on His people. If spiritual gifts per se are the problem, the problem is with the God who authored them. Surely no one would want to say the latter.

3. Sam Storms, *Practicing the Power: Welcoming the Gifts of the Holy Spirit in Your Life* (Grand Rapids, MI: Zondervan, 2017), 252–253.

4. Storms, *Practicing the Power*, 253.

5. D. A. Carson, *Exegetical Fallacies*, 2nd ed. (Grand Rapids, MI: Baker Academic, 1996), 77.

6. Says Gordon Fee: "The change of verbs is purely rhetorical [i.e., it is merely a stylistic variation that carries no special theological significance]; to make it otherwise is to elevate to significance something in which Paul shows no interest at all. Just as one can scarcely distinguish between 'cease' and 'pass away' when used in the same context, neither can one distinguish between *katargeō* [translated "pass away"] and *pauō* [translated "cease"] in this context (although NIV's choice of 'be stilled' for tongues is felicitous). The middle voice came along with the change of verbs" (Fee, *The First Epistle to the Corinthians*, 713, n. 375).

7. Richard B. Gaffin, "A Cessationist View," in *Are Miraculous Gifts for Today?*, 55, n. 81.

8. Gaffin, "A Cessationist View," in *Are Miraculous Gifts for Today?*, 55.

9. Says Fee, "It is a primary exegetical axiom that what neither Paul himself nor the Corinthians could have understood can possibly be the meaning of what Paul was writing to them" (Fee, *The First Epistle to the Corinthians*, 715, n. 381).

10. Turner, *The Holy Spirit and Spiritual Gifts*, 294.

11. Turner, *The Holy Spirit and Spiritual Gifts*, 295.

12. Fee, *The First Epistle to the Corinthians*, 715.

13. Garland, *1 Corinthians*, 623.

14. Fee, *The First Epistle to the Corinthians*, 716.

CHAPTER 13:
TONGUES IN EARLY CHRISTIANITY, PART II

1. D. A. Carson, *Showing the Spirit: A Theological Exposition of 1 Corinthians 12–14* (Grand Rapids, MI: Baker Book House, 1987), 166.

2. See Cyprian Bishop of Carthage, *The Epistles of Cyprian*, Epistle vii, 3–7; and Epistle lxviii, 9–10, accessed February 12, 2019, https://biblehub.com/library/cyprian/the_epistles_of_cyprian/index .html.

3. James L. Ash Jr., "The Decline of Ecstatic Prophecy in the Early Church," *Theological Studies* 37, no. 2 (May 1976): 252, https://doi.org/10.1177/004056397603700202.

4. Portions of this chapter, especially this section, were drawn from my book *Practicing the Power*. Used with permission.

5. For helpful documentation, see Stanley M. Burgess, *The Spirit and the Church: Antiquity* (Peabody, MA: Hendrickson Publishers, 1984); Ronald A. N. Kydd, *Charismatic Gifts in the Early Church* (Peabody, MA: Hendrickson Publishers, 1984); Jeff Oliver, *Pentecost to the Present: The Holy Spirit's Enduring Work in the Church*, 3 vols. (Newberry, FL: Bridge Logos, 2017); Eddie L. Hyatt, *2000 Years of Charismatic Christianity* (Lake Mary, FL: Charisma House, 2002); Kilian McDonnell and George T. Montague, *Christian Initiation and Baptism in the Holy Spirit: Evidence From the First Eight Centuries* (Collegeville, MN: The Liturgical Press, 1991); Stanley M. Burgess, ed., *Christian Peoples of the Spirit: A Documentary History of Pentecostal Spirituality From the Early Church to the Present* (New York: New York University Press, 2011), 177–186; Cecil M. Robeck Jr., *Prophecy in Carthage: Perpetua, Tertullian, and Cyprian* (Cleveland, OH: The Pilgrim Press, 1992); and J. D. King, *Regeneration: A Complete History of Healing in the Christian Church, Volume One: Post-Apostolic Through Later Holiness* (Lee's Summit: MO, Christos Publishing, 2017). Then, of course, one must reckon with the massive documentation of miraculous gifts throughout the course of church history as compiled by Craig S. Keener in his two-volume work, *Miracles: The Credibility of the New Testament Accounts* (Grand Rapids, MI: Baker Academic, 2011).

6. Barnabas, *The Epistle of Barnabas*, xvi, 9; *Ancient Christian Writers*, 6:61.

7. Justin Martyr, *Dialogue With Trypho*, 39, accessed February 12, 2019, http://www.ccel.org/ccel/schaff/anf01.pdf.

8. Martyr, *Dialogue With Trypho*, 82, accessed February 12, 2019, http://www.ccel.org/ccel/schaff/anf01.pdf.

9. Justin Martyr, *The Second Apology of Justin*, vi; Ante-Nicene Fathers 1:190.

10. Saint Irenaeus, *Against Heresies*, Book 2, ch. 32, 4, accessed February 12, 2019, http://www.ccel.org/ccel/schaff/anf01.pdf.

11. Irenaeus, *Against Heresies*, Book 2, ch. 32, 5, accessed February 12, 2019, http://www.ccel.org/ccel/schaff/anf01.pdf.

12. Irenaeus, *Against Heresies*, Book 5, ch. 6, 1; Euseb. H. E. 5.7.6.

13. Tertullian, *A Treatise on the Soul*, xlvii, ANF, 3:225–226, accessed February 12, 2019, https://www.biblestudytools.com/history

/early-church-fathers/ante-nicene/vol-3-latin-christianity/tertullian
/a-treatise-soul.html.

14.   Tertullian, *A Treatise on the Soul*, ix, ANF, 3:188, accessed
February 12, 2019, https://www.biblestudytools.com/history
/early-church-fathers/ante-nicene/vol-3-latin-christianity/tertullian/a-
treatise-soul.html.

15.   Tertullian, *Against Marcion*, viii, ANF, 3:446–447, accessed
February 12, 2019, http://www.ccel.org/ccel/schaff/anf03.v.iv.vi.viii.html.

16.   See Robeck, *Prophecy in Carthage*, 11–94; J. E. Salisbury,
Perpetua's Passion: The Death and Memory of a Young Roman Woman
(New York: Routledge, 1997).

17.   The most helpful and fair-minded treatment of Montanism is
the book by Christine Trevett, *Montanism: Gender, Authority and the
New Prophecy* (New York: Cambridge University Press, 1996).

18.   Didymus, *On the Trinity*, 3:41, quoted in Kydd, *Charismatic
Gifts in the Early Church*, 32.

19.   Epiphanius, *Panarion*, 48:12; col. 873, quoted in Kydd,
Charismatic Gifts in the Early Church, 32.

20.   Epiphanius, quoted in Kydd, *Charismatic Gifts in the Early
Church*, 32.

21.   Athenagoras, *A Plea for the Christians*, ch. 9, accessed February
12, 2019, http://www.ccel.org/ccel/schaff/anf02.v.ii.ix.html.

22.   Eusebius, *Ecclesiastical History*, 5, 16:7, trans. Kirsopp
Lake (London: William Heinemann, 1926), 1:475; quoted in Kydd,
Charismatic Gifts in the Early Church, 35.

23.   Eusebius, *Ecclesiastical History*, 5, 16:9, 1:477; quoted in Kydd,
Charismatic Gifts in the Early Church, 35.

24.   Eusebius, *Ecclesiastical History*, 5, 16:12, 1:479. Quoted in
Kydd, *Charismatic Gifts in the Early Church*, 35.

25.   Trevett, *Montanism*, 95–105.

26.   Trevett, *Montanism*, 60–62; McDonnell and Montague,
Christian Initiation and Baptism in the Holy Spirit, 136.

27.   McDonnell and Montague, *Christian Initiation and Baptism in
the Holy Spirit*, 136–137.

28.   McDonnell and Montague, *Christian Initiation and Baptism in
the Holy Spirit*, 137.

29.   McDonnell and Montague, *Christian Initiation and Baptism in
the Holy Spirit*, 137.

30.   Clement of Alexandria, *Excerpta ex Theodoto*, 24:1

31.   Clement of Alexandria, *The Instructor*, iv.21, ANF, 2:434.

32.   Origen, *Against Celsus*, ch. 46, ANF, 4:415, accessed February 12, 2019, http://www.ccel.org/ccel/schaff/anf04.vi.ix.i.xlvii.html.

33.   Alexander Roberts and James Donaldson, eds., *Ante-Nicene Christian Library: Translations of the Writings of the Fathers, vol. X, The Writings of Origen*, "Origin Against Celsus" (Edinburgh, UK: T&T Clark, n.d.), 399–400.

34.   Origen, *Against Celsus*, ch. 2, ANF 4:397–398, accessed February 12, 2019, http://www.ccel.org/ccel/schaff/anf04.vi.ix.i.v.html.

35.   Origen, *Against Celsus*, 7.9; quoted in Jeff Oliver, *Pentecost to the Present: The Holy Spirit's Enduring Work in the Church, Book One* (Newberry, FL: Bridge-Logos, 2017), 84.

36.   Burton Scott Easton, ed., *The Apostolic Tradition of Hippolytus* (Cambridge: Cambridge University Press, 1934), 41.

37.   Novatian, *Treatise Concerning the Trinity*, 29.10.

38.   Cyprian, *The Epistles of Cyprian*, vii.3–6, ANF, 5:286-287; vii.7, ANF, 5:287; lxviii.9-10, ANF, 5:375; iv.4, ANF, 5:290.

39.   Philip Schaff and Henry Wace, eds., "Catechetical Lectures" in *A Select Library of Nicene and Post-Nicene Fathers of the Christian Church, Second Series* (New York: The Christian Literature Series, 1894), 118.

40.   Oliver, *Pentecost to the Present*, 124.

41.   Basil the Great, *The Longer Rules*, vii.

42.   Philip Schaff and Henry Wace, eds., "On the Holy Spirit" in *A Select Library of Nicene and Post-Nicene Fathers of the Christian Church, Second Series*, vol. 8 (New York: The Christian Literature Series, 1895), 25.

43.   Basil the Great, *The Longer Rules*, xxiv, xxxv, xlii, lv.

44.   Saint Gregory of Nyssa, "On the Christian Mode of Life" in *Ascetical Works* (The Fathers of the Church, Volume 58), trans. Virginia Woods Callahan (Washington, DC: The Catholic University of America Press, 1967, 1990), 141.

45.   See Gregory of Nazianzen, *On the Death of His Father*, xxviii–xxix, NPF 2nd Series 7:263–264; xxxi, NPF 2nd Series 7:264, accessed February 12, 2019, https://www.ccel.org/ccel/schaff/npnf207.iii.x.html.

46.   Hilary of Poitiers, *On the Trinity* in Philip Schaff and Henry Wace, eds., *A Select Library of Nicene and Post-Nicene Fathers of the Christian Church*, second series, vol. 9 (New York: The Christian Literature Series, 1908), 146.

47.	Ambrose, who highly influenced Augustine, also believed in the operation of tongues in his day (*The Holy Spirit*, 2.150).

48.	Augustine, *City of God*, Book 22, chapter 8, 489, accessed February 12, 2019, https://www.ccel.org/ccel/schaff/npnf102 .iv.XXII.8.html.

49.	Saint Augustine, *The Works of Saint Augustine: Revisions* (Hyde Park, NY: New City Press, 2010).

50.	Cited by Oliver, *Pentecost to the Present*, 142–143.

51.	For extensive documentation see Stanley M. Burgess, *The Holy Spirit: Medieval Roman Catholic and Reformation Traditions (Sixth-Sixteenth Centuries)* (Peabody, MA: Hendrickson Publishers, 1997). See also Paul Thigpen, "Did the Power of the Spirit Ever Leave the Church?," *Charisma* (September 1992): 20–29; and Richard M. Riss, "Tongues and Other Miraculous Gifts in the Second Through Nineteenth Centuries," *Basileia* (1985).

52.	This list was included in my book *Practicing the Power*. It is used here with permission.

53.	Stanley M. Burgess, ed., *Christian Peoples of the Spirit: A Documentary History of Pentecostal Spirituality from the Early Church to the Present* (New York: New York University Press, 2011), 177–186.

54.	Rufus M. Jones, ed., *George Fox: An Autobiography* (Richmond, IN: Street Corner Society, 1976).

55.	Jack S. Deere, *Surprised by the Voice of God* (Grand Rapids, MI: Zondervan, 1996), 64–93.

56.	See Deere, *Surprised by the Voice of God*, 64–93.

57.	See Deere, *Surprised by the Voice of God*, 64–93.

58.	Charles Spurgeon, *The Autobiography of Charles H. Spurgeon* (Curts & Jennings, 1899), 226–227.

59.	Spurgeon, *The Autobiography of Charles H. Spurgeon*, 227.

60.	*C. H. Spurgeon's Autobiography: The Full Harvest* (Carlisle, PA: Banner of Truth Trust, 1973), 2:60.

CHAPTER 14:
ENCOURAGING TESTIMONIES OF
OTHERS WHO SPEAK IN TONGUES

1.	Much of what I share about Jackie Pullinger is taken from her book, *Chasing the Dragon: One Woman's Struggle Against the Darkness of Hong Kong's Drug Dens*. If you haven't read it, I encourage you to do so.

2.	Jackie Pullinger and Andrew Quicke, *Chasing the Dragon: One Woman's Struggle Against the Darkness of Hong Kong's Drug Dens* (Bloomington, MN: Chosen Books, 1980, 2014), 34.

3.	Pullinger and Quicke, *Chasing the Dragon*, 35.

4.	Again, if you haven't read Jackie's autobiography, *Chasing the Dragon*, do so now.

5.	Pullinger and Quicke, *Chasing the Dragon*, 61.

6.	Pullinger and Quicke, *Chasing the Dragon*, 62.

7.	Pullinger and Quicke, *Chasing the Dragon*, 64.

8.	Storms, *The Beginner's Guide to Spiritual Gifts*, 191–192. Used with permission.